RIGHTS AND DUTIES

RUSSELL KIRK

RIGHTS AND DUTIES

Reflections on Our Conservative Constitution

Edited by Mitchell S. Muncy
Introduction by Russell Hittinger

SPENCE PUBLISHING COMPANY · DALLAS
1997

To the memory of Edmund Burke,

the philosopher in action,

on the bicentennial of his death

Published in the United States by
Spence Publishing Company
501 Elm Street, Suite 450
Dallas, Texas 75202

Library of Congress Cataloging-in-Publication Data

Kirk, Russell.
    Rights and duties : reflections on our conservative constitution /
Russell Kirk ; edited by Mitchell S. Muncy ; introduction by Russell
Hittinger.
        p. cm.
    Rev. ed. of: The conservative constitution. c1990.
    Includes bibliographical references and index.
    ISBN 0-9653208-2-0 (hardcover)
    1. Constitutional law—United States.   2. Conservatism—United States.
I. Muncy, Mitchell S. (Mitchell Shannon), 1968- .
II. Kirk, Russell. Conservative constitution.   III. Title.
KF4550.K543 1997
342.73'02—dc21   97-22262

All chapters except 6, 10, 11, and 13 previously published
by Regnery Publishing as *The Conservative Constitution*
© 1990 by Russell Kirk.

Contents

Preface

ADDRESSED TO THE COMMON READER, this book is a desultory examination of the Constitution of the United States, emphasizing its conservative purpose. This is not a systematic history of interpretations of the Constitution. Rather, it is an endeavor to examine the conservative ends of our basic federal law, the relationship between political economy and the Constitution, and the varying fortunes of conservative constitutional concepts over the years.

I have not hesitated to introduce into my chapters some mordant observations on judicial decisions regarding religion, property, and other bones of contention during recent decades; and I hope that no reader may be offended at the occasional intrusion of the author's experiences, by way of illustration of arguments advanced.

There runs through these chapters an especial attention to Edmund Burke, who was much more in the mind of the Framers than was John

Locke. At once the champion and the improver of the British Constitution, Burke was read attentively by such Framers and Founders as John Dickinson, Alexander Hamilton, Fisher Ames, and John Marshall. More important, Burke's views on law, constitutions, and much else came to permeate the opinions and the books of those eminent commentators on American constitutional law Justice Joseph Story and Chancellor James Kent. Burke's speeches and pamphlets were read by the men of 1776 and the men of 1787—and studied with yet closer attention from 1790 to 1815, and later. In divers ways—some obvious, some subtle—Burke's rhetoric, Burke's politics, and Burke's constitutional principles were woven, generation after generation, into American modes of thought and American understanding of constitutional law. One can trace Burke's influence upon American law and politics down into the twentieth century.

On Massachusetts Avenue in Washington, D.C., stands a statue of Burke. Why is it there? Because Burke was a principal defender of that world of reason and order and peace and virtue in which the United States participates. Constitution, custom, convention, and prescription give society continuity, Burke perceived. And he pointed out that prudent change is the means of our preservation; he understood how the claims of freedom and the claims of order must be kept in a tolerable tension. Such truths he taught not as a coffee-house philosopher, but as a practical statesman and manager of a political party.

In short, the convictions of Burke remain relevant to our present discontents. This book is not all about Edmund Burke; yet it is an attempt to understand the Constitution of the United States as a framework for a conservative political order. I invite the reader to look at America's basic law, and America's politics today, through Burke's eyes, through the eyes of a great conservative.

To seek political wisdom from Burke is no more exotic for Americans than it is to seek humane insights from Shakespeare or spiritual insights from St. Paul. In many respects, the American Republic today is more like the imperial Britain of 1790 than the infant federation of liberated British North American provinces early in 1790. The problems of modern society transcend simple questions of governmental structure. An appeal to the pristine purity of the Constitution of the United States will not suffice as a barrier against the destructive power of fanatic ideology. To Burke, "the philosopher in action," we need to turn for analysis of the first principles of order, justice, and freedom.

Today the United States is the great conservative power in a world that has been falling to ruin since 1914. To apprehend this country's conservative duties and opportunities in defense of civilization, it is well first to become acquainted with the conservative intent and function of America's Constitution, both written and unwritten. Then, granted prudence, we may begin to work our way out of our time of troubles.

RUSSELL KIRK

Acknowledgements

MOST OF THESE LECTURES AND ESSAYS were published in 1990 as a collection entitled *The Conservative Constitution*, but this new volume differs in important respects from its predecessor. It contains additional chapters on the character of the Founders, the sources of law, and the relation of church and state, as well as a new introduction and substantial revisions in the order and presentation of the original chapters. I am hopeful that through these additions and revisions the lineaments of Russell Kirk's legal thought may emerge fully and clearly and his arguments renew their strength.

These differences notwithstanding, it is appropriate to acknowledge here contributions to the publication of *The Conservative Constitution*. The original volume was made possible in part by a grant from the National Endowment for the Humanities and incorporated two series of lectures: one series at The Heritage Foundation in Washington,

D.C., the other at the University of Detroit. The latter series, concerned with political economy and the Constitution, was sponsored by the American Council on Economics and Society. An appointment as a Fulbright Lecturer at the University of St. Andrews in Scotland enabled Dr. Kirk to lecture on constitutional questions at St. Andrews, the University of Trier, the University of Groningen, and at Zurich to a gathering of Swiss university students.

This volume also contains Dr. Kirk's 1991 Henry Salvatori Lecture, "The Marriage of Rights and Duties," sponsored by the Intercollegiate Studies Institute; a Maurice Stans Lecture to the Minnesota Historical Society on "A Revolution Not Made, but Prevented"; a lecture on "The Declaration of the Rights of Man versus the Bill of Rights" to the Academy of Senior Professionals at Eckerd College, and a variation on that theme to a Center for the Study of the Presidency meeting at Fordham University; several lectures on constitutional subjects to the law schools of the University of Notre Dame, Loyola University Chicago, Catholic University, Harvard University, and Yale University; and other lectures at the University of Colorado, Albion College, the University of Virginia, Madonna College, Lake Superior State University, Grand Valley State University, Hillsdale College, Yale University, the George Washington University, Princeton University, Alfred University, Dartmouth College, and elsewhere. Several of these lectures were sponsored by Young America's Foundation, with support from the John M. Olin Foundation. Others were sponsored by the Intercollegiate Studies Institute.

Portions of this volume have been published previously in a somewhat different form in *The Notre Dame Law Review*, *The Journal of Christian Jurisprudence*, *Law and Contemporary Problems*, *The World & I*, *Modern Age*, *The Intercollegiate Review*, *The Woods-Runner*, *The Presidential Studies Quarterly*, Special Report Number 40 of the Public Policy Education Fund, and *The Political Theory of the Constitution*, Vol. III (University Press of America, 1990).

Dr. Kirk was assisted in the preparation of *The Conservative Constitution* by Professor Forrest McDonald and the late Professor M. E. Bradford, as well as by Dr. Marjorie Haney, Mr. Edward Giles, Mr.

Robert Roach, and Mr. Andrew Shaughnessy, who were fellows of the Wilbur Foundation. In the preparation of *Rights and Duties*, I received invaluable assistance from Mrs. Annette Y. Kirk, Mr. Jeffrey O. Nelson, Professor Russell Hittinger, Mrs. Mary Z. Hittinger, Mr. Michael Muncy, Dr. Bruce Frohnen, Mr. Thomas Spence, Dr. James McClellan, Mr. Charles Brown, Mrs. Analeslie Muncy, and once again, Dr. Haney and Mr. Shaughnessy.

The additions and revisions described above required that I edit for consistency and to eliminate repetition and anachronisms. Where it was necessary to alter Dr. Kirk's words, I attempted to avoid altering their substance or effect and to conform rigorously to his tone and style.

The preparation for publication of a collection of lectures and essays, especially that of an author who cannot approve its final draft, is a hazardous undertaking. Any imperfections in this volume should be attributed to its editor, rather than to its distinguished author or those who generously assisted in its publication.

MITCHELL S. MUNCY

Introduction

I N *The Conservative Mind* (1953) and in *The Roots of American Order* (1974), Russell Kirk locates the American constitutional order in the broad history and institutional habits of western civilization. *Rights and Duties* reflects the same general approach, carried out here in the form of discrete essays and lectures. In this work, Kirk engages in both the celebration and analysis of the social, cultural, and political inheritance of the Constitution of the United States—a tradition that is only partially expressed in the written artifact of the Constitution. Forever the Burkean, he had an abiding suspicion of the theorist who would purport to explain the complex habits and institutions of a people on the basis of a single theory. Like any great civilization, the American order cannot be reduced to a single, actuating principle. As Kirk protests in chapter eight, the Constitution is not "Lockean" in the sense that some theorists are wont to insist. Nor, for that matter, is it Montesquiean, or Madisonian, or Rawlsian. Rather, the constitutional order is like "some immense tree" having many roots of order.[1] Although he calls these essays a "desultory examination" of the Constitution, each relates to his theme of the unwritten constitution.

The previous edition of this book, *The Conservative Constitution*, was published three years after the bicentenary of the ratification of the U. S. Constitution, one year before the bicentenary of the Bill of Rights, and on the exact bicentennial of Edmund Burke's *Reflections on the Revolution in France*. Kirk invites us to "look at America's basic law, and America's politics today, through Burke's eyes."[2] From this perspective, the question today is much the same as it was two centuries ago: Why do some constitutions resist "the tooth of time," while other constitutions come and go with the season? The ideals of constitutional democracy, commitment to the transcendent rights of man, and even the soundness of a written constitution do not sufficiently explain why the basic law of the United States, almost alone among the constitutions of the modern period, has remained relatively unchanged over these centuries. History shows that in Europe and its former colonies, constitutions have not so endured; and this, despite the fact that they were often enough written in light of virtuous ideals of justice.

Kirk maintains that the success of the American Constitution is due to its "conservative purposes," both written and unwritten. By "conservative," Kirk does not mean resistance to any change; nor does he mean the legal hallowing of traditional precepts of morality or religion. On the first score, conservatism is not neophobia. Kirk's models of conservatism were Whigs rather than Tories. The last great Whig, Edmund Burke, wrote: "Change is the means of our preservation."[3] We Americans are avid for social, technological, and economic change; yet, as Kirk points out, even the most abrupt changes have rarely led to an alteration of the written Constitution. In the twentieth century, the Constitution has been amended only twelve times, and two of these involved the adoption and repeal of Prohibition. Arguably, only the Sixteenth Amendment (1913), empowering Congress to tax incomes, and the Nineteenth Amendment (1920), extending suffrage to women, have had a lasting effect upon our institutions and culture.

On the second score, Kirk does not credit Americans of any period with being especially virtuous. In *The Conservative Mind*, he writes: "American character, individualistic, covetous, contemptuous of restraint, always had been stubborn clay for the keepers of tradition to mould into civilization."[4] Like John Adams and Alexis de Tocqueville, Kirk appreciated the "stubborn clay" of American society. Alongside the roots of order are seeds of disorder. Throughout his writings, including these pages, he often uses the word "tolerable" to describe the kind of public order secured by law. Indeed, he rejects the idea that the written Constitution should be much used as an instrument for "improving public morality,"[5] and even less that it should be an all-purpose platform for moralistic rhetoric. John Randolph of Roanoke decried "making the extreme medicine of the Constitution our daily food."[6] It is a sentiment with which Kirk agreed. The Constitution, after all, does not embrace the entirety of the constitutional order.

For Kirk, to call the Constitution and its purposes "conservative" means that the basic law preserves the pattern of political order through time and change. This conserving propensity is rooted chiefly in the "unwritten constitution," consisting of many different ideals, purposes, habits, and practices which are only partially expressed in the written artifact. The written Constitution, for example, prescribes the ways that changes are to be enacted; it does not prescribe any particular amendment, and it gives no advice on how deeply or how often amendments ought to be adopted. During the era of the New Deal, the Constitution was amended only twice (neither amendment concerned the agenda of the New Deal), even though the party of reform eventually controlled all three branches of the United States government and had ample opportunity to embed its political aims in the basic law. However important, constitutional texts, legal mechanics, and political power cannot themselves explain the fact that Americans have so rarely altered the frame of the basic law.

Drafted and ratified in an age of revolution just two years before the Constituent Assembly in France adopted the "Rights of Man and of the Citizen," the Constitution of the United States expressed the people's interest in the ordinary tasks of government, such as responsibility for public debts, the orderly transmission of authority, and creation of a postal service. In the unamended Constitution ratified in 1787, the word "liberty" is used but once, in the Preamble; the word "right[s]" is also used once, in Article I Section 8, where Congress is given power to secure "for limited Times to Authors and Inventors the exclusive Right to their respective Writings and Discoveries." In France, state law became an instrument for radical social change, while in the United States, the Constitution, though amenable to such purposes, rarely has been used *deliberately* to attack or change the inherited social order. In his *Commentaries*, Justice Joseph Story wrote: "Indeed, the rage of theorists to make constitutions a vehicle for the conveyance of their own crude, and visionary aphorisms of government, requires to be guarded against with the most unceasing vigilance."[7] Such vigilance, however, is not found ready-made in the written text of the Constitution. It is rooted in the habits and experiences of the people who inherited from the Framers both written and unwritten rules about how this powerful instrument is to be used.

From the beginning to the end of his literary career, Kirk insisted that the United States is unique among the great powers for preserving both the written and unwritten constitutions over time. In *The Conservative Mind*, he remarks: "As for political institutions, the outward shape of things has altered little in either Britain or the United States; and even the inward constitution has changed only in an orderly fashion, with a few exceptions."[8] In *The Roots of American Order*, having noted the changes wrought by the Civil War amendments, he states: "And yet the general character of that American order remains little altered. The circumstances have changed markedly, from time to time, but the laws and the mores have endured."[9]

In *Rights and Duties*, Kirk is somewhat more cautious in his verdict. For example, in contrast to earlier statements on the solidity and continuity of the American constitutional order, he now says that the Constitution has not been *deliberately* changed by the people.[10] "Among the great powers, only the American Republic has not *deliberately* altered its general frame of government—neither the formal written Constitution of the United States nor the unwritten constitution. . . ."[11] This qualification is important, because Kirk understood that the lack of material changes in the written Constitution does not tell the whole story. Change can also take place through official interpretations and usages, and can profoundly alter the myriad of beliefs and practices, purposes and expectations, which constitute the unwritten part of the constitutional order.

Although he sets out to celebrate the conservative Constitution, Kirk voices his alarm that the federal courts are using the Constitution to effect precisely the kind of radical change that has afflicted other regimes. In the Epilogue, he notes: "In my seemingly complacent account of America's conservative ways, then, I have omitted something important: the strong tendency of our courts of law, the Supreme Court of the United States in particular, to remold our political and social institutions nearer to the judges' hearts' desires."[12] Indeed, he quotes Burke's *First Letter on a Regicide Peace*: "Let us not deceive ourselves; we are at the beginning of great troubles."[13]

IS IT POSSIBLE for a Constitution to be relatively unchanged in the material sense but remain only a shell of its former self? If we take seriously the distinction between the unwritten and written Constitution, the answer is yes. Devotion to an unwritten constitution provides for conservative virtues, but it also presents opportunity for great mischief on the part of those who would ignore the positive law of the Constitution in favor of its unwritten ideals. Over time, a people can lose its Constitution even without changing its written provisions. Kirk does not hold that this is the present condition or the ultimate fate of the American constitutional order. But he does worry about a disposition in the direction of radical and deformative change. Hence, we detect that Kirk's mind is working in the vicinity of more shadows than in earlier books. Here and there, he is feeling his way into this territory, trying to take an accurate measure of disturbing changes in the moral and legal culture.

Kirk understood that these changes are not merely cultural, but have become, as it were, constitutionalized. Things can be said to be constitution*alized* even when they are not formally made constitution*al*. Issues of moral and social order, which in past generations were not considered fit subjects of Constitutional deliberation, today are routinely litigated as problems which the Constitution must resolve. These include many, if not most, of the issues we might include under the rubric of the culture wars—from court-ordered school busing to relations between the sexes. As Kirk found with his own experience as an expert witness in the Mobile textbook trial, federal courts have made the religion clauses of the First Amendment speak a language of secular humanism that reminds one of nothing so much as the revolution in eighteenth-century France.

Are the changes of the past forty years, more or less, due chiefly to the excesses of the courts, or do they augur a spiritual change in the people? Whatever the answer, it will have to be formulated in reference to the unwritten constitution. For, as Kirk shows, the American people have been remarkably reluctant to change the written Constitution.

Let us turn, then, to Kirk's understanding of the unwritten constitution. As we might suspect, the unwritten constitution is not easily defined. In his various works, Kirk approaches the idea from more than one direction. At the outset of *Rights and Duties*, he remarks: "For it has been said that every country possesses two constitutions, existing side by side, yet distinct. One of those two is the formal written constitution of modern times; the other constitution is the old 'unwritten' one of political compromises, conventions, habits, and ways of living together in the civil social order that have developed among a people over the centuries." [14]

This notion of the unwritten constitution Kirk celebrates and expounds at length in *The Roots of American Order*, where he maintains that "an order is bigger than its laws, and many aspects of any social order are determined by beliefs and customs, rather than being governed by positive laws." [15] Kirk traces the roots of the unwritten constitution back to ideas, habits, and institutions drawn from ancient Jerusalem, Athens, and Rome, medieval England, and the Protestant Reformation.

The unwritten constitution, however, is not just the roots or sources, but the order that obtains once those sources are filtered through the practices of an actual people. In his *History of the Common Law of England*, Sir Matthew Hale surveys the many historical origins of the common law, from Moses to the ancient Danes, and concludes that they all partake of the common law "by Virtue only of their being received and approved here." So, too, the American order is not an amalgam of western civilization, but an active reception of those sources in a people's practices. It is, in a manner of speaking, a living constitution.[16]

In yet another approach to the unwritten constitution, Kirk calls attention to Orestes Brownson's distinction between "the providential constitution of the people" and "the constitution of the government."[17] Brownson held that the American republic "has been instituted by Providence" to reconcile natural rights and the common good: "Yet its mission is not so much the realization of liberty as the realization of the true idea of the state, which secures at once the authority of the public and the freedom of the individual—the sovereignty of the people without social despotism, and individual freedom without anarchy. In other words, its mission is to bring out in its life the dialectic union of authority and liberty, of the natural rights of man and those of society."[18]

On this view, the unwritten constitution is not just the historical sources, but a forward-looking *telos* that shapes the very form of a society, including its written laws. Brownson pronounced the American Constitution—written and unwritten—"the least imperfect that has ever existed."

Whether we approach the unwritten constitution according to Matthew Hale's common law model, where history streams from the past through the present, or the forward-looking perspective of Orestes Brownson, the unwritten constitution is the immediate creature neither of nature nor of human art. It is an order that includes both, without being reducible to either.

Every constitution can be said to consist of rules that govern the making of rules. That a constitution consists of such ground rules, as it were, is very clear in the written Constitution. The U. S. Constitution delegates and enumerates the powers of government, and in a tolerably clear way establishes those conditions according to which further laws and policies can be adopted. We know, for example, that Congress can make no law respecting an establishment of religion, but that it can establish post offices and post roads. Kirk maintains that the unwritten constitution, like the written Constitution, consists of certain ground rules.

The unwritten constitution functioned as a kind of rule and measure of what can or ought to be contrived by and committed to positive law. For instance, as we pointed out earlier, the Constitution gives Congress power to secure "for limited Times" exclusive rights to authors and inventors for their respective writings and discoveries.[19] The Constitution does not, however, tell Congress whether it ought to award such a right to the inventor of a suicide machine. That judgment, leading to law or policy, is not constitutionalized. Other rules of order will influence such judgments, some of them moral, others scientific. Changes by amendment, of course, are constitutionalized. But even here, the Constitution prescribes only the manner not the substance of changes.

Kirk's point is that the Constitution, taken as "a whole," is an order written and unwritten. The conservative appreciates both, without confusing or separating the two. This is why Kirk was annoyed by those "conservatives" who so emphasize the blackletter law of the Constitution that they denigrate the unwritten order. If the Constitution leaves a judgment to the political branches, the judgment is not necessarily a matter of indifference, nor is just any law or policy appropriate, even with respect to the written Constitution.

This subject arose during the Senate hearings on the nominations of Robert Bork and Clarence Thomas to the Supreme Court. Does the natural law figure at all in constitutional interpretation? We shall return to this problem later. Here it will suffice to point out that Kirk was troubled by the fact that some conservatives confuse two quite different propositions: first, that the judiciary must settle disputes according to the positive law of the Constitution; second, that natural law forms no part of the organic laws of the country. Kirk approved of the first, and criticized the second.[20] He worried that the conservative reaction against judicial uses of natural law would lead to the extreme view that there is no unwritten constitution, that American order is created from scratch in every respect by positive law, and that once it is determined that the Constitution leaves a judgment to the political branches or state governments, the only remaining rule is the fiat (or preferences) of the majority or the fiat of the individual.

Without an unwritten constitution, the political order would only represent juxtapositions of power: first, the specific powers and absence of governmental powers spelled out by the Constitution; second, the powers exercised by the people to legislate, at their discretion, where they are not forbidden to do so by the Constitution; and third, the liberty of individuals to proceed at will in the absence of any positive law pertaining to the choice at hand. So put, this scheme captures fairly well how a written Constitution of enumerated and delegated powers delineates powers and liberties. The social order, however, can only be described misleadingly in the language of powers and liberties. Few would deny this truth. Some conservatives, however, are so eager to close off every path of judgment beyond the text of the positive law of the Constitution that they can fall inadvertently into a kind of operational positivism, or at least into a myopia that narrows constitutional order to the problem of judicial conduct and theories about it.

SUCH MYOPIA is difficult to avoid altogether, because the federal courts have made it their business to teach that the Constitution is chiefly the Bill of Rights, which is, in turn, what the courts determine—not infrequently in the name of unwritten norms.[21] In *Griswold v. Connecticut* the Court discovered an unenumerated right of privacy in the "penumbras, formed by the emanations," of the Bill of Rights. It is not the written text, but the penumbras which, as Justice Douglas insisted, give the Bill of Rights "life and substance."[22] In his concurring opinion, Justice Goldberg proposed that such unenumerated rights are "rooted in the traditions and conscience of our people."[23]

We might ask how Kirk's understanding of the conservative constitution differs from the jurisprudence of liberal judges who also insist that the Constitution as a whole consists of more than the written text. In an article originally delivered as a speech at Georgetown University in 1985, Justice William J. Brennan asserts that when a judge "draws meaning" from the text of the Constitution, he does not speak for himself alone, but seeks "the community's interpretation."[24] When a decision countermands the will of a majority, the justices must render "constitutional interpretations that are received as legitimate."[25] Brennan avers that interpretations can be received as legitimate so long as they are framed, first, in light of the perennial values embodied in the Constitution and the Bill or Rights, and second, insofar as they are adapted to the social condition of the people—a condition that evolves over time.

Brennan does not use the exact language of the "unwritten constitution," but one notes at least a superficial similarity to the idea espoused by Kirk. For Brennan, as for Kirk, constitutional order preserves the pattern of politics through change. Brennan and Kirk agree that the relative infrequency of formal amendments to the Constitution is a virtue rather than a vice. Neither is a reductionist, for each believes that the Constitution, taken as a whole, evinces a complex interplay between written and unwritten norms, including certain transcendent principles of right.[26] Both can approve Calhoun's famous dictum: "[a] constitution, to succeed, must spring from the bosom of the community, and be adapted to the intelligence and character of the people. . . ."[27]

Does the difference between them come down to their respective positions on the substantive values allegedly embedded in the Constitution, or perhaps to their different views on how those values should be applied by the courts? Undoubtedly, on such issues as abortion, school prayer, and the death penalty, Brennan is a liberal and Kirk a conservative. While it is beyond the scope of an introduction to develop their differences at a proper level of detail, two principal differences ought to be mentioned here. The first is broadly philosophical in nature and concerns what Orestes Brownson called "the dialectic union of authority and liberty." The second is chiefly a question of institutional authority, particularly that of the judiciary.

For Justice Brennan, the Constitution as a whole is rather like a piece of music that has a single theme: the steady advancement of human rights, which must be won in every generation against the status quo that majorities are inclined to preserve. By its very nature, this story is incomplete, and thus one can say that it is partially written and unwritten. In his Georgetown speech, Brennan borrows a page from Jefferson's letter to James Madison in the early months of the French Revolution. Jefferson announced that "the earth in usufruct belongs to the living," and that each generation must undergo its own revolution to emancipate itself from the past. This, for Jefferson, represented one of "the elementary principles of society." [28] For his part, Justice Brennan writes: "Our Constitution was not intended to preserve a pre-existing society but to make a new one, to put in place new principles that the prior political community had not sufficiently recognized." [29]

In this view the *telos* of the Constitution is nothing less than the remaking of society generation by generation, and the constitutional order should always be interpreted to defer to the dignity of individual liberty rather than to government—government, that is, not only in its ordinary legislative and administrative functions, but also in its judicial rulings. Explaining the limits of stare decisis, Brennan remarks "our views must be subject to revision over time, or the Constitution falls captive, again, to the anachronistic views of long-gone generations." [30] The standing of a previous decision therefore is not to be corrected in the light of the Constitution, but rather in the light of the needs of the present generation—needs which include the creation "new principles." This method does not exhibit a subtle interplay of written and unwritten constitutions. [31] Instead, the written Constitution is the occasion for, and not the norm of, judgments in favor of social change.

In his oft-quoted dissenting opinion in *Michael H. v. Gerald D.* (1989), Brennan writes: "[In] construing the Fourteenth Amendment to offer shelter only to those interests specifically protected by historical practice, moreover, the plurality ignores the kind of society in which our Constitution exists. We are not an assimilative, homogeneous society, but a facilitative, pluralistic one, in which we must be willing to abide someone else's unfamiliar or even repellent practice because the same tolerant impulse protects our own idiosyncrasies." [32] This case involved a challenge to a California law making the legitimacy of a child irrebuttable by anyone but the lawfully married parents. The precedent for statutes of this sort goes back to English common law, where dubious paternity was resolved in favor of the legal and socio-logical family rather than natural parentage. In short, it protects the family against the indiscretions of adultery. When the majority of the Court refused to find an unenumerated right on the part of the adulterer to enjoy filiation of the child, Brennan scolded his fellow justices for deferring to the state's estimation of the legitimate interests of the family. For Brennan, then, it is not merely the written Constitution that serves as an occasion (rather than a norm) of social change; society itself is to be viewed as an occasion for the advancement of individual dignity. This is why rights, in Brennan's jurisprudence, are not simply claims against the government. Granted that a court cannot adjudicate rights claims until they are lodged against an action of government, the nature of the rights is best seen as claims against society.

It is not difficult to see where the superficial similarities between Kirk's and Brennan's understanding of the unwritten constitution end and the real differences begin. Brennan's "facilitative" society is very nearly the opposite of Burke's trans-generational "partnership"—the "primaeval contract of eternal society." Whereas Kirk, following Burke, holds that society is wiser than the individual, Brennan suggests that the unwritten principle governing the Constitution is that society has no such wisdom. The unwritten constitution does not consist of rules and measures. Or, to put it another way, Brennan does indeed believe that there exists a social wisdom; but on his view it is an abstract wisdom vested in constitutional ideals, not a truly concrete and mediating wisdom of a flesh-and-blood society. For this reason, Brennan sees no contradiction in upholding individual rights as so many immunities against the concrete society in the name of "society" itself.

From Kirk's perspective, Brennan's theory follows the path taken by the French Revolution. It makes the social order the direct object of deliberate change. It is important to note that Kirk disapproved of this revolutionary mentality whether it is effectuated by judges or by legislators, and indeed whether the retooling of the social order is done for putatively conservative ends.[33] Either way, it must produce a Constitution that is "all sail and no anchor," in Lord Macaulay's words.[34] As Kirk points out, there is no good reason to believe that the "personal and shifting" judgments of nine justices can suffice for the "enduring moral standards derived from religion, philosophy, and a people's customs and conventions."[35]

Kirk's brief against such radicalism is not just epistemological. For Kirk, the unwritten societal constitution cannot be understood by opposing the power of government and individual liberty. The liberal will concede that government must exercise such power as is necessary to secure individual liberties. The liberal might also concede that any government that does not plan to be at war with the people must make use of societal conventions to secure individual liberty. The liberal differs from the conservative most deeply on the question of whether the social order has inherent value. Thus, Brennan regards the great drama of constitutional history as the struggle between the individual and the power of society (most potently expressed in the law of the state). Since only individuals have "dignity," deference should be given to the individual unless the government can show a compelling interest in restrictions of his liberty; since society is merely "facilitative" of individual choices and well-being, when individual rights are at stake the government may not appeal to the inherent goods of society as a compelling interest.

In this respect, Brennan's notion of the living and adaptable Constitution, despite some superficial similarites, differs considerably from Brownson's "providential constitution." Brownson spoke not only of the "dialectic union of authority and liberty" (which is superficially similar to Brennan's notion), but also of the reconciliation of the "natural rights of man and those of society." Where Brennan underscores the drama of emancipation, Brownson also emphasizes reconciliation; where Brennan calls attention to the power of the state, Brownson refers also to authority; where Brennan speaks of society as a facilitator of individual rights, Brownson also speaks of societal rights; and where Brennan refers to the common good primarily as abstract and procedural, Brownson has in mind a substantive common good.[36]

In sum, Kirk and Brennan have very different and, in most important respects, opposite understandings of the unwritten constitution.
The one, vested in concrete society, is the source of genuine though
unwritten norms reconciling authority and liberty; the other, vested
abstractly in constitutional ideals, is also the source of unwritten norms,
but its *telos* is the emanicipation of the individual from society.

SOME CONSERVATIVES might respond that although it is certainly true
that conservatives and liberals differ in typical and predictable ways on
a wide range of substantive values, unwritten constitutions of either
sort allow judges to give precedence to natural law or natural rights
over the written Constitution. As Robert Bork once put it, there is no
good reason to believe that "good natural law will drive out the bad."[37]

Kirk's answer to this question is twofold. First, the unwritten
constitution consists of real norms, both natural and customary. To
deny authority to the unwritten constitution is to say that neither the
natural law nor custom has any legal status, except perhaps in a
metaphorical sense. Kirk rejects this position in no uncertain terms.
Notice in *The Conservative Mind*, for example, that the first canon of
conservatism is belief in a body of natural law that "rules society as
well as conscience."[38] Kirk subscribed to the dicta of Roman and English-speaking jurisprudents, who held that the natural law enters into
the organic laws of a people through customs and usages, and eventually
through the many judgments which go into the making of statutory
law.[39] It follows, therefore, that the unwritten constitution does possess
authority.

Kirk makes it equally clear, however, that "[w]hat the natural law
provides is the *authority for* positive law, not an alternative to positive
law."[40] Since positive law grows out of a people's experience in community, "the natural law could not conceivably supplant judicial
institutions." Otherwise, the natural law would speak with a forked
tongue, guiding men to actions in accord with the common good
(including the creation of a system of positive law), while providing
justification for jettisoning those very actions, laws, and institutions

meant to secure that end. Affirming natural law does not imply that legal officials are authorized to transgress the limits fixed to their offices by the positive law.

"We are safe in saying," Kirk writes, "that the Framers, with few conceivable exceptions, believed in the reality of natural law and had no intention of contravening natural law by the instrument they drew up in Philadelphia."[41] Even so, the Constitution of the United States is not "a natural law document."[42] The Constitution, he says elsewhere, "makes no reference to natural and imprescriptible rights, nor indeed to any body of political thought: it is not a philosophical discourse."[43] The proximate rule and measure for the judge is the positive law.

For the relationship between the natural law and the written Constitution, Kirk drew guidance from Orestes Brownson's 1851 essay "The Higher Law."[44] The proximate occasion for the essay was a speech made by William Henry Seward of New York, who argued on the floor of the Senate that the Fugitive-Slave Bill was contrary to the "higher law" and, despite the fact that it carried out an express constitutional provision, should not have been voted for or executed. As Brownson understood the position of Seward and the abolitionists, two propositions were advanced. First, that every human enactment incompatible with the higher law is null and void. So put, Brownson did not dispute this proposition. Second, that one is entitled to hold a seat of authority by virtue of the positive law that one may (at the same time) nullify—albeit, in part. Brownson rejected this proposition.

Brownson contended one must avoid two extremes which attend such disputes. "Mr. Seward and his friends asserted a great and glorious principle, but misapplied it. Their opponents, the friends of the constitution and the Union, seeing clearly the error of the application, have, in some instances at least, denied the principle itself, and their papers North and South are filled with sneers at the higher law doctrine." We recall that Brownson would hold that the "providential constitution" of the American people is the goal of reconciling the natural rights of individuals with those of society. Brownson, then, had to affirm both natural rights and the authority of the written Constitution against those who affirm one to the detriment of the other. Holding these two truths together is no small task in a country that tends to oscillate between these two extremes.

We can appreciate why Kirk so often repaired to Brownson on this specific issue. Kirk too wished to steer a middle course between those who would use the offices of the government as a platform for private judgment, and those who so recoil from using the higher law as an excuse for private judgment that they deny altogether the authority of the natural law. Both extremes end in forms of willfulness which make the human mind the final arbiter of justice. [45] It throws us back into the Brennan problematic of whether the judge ought to defer to the individual or to society. If the laws of society and the judgments of the individual are equally willful, why not defer to the idiosyncrasies of the individual, who is less the bully, and who is bearer of natural rights?

Like Brownson, Kirk refused to settle the problem of natural law along either extreme. On the dispute over Robert Bork's jurisprudence, Kirk held that Bork's understanding of judicial restraint and original intent is correct; he also held that Bork underestimates the history and authority of the natural law in the development of American laws.[46] Those who make the positive law are entitled, indeed obliged, to secure justice according to the general dictates of the natural law. But judges have no natural right to bind the polity apart from the provisions of the positive law of the Constitution. The positive law binds the judge to judge according to the positive law. Judicial decisions are not the fundamental law, but are inferior to it.[47] Whereas Justice Brennan claims to "draw meaning" from the text of the Constitution, Kirk expects courts to find and apply the law according to the text and the original intent of the framers and ratifiers. In one sentence, Kirk mentions that "we have recourse to natural law, as opposed to the letter of the Constitution, only as a last resort, ordinarily." [48]

WE HAVE SHOWN how Kirk's understanding of the unwritten constitution differs considerably from the liberal idea of an evolving constitution overseen by judges. We have also indicated how Kirk differed in a few subtle ways from conservatives who tend toward the opposite extreme. Let us return to the question raised earlier. Can a constitution undergo profound and deformative alteration even though the written Constitution is left, more or less, intact? Kirk himself poses this question in the following way: "Yet how much of the providential constitution, the unwritten constitution, still operates within American society? Is the providential constitution a ghost merely? If so, can the written Constitution be long for this world?" [49]

Kirk leaves little doubt that the main cause of the deformative alterations in the Constitution is the Supreme Court—"the Ephors of Washington": "there exists no clear and present danger of a discarding of the old Constitution by the people, by the Congress, or by the executive branch. Innovative alteration of the Constitution has been the work, instead, of a majority of the justices of the Supreme Court, within the past forty years, chiefly." [50] Having abandoned a "reasonable attachment" to the written text of the Constitution, the Court's "eccentric" jurisprudence undermines the unwritten constitution. [51] For Kirk, the unwritten constitution does not consist of transient perceptions of social needs and policies. He worried, therefore, that once the written Constitution is cast aside, the unwritten constitution becomes amenable to ideologies of the moment, which are in turn constitutionalized through judicial decrees. Under such circumstances, the fact that the written text is not changed does not bespeak a conservative respect for the basic law, but rather a haughty disregard for a Constitution not even worth changing.

Kirk describes the prospects of living under a judicial aristocracy as "bleak," and prospects of fixing the situation as "melancholy." A conservative like Kirk could find no reason to celebrate living under an ersatz constitution created by the courts; on the other hand, he could not relish the kind of agitation that would be required to check the judicial usurpation of authority. With regard to the latter, Kirk considers impeachment of judges and even Congressional action to change the appellate jurisdiction of the Court. [52] Some readers may be disappointed that Kirk provides no detailed policy recommendations for reform of the federal judiciary. Yet Kirk was not a policy analyst and was perfectly content to leave that work to others. Moreover, these lectures and essays were written and delivered during years in which the Republican party had pledged to undertake reform of the courts. He hoped that a political constituency for that reform was gradually emerging.

If Kirk is to be criticized, it might be for his rather sketchy historical account of how the courts acquired such enormous power. One wonders, for example, whether he fully thought through the problem of the Fourteenth Amendment, which he himself concedes was the deepest alteration in the basic law.[53] He mentions, approvingly it seems, Orestes Brownson's rather vehement denunciation of the Fourteenth Amendment.[54] Elsewhere he speaks of the Court "snatching jurisdiction" from state governments on matters of religion[55]; and he concludes that "[a]bout the Fourteenth Amendment, then, there still hangs a cloud."[56] There is not much reason to doubt that Kirk rejected the doctrine of "incorporation" insofar as it is used to impair the reserved powers of the states in matters religious. The Mobile textbook case, mentioned earlier, involved a sidelong challenge to incorporation of the Establishment Clause of the First Amendment.

What was his final and considered judgment of the Fourteenth Amendment, apart from the specific controversy over incorporation of the religion clauses? Was the amendment constitutionally flawed from the outset, evincing a Jacobin moment in the American constitutional experiment, or are the problems due to misapplication by the courts, or perhaps due to the neglect of Congress in supervising the courts? What are we to make of the fact that the American people have generally acquiesced in the unwritten regime of judicial interpretation based on the Fourteenth Amendment, despite its being used almost every season to sweep away the conservative constitution? The Constitution of 1787 worked, Kirk says, not because it was "far-sighted," but because it reflected the "social realities and necessities in the new Republic."[57] Can we say the same today?

In *The Roots of American Order*, Kirk concluded (in 1973) that "whatever America's incertitudes today, it is difficult to find American citizens who can sketch any convincing ideal new order as an alternative to the one long rooted here."[58] The conservative agrees that there is no "convincing" alternative. Yet the flesh-and-blood of culture has a life of its own, and there is no guarantee that the conservative's understanding of right reason will remain a part of the body of unwritten propositions. "And no matter how admirable a constitution may look on paper," Kirk insists at the end of *Rights and Duties*, "it will be ineffectual unless the unwritten constitution, the web of custom and convention, affirms an enduring moral order of obligation and personal responsibility. . . . It is not accident that will preserve them for posterity."[59] Each generation must grasp and defend the sources of law anew. "Of those Americans who dabble in politics at all," Kirk concludes, "many think of such activities chiefly as a game, membership on a team, with minor prizes to be passed out after the latest victory. Yet a few men and women, like Burke, engage in politics not because they love the game, but because they know that the alternative to a politics of elevation is a politics of degradation. Let us try to be of their number."[60] The task of intellectual and cultural renewal is too important to be left to lawyers, much less to the "Ephors of Washington."

RUSSELL HITTINGER

Part I

All Sail and No Anchor?

I

Conserving Order, Justice, and Freedom

I N THE SPRING OF 1789, with the inauguration of President Washington and Vice President Adams, the federal government commenced to function under the Constitution of the United States. That Constitution had been designed by its Framers, in 1787, to conserve the order and the justice and the freedom to which Americans had grown accustomed. And most of the time, during the two centuries since George Washington took his oath of office, the Constitution has succeeded as a restraint upon arbitrary power, rash innovation, and what Tocqueville called "the tyranny of the majority." In short, the American nation has prospered under a conservative constitution.

First, some words of definition. What is meant by this term *constitution*? In politics, *constitution* signifies a system of fundamental institutions and principles, a body of basic laws, for the governing of a commonwealth. It is a design for permanent political order.

Every society develops a constitution of some sort. For without a regular pattern of basic law, a people could not live together in peace. Lacking a tolerable constitution, they never would know personal safety or protection of their property or the love of neighbor. Even savage tribes may be said to be governed by simple constitutions, expressed in custom and convention.

The Constitution of the United States was and is rooted in the experience and the thought of earlier times—which is a major reason why the American Constitution has not perished or been supplanted by some different political system. No civilization could survive for a great while if somehow its political constitution should be swept away and no tolerable new constitution substituted. Deeply rooted, like some immense tree, the American Constitution grew out of a century and a half of civil social order in North America and more than seven centuries of British experience.

The general public thinks of a constitution as a written document. But actually constitutions may be wholly or partially unwritten—that is, not comprehended in a single document, but instead made up of old customs, conventions, charters, statutes, and habits of thought. The British Constitution, ill understood by most Americans, is the principal surviving example of this sort. And even the Constitution of the United States is not wholly set down on paper.

For it has been said that every country possesses two constitutions, existing side by side, yet distinct. One of those two is the formal written constitution of modern times; the other constitution is the old "unwritten" one of political compromises, conventions, habits, and ways of living together that have developed among a people over the centuries. Thus, for instance, certain important features of America's national political structure are not even mentioned in our written Constitution. What does the written Constitution of the United States say about political parties? Nothing; yet political parties direct the course of our national affairs. What does our written Constitution say about the president's cabinet, with its secretaries of state, treasury, agriculture, defense, education, and the like? Next to nothing; yet the executive branch of the federal government could not function without that cabinet. What does our Constitution say about presidential primary elections, nowadays the principal means for nominating candidates for the presidential office? Nothing whatsoever; yet the primaries have quite supplanted the method of selecting presidents intended by the Constitution's Framers.

The aim of a good constitution is to achieve in a society a high degree of political harmony, so that order and justice and freedom may be maintained. No commonwealth ever has attained perfect order, justice, and freedom for everybody, and the Framers did not expect to achieve perfection of human nature or government. Yet they did expect "to form a more perfect union" and to exceed other nations of their time, and of earlier eras, in establishing a good political order.

Over the centuries, political constitutions have come into existence in a variety of ways. They may be decreed by a king or an emperor; they may be proclaimed by some conqueror or tyrant; they may be given to a people by religious prophets, as Moses gave laws to the wandering Israelites; they may be designed by a single wise man, as Solon gave the Athenians a new constitution early in the sixth century before Christ; they may grow out of the decisions of judges and popular custom, as did the English common law; they may be agreed upon by a convention. Those constitutions which have been accepted willingly by the leaders of a people generally have been the constitutions that have endured for a tolerable length of time.

But humankind being restless and quarrelsome, and because for the past three centuries the conditions of society have altered mightily in many countries, few constitutions have lasted a great many years. Nearly all the national constitutions that were promulgated in Europe after the First World War had collapsed by the end of the Second World War, if not earlier; most of the new constitutions proclaimed in Europe, Asia, and Africa not long after the Second World War already have been tossed aside or else do not really function. The elaborate constitution of the old Soviet Union was ignored in practice from the time it was drawn up.

Of those constitutions which have endured for some generations or some centuries—the British Constitution being the most venerable of these—all have changed somewhat with the passage of time, neces-sarily. Yet enduring constitutions contain provisions and assumptions which are permanent, preserving a society's continuity through many generations. The spirit of such a constitution resists the tooth of time. Such has been the Constitution of the United States.

So much by way of succinct definitions. We turn to the question of the Constitution's conservatism.

IN THE SENSE that all constitutions are formed with the purpose of maintaining some sort of political order—or at least in that pretense—*all* constitutions are conservative. But the Constitution of the United States, over two centuries old, is especially and deliberately conservative of a social inheritance. This truth has been commented upon by several eminent observers from abroad.

Less than half a century after the Constitutional Convention of 1787, Alexis de Tocqueville described the United States Constitution as a work of political wisdom uniquely successful in maintaining in a healthy tension the claims of central authority and the claims of state and local freedom. He found in the Constitution restraints upon the egalitarian impulse, helping to preserve America from what he called "democratic despotism." In his lengthy analysis of the Constitution's articles, Tocqueville indeed points to several grave flaws, especially the possibility of presidential re-elections, with consequent dangers. But in general Tocqueville heartily approves the Constitution as a strong means for maintaining liberty under law—a device very different from the several French constitutions that had arisen and fallen in his own lifetime.

Throughout the first half of the nineteenth century, European and British observers often remarked with a degree of wonder the stability of the Americans' constitutional structure, in contrast with the up-heavals of 1830 and 1848 in Europe, and even in Britain the violence that preceded the Reform Bill of 1832 and the Chartist riots. But this approbation had some strong exceptions, notably that of Thomas Babington Macaulay. In 1857, old Lord Macaulay wrote to Henry S.

Randall, the American biographer of Thomas Jefferson, that Jeffersonianism would bring about the ruin of the American Republic. The paper Constitution would be of no avail in an hour of social crisis. America, unlike Britain, having no ruling class of educated and propertied gentlemen accustomed to command and to restrain popular appetites, had no body of customs and usages that could allay popular discontent. This passage from Macaulay's letter is well known:

> It is quite plain that your government will never be able to restrain a distressed and discontented majority. For with you the majority is the government, and has the rich, who are always a minority, absolutely at its mercy. The day will come when, in the State of New York, a multitude of people, none of whom has had more than half a breakfast, or expects to have more than half a dinner, will choose a Legislature. Is it possible to doubt what sort of a Legislature will be chosen? On one side is a statesman preaching patience, respect for vested rights, strict observance of public faith. On the other is a demagogue ranting about the tyranny of capitalists and usurers, and asking why anybody should be permitted to drink Champagne and to ride in a carriage, while thousands of honest folk are in want of necessities. Which of the two candidates is likely to be preferred by a working man who hears his children cry for more bread? I seriously apprehend that you will, in some such season of adversity as I have described, do things which will prevent prosperity from returning; that you will act like people who should in a year of scarcity, devour all the seed corn, and thus make the next year, not of scarcity, but of absolute famine. There will be, I fear, spoliation. The spoliation will increase the distress. The distress will produce fresh spoliation. There is nothing to stop you. Your Constitution is all sail and no anchor. As I said before, when a society has entered on this downward progress, either civilization or liberty must perish. Either some Caesar or Napoleon will seize the reins of government with a strong hand, or your republic will be as fearfully plundered and laid waste by barbarians in the twentieth century as the Roman Empire was in the fifth;—with this difference, that the Huns and Vandals who ravaged the Roman Empire came from without, and that your Huns and Vandals will have been engendered within your own country by your own institutions.[1]

What Macaulay predicted has not yet come to pass—although we have now in America a genuine proletariat of the sort Macaulay dreaded, though that proletariat as yet is a minority in any state. Is the American Constitution indeed "all sail and no anchor"? Four years after Macaulay wrote to Randall, the Union fell apart and the Constitution, in effect, was suspended for four years. Yet whatever the weaknesses of the Constitution, and by whatever favorable circumstances it has been assisted, still it has endured as a conservative power when every other country's written constitution has been discarded or else revised out of recognition. It has been altered far less, over the generations, than has the British Constitution. Much that Macaulay thought essential to the Constitution of England has been effaced. While the American Constitution, despite its Reconstruction Amendments, despite grand changes by decisions of the Supreme Court, remains long after Macaulay's warning a barrier to radical alteration of American society.

By 1885, when Sir Henry Maine published *Popular Government*, it had become clear enough that the Constitution of the United States was more of a conservative power than the British Constitution had become. The august historical jurist allotted a fourth of his book to an examination of the American Constitution, and as Sir Ernest Barker remarked half a century later, for Maine it was *ex America lux*.

In Britain, by 1885, thoughtful men had taken alarm at the dissemination of socialist ideas. The total exclusion of king or queen from politics, the diminishing of the authority of the House of Lords, the admitting to the franchise of most workingmen, the fact (first made plain by Walter Bagehot) that in effect Britain was now governed by a committee of the House of Commons called the cabinet—these and other large alterations in the old British Constitution had opened the way for the radical egalitarians. Separation of powers no longer prevailed in Britain: the House of Commons was supreme, judicial restraint upon Parliament never had existed, and altogether the British Constitution in the closing decades of the nineteenth century had lost many of the features that Montesquieu had praised at the middle of the eighteenth century.

"The Federal Constitution has survived the mockery of itself in France and in Spanish America," Maine wrote. The American Constitution's success, he went on, has been "great and striking."[2] Especially Maine emphasized the conservative function of the Supreme Court, the indirect creation of Montesquieu, but also founded in part on English methods of adjudication.

Constitutional protections of property and contract, reinforced by Supreme Court rulings, are praised by Maine:

> I have seen the rule which denies to the several States the power to make any laws impairing the obligations of contracts criticized as if it were a mere politico-economical flourish, but in point of fact there is no more important provision in the whole Constitution. Its principle was much extended by a decision of the Supreme Court [*Dartmouth College v. Woodward*, 1819] which ought now to interest a large number of Englishmen, since it is the basis of the credit of many of the great American Railway Incorporations. But it is this prohibition which in reality secured full play to the economical forces by which the achievement of cultivating the soil of the North American Continent has been performed; it is the bulwark of American individualism against democratic impatience and Socialistic fantasy.[3]

Maine's analysis of the root assumptions behind the American Constitution, and of the British origins of American constitutionalism, are as valid today as they were in 1885, three years before Maine's death. No one ever understood *The Federalist* better than did Maine; and no writer better explains the Constitution's conservative functions. His concluding sentences must suffice us here:

> When the American Constitution was framed, there was no such sacredness to be expected for it as before 1789 was supposed to attach to all parts of the British Constitution. There was every prospect of political mobility, if not of political disorder. The signal success of the Constitution of the United States in stemming these tendencies is, no doubt, owing in part to the great portion of the British institutions which were preserved in it; but it is also attributable to the sagacity with which the American

statesmen filled up the interstices left by the inapplicability of certain of the then existing British institutions to the emancipated colonies. This sagacity stands out in every part of *The Federalist*, and it may be tracked in every page of subsequent American history.[4]

Three years after the publication of *Popular Government*, James Bryce, British ambassador to the United States from 1907 to 1913, brought out the first edition of his famous two volumes entitled *The American Commonwealth*, which were to pass through many editions and printings. In Bryce's chapters one encounters the fullest recognition of the conservative character of the American Constitution. The passages I shall quote here are from the edition of 1919.

Bryce describes two general types of constitutions, the "Flexible" and the "Rigid." England's constitution is flexible: "The Constitution of England is constantly changing, for as the legislature, in the ordinary exercise of its powers, frequently passes enactments which affect the methods of government and the political rights of the citizens, there is no certainty that what is called the Constitution will stand the same at the end of a given session of Parliament as it stood at the beginning."[5] As Bryce points out, the first statesman clearly to understand this point was James Wilson, one of the principal framers of the Constitution of the United States. During the Pennsylvania debates on ratification of the Constitution drawn up in 1787, Wilson emphasized that the British Constitution existed wholly at the will of Parliament:

> The idea of a constitution limiting and superintending the operations of legislative authority, seems not to have been accurately understood in Britain. There are at least no traces of practice conformable to such a principle. The British Constitution is just what the British Parliament pleases. When the Parliament transferred legislative authority to Henry VIII, the act transferring could not, in the strict acceptation of the term, be called unconstitutional. To control the powers and conduct of the legislature by an overruling constitution was an improvement in the science and practice of government reserved to the American States.[6]

In a public lecture at the University of St. Andrews in Scotland, comparing the British and the American constitutions, I touched upon this somewhat perilous flexibility of positive law in the United Kingdom: even the greatest statutes and charters would not be proof against a radical and reckless majority in the House of Commons today. I found that my British auditors were painfully aware, most of them, of this clear and present danger to the British Constitution. The shift of fifty or sixty seats in a general election might conceivably bring about "nationalization" of the land, abolition of the famous boarding schools, and the ruin of the British economy, not to mention other permanent damage to the rule of law in Britain.

But let us turn from the flexible constitution of Britain to the rigid constitution of the United States—for so Bryce styles the American Constitution, declaring that "As the English Constitution is the best modern instance of the flexible type, so is the American of the rigid type." [7] In countries with rigid constitutions, Bryce tells us,

> the laws and rules which prescribe the nature, powers, and functions of the government are contained in a document or documents emanating from an authority superior to that of the legislature. This authority may be a monarch who has *octroyé* a charter alterable by himself only. Or it may be the whole people voting at the polls; or it may be a special assembly, or combination of assemblies, appointed *ad hoc*. In any case we find in such countries a law or group of laws distinguished from other laws not merely by the character of their contents, but by the source whence they spring and by the force they exert, a force which overrides and breaks all conflicting enactments passed by the ordinary legislature. [8]

Even a rigid constitution, Bryce remarks, must undergo gradual alteration. In his words, "No constitution can be made to stand unsusceptible of change, because if it were, it would cease to be suitable to the conditions amid which it has to work, that is, to the actual forces which sway politics. And being unsuitable, it would be weak, not rooted in the nature of the State and in the respect of the citizens for whom it exists; and being weak, it would presently be overthrown." [9]

The Constitution of the United States, however, remained suitable in 1914—and, one may add, remains suitable today—because it has changed and developed in response to national necessities.

Bryce lists three ways in which such change has occurred: formal amendment, interpretation, and usage. Altogether, he calculates, the constitutional changes which occurred in the United States between 1789 and 1914 were far smaller than those which the British Constitution underwent during the same century and a quarter. As he puts it, "So far, therefore, the Rigid Constitution has maintained a sort of equilibrium between the various powers, whereas that which was then supposed to exist in England between the king, the peers, the House of Commons, and the people (i.e., the electors) has vanished irrecoverably." [10]

Bryce recognizes certain weaknesses, or potential weaknesses, in the American Constitution, reminding his readers that "To expect any form of words, however weightily conceived, with whatever sanctions enacted, permanently to restrain the passions and interests of men is to expect the impossible. Beyond a certain point, you cannot protect the people against themselves any more than you can, to use a familiar American expression, lift yourself from the ground by your own bootstraps." [11] But he concludes his lengthy examination of the American national government with hearty and specific praise of the conservative character of the Constitution of the United States, the more noteworthy because Bryce was a pillar of British Liberalism:

> Nevertheless the rigid Constitution of the United States has rendered, and renders now, inestimable services. It opposes obstacles to rash and hasty change. It secures time for deliberation. It forces the people to think seriously before they alter it or pardon a transgression of it. It makes legislatures and statesmen slow to overpass their legal powers, slow even to propose measures which the Constitution seems to disapprove. It tends to render the inevitable process of modification gradual and tentative, the result of admitted and growing necessities rather than of restless impatience. It altogether prevents some changes which a temporary majority may clamour for, but which will have ceased to be de-

manded before the barriers interposed by the Constitution have been overcome.

It does still more than this. It forms the mind and temper of the people. It strengthens their conservative instincts, their sense of the value of stability and permanence in political arrangements. It trains them to habits of legality as the law of the twelve tables trained the minds of the educated Romans. It makes them feel that to comprehend their supreme instrument of government is a personal duty, incumbent on each one of them. It familiarizes them with, it attaches them by ties of pride and reverence to, those fundamental truths on which the Constitution is based.[12]

Bryce's sentences form a fitting conclusion to my remarks on the analysis of the American Constitution by observers from abroad. One might easily extend the citing from other visitors to the American Republic down to the present year.

TOCQUEVILLE, MAINE, AND BRYCE concluded that the Constitution of the United States was sound—and unique. Discernment of the conservative virtues of the United States Constitution does not mean that America's fundamental law may be transplanted readily to other lands: attempts at that generally have failed. As Tocqueville pointed out forcefully, the American constitution is the product of American mores, convictions, customs, and previous political experience; it was formed out of peculiar American circumstances; other democracies could not well adopt it. As Daniel Boorstin put this point more than forty years ago, "The Constitution of the United States is not for export."[13] Nevertheless, in both Democratic and Republican national administrations, the Department of State and major media of opinion have behaved as if the troubled states of Asia, Africa, and Latin America, not to mention Europe, could readily frame constitutions very like that of the United States. Doubtless it would be well for "emergent nations" to take heed of the conservative spirit of the American Constitution. Yet it is not possible for the politicians of very different cultures to emulate thoroughly the American framework of institutions, for their circumstances and necessities are very different from ours. Even if they were so to copy the details of the American Constitution, that house of cards would fall to its ruin within a few years, at most.

On what principles, then, may a constitution be assessed for soundness? Aside from the general object of protecting order, justice, and freedom, one may set down, I think, four primary characteristics of a desirable constitution.

First, a good constitution should provide for stability and continuity in the governing of a country. The subjects or citizens of a political state should be assured by their constitution that the administration of the laws and of major public policies will not change abruptly from one year to the next. What was lawful yesterday should not arbitrarily be declared unlawful tomorrow without formal and prudent amendment of the constitution. The people must be able to live their lives in the confidence that if they obey certain rules, they will not be made to suffer. Such a constitution encourages the growth of economic prosperity, among other benefits. When a country's constitution does not provide a reasonable degree of political stability and continuity, no man or woman may make major decisions without fear of unhappy consequences—as in the Soviet Union under Stalin or in Germany under Hitler.

Second, a good constitution should divide political power among different branches of government and should restrain government from assuming powers that belong to other social organizations, social classes, or individuals. A wise constitution may allocate certain powers to a central government and other powers to regional or local governments; or it may assign certain functions and prerogatives to each of the major branches of government—the executive, the legislative, the judicial. Certainly a prudent constitution will provide safeguards against arbitrary and unjust actions by persons who hold power temporarily.

Third, a good constitution should establish a permanent arrangement by which holders of political authority are representative of the people they govern. To put this another way, under a constitutional order the people ought not to be ruled by a group or class of persons quite different from themselves, who do not at least have the best interests of the majority of the people at heart. This does not necessarily mean that a constitutional government has to be democratic, and still less that it necessarily must provide for one man, one vote. There have been decent constitutional systems, in various times and lands, that were monarchical, or aristocratic, or formed without popular elections. What matters is that the persons who make public decisions and hold political authority should represent the general public interest and usually be accepted by most of the people of a country.

Fourth, a good constitution should hold accountable the persons who govern a state or a country. That is, a governing class or body of public officials should be held responsible, under the constitution, for their actions while in public office, and should give an account of their performance when they leave office. Under a truly constitutional government, no man or woman can be permitted to exercise arbitrary power—that is, to do much as he likes, without regard for laws or popular rights. All officials must be accountable to regular authorities—to courts of law, to some representative or legislative body, to the voting public at election time, to fiscal inspectors, to such devices as impeachment and recall, to some other group or organization competent to judge of performance in office and, if need be, to remove even very powerful persons from office or to punish them for abuse of power or misuse of public funds.

Tocqueville, Maine, Bryce, and other European or British political critics found in the Constitution of the United States the four virtues discussed above. They discerned that the American Constitution was no declaration of abstractions, but instead a practical instrument for governance.

A sound national constitution does not lay down some system of theology or moral philosophy, even though certain constitutions drawn up since the French Revolution have been attempts to do precisely that. A constitution is a design for government, a general plan for the political order of a state. A constitution—that is, a good constitution—distinctly is not a treatise on political and economic and moral theory. Any constitution, or its framers, may be influenced by religious belief or philosophical principles, of course; yet the chief practical purpose

of a political constitution ought not to be confused with the imparting
of a religion or a philosophy. Although in every era the moral order of
a culture affects the political order, it does not follow that preaching a
moral creed in the constitution would be an effective method for improving public morality.

Thus the Constitution of the United States was adjudged sound
in what it refrained from attempting, as well as praiseworthy in its
conformity to the general principles of constitutional purpose. But in
what sense was that Constitution unique?

The really distinctive feature of the Constitution was and is the
Supreme Court, intended to be a conservative tribunal. Without the
justices of the Supreme Court, Tocqueville found,

> the Constitution would be a dead letter; it is to them that the
> executive appeals to resist the encroachments of the legislative
> body, the legislature to defend itself against the assaults of the
> executive, the Union to make the states obey it, public interest
> against private interest, the spirit of conservation against demo-
> cratic instability . . . The President may slip without the state
> suffering, for his duties are limited. Congress may slip without
> the Union perishing, for above Congress there is the electoral
> body which can change its spirit by changing the members. . . .
>
> But if ever the Supreme Court came to be composed of rash
> or corrupt men, the confederation would be threatened by anarchy
> or civil war.[14]

Tocqueville goes on to emphasize the need for a strong and independent Supreme Court—a court of broad scope, the powers of
which, if abused, must be highly dangerous. That peril, indeed, has
come to pass during the latter half of the twentieth century, with the
Court's abandoning of Justice Frankfurter's doctrine of judicial self-
restraint, and its assumption of jurisdiction over matters formerly regarded as "political."

To sum up this first chapter, whatever may be said of certain Supreme
Court decisions since the Second World War, the Constitution con-

tinues to function today as a conservative framework for the Republic. The British Constitution now lies at the mercy of any majority in the House of Commons; and the British population, still a "deferential people" when Walter Bagehot wrote his famous book on the British Constitution, are by no means so attached nowadays to custom and convention as they then were.

Today, no other written constitution is very old, and few can be expected to endure very long. All constitutions drawn up in recent years pretend to be democratic, but some of them are whited sepulchres. Certain constitutions are mostly ideological pronunciamentos, full of sound and fury, signifying nothing; others are lengthy and tedious administrative documents, expressing in fundamental law what ought to be left to statute and administrative rules. Yet others are mere political facades, ignored in practice, all power actually being exercised by a ferocious party or a set of squalid oligarchs. What reasonable constitutions survive to our time are rooted, most of them, in the British constitutional experience—as is the Constitution of the United States.

The Framers of 1787, and President Washington in 1789, did not employ the word *conservative* to describe the Constitution they had shaped. That word did not become a term of politics until the first decade of the nineteenth century and was not much employed in North America until the 1840s. Nevertheless, the Constitution's purpose was thoroughly conservative, and the succeeding chapters of this book are intended to make clear certain aspects of that conservative character.

2

The Controversy over Original Intent

N O MATTER HOW PLAINLY and lucidly written, any statute—let alone any constitution—requires interpretation by judges. It is presumed that judges must govern themselves in their interpretation by the intentions of the Framers of constitution or statute: for judges are not supposed to exercise legislative or executive functions.

Such concerns arise frequently, one jurist expounding the doctrine of "original intent," one justice of the Supreme Court declaring that the Constitution is whatever the Supreme Court wishes to make it. Hot disputes of this sort have occurred ever since the clash between Federalists and Republicans in the first decade of the Republic. In this "original intent" debate there arises the question, "Is the Constitution an instrument for preservation or an instrument for change?"

In this chapter I discuss first the necessity for a doctrine of original intent; second, the difficulties of ascertaining such intent; third, the means which were employed in the past for interpreting the Constitution in the light of original intent. Finally, I shall touch upon the alternatives to conformity to original intent.

THE LEAST CONTROVERSIAL portion of the proposed new Constitution, in 1788, was Article III, concerning chiefly the federal judiciary. Who could obdurately oppose the establishment of federal courts, even though such had not existed under the Articles of Confederation? Obviously any effective general government must have judges to apply its laws. Few at the state ratifying conventions, or in the first Congress under the Constitution, could have fancied how powerful those federal judges might become two centuries later.

Certain Anti-Federalists, nevertheless, objected that federal courts might overshadow or overrule state courts and that federal judges might impede the federal legislative branch, the Congress. Alexander Hamilton replied to these doubting Thomases in *The Federalist*. In Number 81 he declared, perhaps somewhat disingenuously, that never, under Article III, could citizens have recourse to federal courts for suing a state for debts—a point I will take up later. As for judicial usurpation of power, Hamilton endeavored to refute that notion in more than one number of *The Federalist*. As he wrote in Number 77,

> Whoever attentively considers the different departments of power must perceive, that, in a government in which they are separated from each other, the judiciary, from the nature of its functions, will always be the least dangerous to the political rights of the Constitution; because it will be least in a capacity to annoy or injure them. . . . The judiciary . . . has no influence over either the sword or the purse; no direction either of the strength or of the wealth of the society; and can take no active resolution whatever. It may truly be said to have neither *force* nor *will*, but merely judgment; and must ultimately depend upon the aid of the executive arm even for the efficacy of its judgments.

As for interpretation of the Constitution, the Federalists argued that judges could not ignore the plain details of a written constitution.

It would be Congress and the state legislatures that would make the laws; the judges of the federal system would be restricted to applying the statutes passed by the Congress.

In 1787 and 1788 no political faction denied that a constitution must possess ascertainable original intentions: for a constitution is the fundamental law of a land. (In no country are the *decisions* and *rulings* of courts of law themselves the fundamental law of the land; rather, they are interpretations and applications of the law.) Clearly the Articles of Confederation had been intended for certain specified purposes and had been interpreted literally. A principal purpose of the Constitutional Convention in 1787 was to define and clarify the purposes and the intentions of the Union of the thirteen original states. Madison, Hamilton, and Jay published *The Federalist* as a systematic explanation and definition of the original intent of the Framers at Philadelphia.

To people unfamiliar with the concept of political and historical continuity, it may not be easy to explain the necessity for a permanent fundamental law—susceptible of change, indeed, but enduring in essence. A country's constitution is a pattern for the maintenance of order in a society. In the case of the Constitution of the United States, it is a written compact, a formal agreement among the people of the United States to "form a more perfect Union, establish justice, insure domestic Tranquillity, provide for the common defence, promote the general Welfare, and secure the Blessings of Liberty to ourselves and our Posterity." It is a binding social compact—not the fanciful contract or compact of Locke or Rousseau, derived from a human "state of nature" which never did exist—a practical, realistic instrument of government resulting from genuine consensus. As Max Farrand and others have remarked, the Constitution is a bundle of compromises: that is how the Framers achieved consensus.

In other words, the Constitution is a solemn agreement on a national scale as to how the American people shall live together in peace. If this solemn pact that we call the Constitution should come to be regarded as a mere formula of words to be set aside for present convenience whenever a temporary majority or strong-willed minority may choose, the peace soon would be breached. For in such circumstances, the terms of the Constitution would fall null and void, the fundamental law would crumble for lack of an enduring consensus, and every faction or interest would feel free, or perhaps obliged, to pursue its own objects in disregard of the general public interest. That condition of society is called anarchy, in which every man's hand is against every other man's, and habitual obedience to the rule of law ceases. Then we can be kept from one another's possessions and one another's throats only by force. Yet as Talleyrand instructs us, "You can do everything with bayonets—except sit upon them." If a generally accepted basic law, a constitution, dissolves in confusion, even an arbitrary master with troops at his disposal cannot long maintain order.

Permanence and continuity in the law are virtually essential to a society's material success. If this need for constancy and enduring precedent is of very high importance in all laws, it is of supreme importance in basic constitutions. That is the case for recognizing and respecting, so far as possible, the original intent of the Framers of the Constitution.

IT IS NO EASY BUSINESS to ascertain precisely the intentions of the Framers in this or that particular. Large differences of opinion existed among factions and individual delegates at the Constitutional Convention; these were bridged over by large and small compromises; but the language of the compromises sometimes remains ambiguous and perhaps sometimes intentionally so, lest awkward inquiries be raised at state ratifying conventions.

Does the power to coin money, conferred upon the Congress in Article I, Section 7, include the power to print paper money? Does the power to "establish Post Offices and post Roads" imply the power to construct turnpikes and canals at the general expense—or later, to subsidize railroads and then airlines? What are the limits, if any, to the authorization "To make all Laws which shall be necessary and proper for carrying into Execution the foregoing Powers"?

In Article II, the President is empowered to "require the Opinion, in writing, of the principal Officer in each of the executive Departments,

upon any Subject relating to the Duties of their respective Offices. . . ."
Has he no greater authority over members of the cabinet than this?
Has the President power to undertake military actions short of a
declaration of war? No such power is specified in Article II.

As for Article III, concerning judicial power, what is meant, for
instance, by its granting to federal courts appellate jurisdiction in actions
"between a State and Citizens of another State"? What about judicial
review of acts of the Congress or of actions by the Executive? Such
powers of the judiciary are not specified.

In other instances as well, the original intent of the Constitution
is not crystal clear. What, for example, is comprehended in the term
"general welfare"? It does not follow that the original intent is quite
impossible to ascertain, but a search must be undertaken, and differences
of opinion are conceivable.

Some light may be obtained through study of Madison's and Yates's
notes on the Convention's proceedings and other fragmentary accounts
by delegates. The correspondence of the men who were Convention
delegates provides some clues. *The Federalist* is a principal source of
information about intent—although in part those newspaper articles
were special pleading—as is St. George Tucker's American edition of
Blackstone's *Commentaries on the Laws of England.* Joseph Story's *Commentaries on the Constitution of the United States* and James Kent's
Commentaries on American Law are of great value. It may be said that
in general the intentions of the Framers may be ascertained by study,
but that some points always have been in dispute.

Considerable latitude as to original intent must be indulged when
courts endeavor to apply provisions of the Constitution to cases that
involve circumstances very different from the circumstances of 1787.
For the United States does not stand still, and occasionally *stare decisis*
must give ground to accommodate technological change. Consider
the power of Congress "to regulate Commerce . . . among the several
States," which eventually produced the multitudinous activities of the
Interstate Commerce Commission. Did the Framers intend to establish
the present jurisdiction of that body? I offer you a simple illustration
of how powers are expanded.

On a warm day late in August 1787, many members of the Constitutional Convention went down to the banks of the Delaware River to observe the demonstration of John Fitch's new contraption, an oared boat propelled by steam. (The Convention had recessed that day so that a committee might discuss proposals to empower Congress to pass navigation acts.) Edmund Randolph, governor of Virginia, and Dr. William Samuel Johnson, the learned delegate from Connecticut, were among the spectators. Both gave to Fitch certificates attesting his experiment's success. It is doubtful whether Randolph, or Johnson, or any other delegate present on the banks of the Delaware, then foresaw that steamboats would become the subject of an action at law which would greatly affect the interpretation of the Constitution they were drawing up that August.[1]

Yet by 1824, Chief Justice Marshall and his colleagues on the Supreme Court would be deliberating over *Gibbons v. Ogden*, the "Steamboat Case," concerning a monopoly granted to Livingstone and Fulton by New York's legislature for commercial navigation of the Hudson River by steamboats. In his opinion, Marshall expounded the doctrine that the Constitution should be liberally construed, not confined to strict limits, as against a previous decision by James Kent in the same litigation that the general government's powers, originating with the sovereign states, ought to be hedged. Marshall's doctrine has prevailed. Incidentally, in this case Marshall ruled that Congress's power extended to vessels propelled by steam as well as to those propelled by wind—even though no practicable commercial steamboats had existed when the Constitution was drawn up.

In such concerns, as the complexity of American life increased, not only the judicial branch, but the legislative and the executive branches of government, would find it necessary or convenient to resort to the doctrines of implied powers and liberal construction. Some extensions of federal jurisdiction or activity seemed extravagant and pernicious to many people in the first half of the nineteenth century, as other such enlargements have seemed yet more baneful to many citizens in the closing half of the twentieth century. As a specimen of protest against liberal construction of the Constitution, take a passage from the long speech of Representative John Randolph of Roanoke in the House of Representatives, on January 31, 1824—only a few days before *Gibbons v. Ogden* was taken up by the Supreme Court.

The Framers of the Constitution had intended to grant Congress only a minimum power over the economy, Randolph declared. Indeed, if when submitted for ratification it had included a specific provision for laying a duty of 10 percent *ad valorem* on imports, the Constitution never would have been adopted. Here are Randolph's sardonic words:

> But, sir, it is said ... we have a right to regulate commerce between the several states, and it is argued that "to regulate" commerce is to prescribe the way in which it shall be carried on—which gives, by a liberal construction, the power to construct the way, that is, the roads and canals on which it is to be carried: Sir, since the days of that unfortunate man, of the German coast, whose name was originally Fyerstein, Anglicized to Firestone, but got, by translation, from that to Flint, from Flint to Pierre-à-Fusil, and from Pierre-à-Fusil to Peter Gun—never was greater violence done to the English language, than by the construction, that, under the power to prescribe the way in which commerce shall be carried on, we have the right to construct the way on which it is to be carried. Are gentlemen aware of the colossal power they are giving to the General Government?...Sir, there is no end to the purposes that may be effected under such constructions of power.[2]

Nevertheless, "literal interpretation" and "original intent" may not always coincide. I have mentioned already the provision in Article III, Section 2 that "The judicial Power shall extend to Controversies;—between a State and Citizens of another State..." On the face of this clause, surely it appears that the Constitution assigns to the Supreme Court an appellate jurisdiction over suits by citizens of one state against another state, "both as to Law and Fact, with such Exceptions, and under such Regulations as the Congress shall make." A literal reading of this provision of Article III would seem to guarantee that a state government might be sued, against its wish, by citizens of other states.

And yet in truth it appears that this clause probably was not so understood by many of the fifty-five delegates to the Constitutional

Convention; and certainly not so understood by the people who elected delegates to the state ratifying conventions, or by most of the delegates to those state conventions. The several states owed huge debts; their governors and legislatures had been insistent that they must not be sued for these debts, against their will, in federal courts. That federal courts might assume jurisdiction over such suits was one of the principal arguments against ratification of the Constitution in several states, New York among them.

Thus Hamilton, eager to persuade citizens of New York to approve the Constitution, wrote in *The Federalist*, Number 81, "It has been suggested that an assignment of the public securities of one State to the citizens of another, would enable them to prosecute that State in the federal courts for the amount of those securities; a suggestion which the following considerations prove to be without foundation." Hamilton went on to declare that

> there is no color to pretend that the State governments would by the adoption of that plan, be divested of the privilege of paying their own debts in their own way, free from every constraint but that which flows from the obligations of good faith. The contracts between a nation and individuals are only binding on the conscience of the sovereign, and have no pretensions to a compulsive force. . . . To what purpose would it be to authorize suits against States for the debts they owe? How could recovery be enforced? It is evident, it could not be done without waging war against the contracting State; and to ascribe to the federal courts, by mere implication, and in destruction of a pre-existing right of the State governments, a power which would involve such a consequence, would be altogether forced and unwarrantable.

That passage from a high Federalist is clear denial of what the offending clause in Article III seems to imply. It appears to have been the understanding at the state ratifying conventions that states could not, under the new Constitution, be sued by citizens of other states.

Hamilton notwithstanding, in the case of *Chisholm v. Georgia* (1793), the Supreme Court ruled that the state of Georgia might be sued by a citizen of another state. The decision was written by Justice James

Wilson, a centralizer and an advocate of democratic political theories, who in his opinion asserted vigorously that the American people formed a nation, transcending state boundaries.

Although this Supreme Court decision might pretend to be a literal interpretation of the pertinent provision in Article III of the Constitution, the ruling in *Chisholm v. Georgia* was received with fury in Georgia and with apprehension in other states. So when Congress convened, the Eleventh Amendment was passed by overwhelming majorities in both Senate and House almost immediately, and speedily ratified in the several states. "The judicial power of the United States shall not be construed to extend to any suit in law or equity, commenced or prosecuted against one of the United States by Citizens of another State, or by Citizens or Subjects of any Foreign State," the amendment read; and so it has stood, unchallenged, to the present day.

Constitutional amendment is one method for overturning a Supreme Court decision believed to contravene the original intent of a constitutional provision. Yet ordinarily the amendment process is an awkward tool, and only in the undoing of *Chisholm v. Georgia* has retribution been so swift. At least the centralizers of 1824, John Marshall among them, endeavored to produce a constitutional warrant for their decisions and policies, while in 1987 at least one justice of the Supreme Court professed to see no need to justify any decision of the Court by reference to the text of the Constitution. There remain today in the law schools, the courts, and the Congress no "strict constructionists," strictly defined. The defense of original intent is carried on in our time by the juristic heirs of Chief Justice Marshall and Justice Story, the early advocates on the Supreme Court of "liberal construction" of the Constitution.

WE TURN NOW to the question of how provisions of the Constitution have been adapted to changed American circumstances without abandoning the doctrine of original intent. "Change is the means of our preservation," Edmund Burke said—meaning that social institutions, like the human body, must experience change and renewal, or else perish. Responding to great social alterations, the law too must change —but gradually, with high regard for continuity, and not "unfixing old interests at once." The executive or the legislative branch of a representative government can work out necessary change by statute or executive order, but such abrupt changes on a grand scale may be too sudden and sweeping, or on the other hand may be effected too tardily. It seems preferable usually to permit judges to modify laws by degrees rather than to take the risk of damaging the whole frame and spirit of law by frequent legislative or executive intervention.

Therefore in every civilized society the judges have enjoyed some degree of latitude in administering and interpreting the laws of the land. Just how far judges rightfully may go in changing the organic law through reinterpretation has become a much-debated question in Britain and the United States. In America, judges have been given a larger share in power than in any other country, ever. A good many people now accuse them of judicial usurpation.

Judges' thirst for power seemed a highly improbable danger in 1787 and 1788: Alexander Hamilton, James Madison, James Monroe, and other gentlemen politicians remarked on the feebleness of the judicial branch, assuring the public that judges never could be a menace to the separation of powers or to public liberties. Yet only fifteen years after the Constitution's ratification, the executive and legislative branches of the American government were at war with the judicial branch, which had begun to assert its independent authority most forcefully. President Jefferson privately urged the House of Representatives, dominated then by Democratic Republicans, to impeach the Federalist Justice Samuel Chase (formerly a radical). John Randolph, leader of the House, passionately did so, winning a large majority for impeachment. But Chase was acquitted in 1805, on his trial by the Senate. Never since then has a justice of the Supreme Court been impeached, although during President Lyndon Johnson's administration Justice Abe Fortas resigned from the Court, rather than face probable impeachment.

The Framers, in 1787, had created a very powerful Supreme Court. It appears probable that most of the delegates at the Convention

expected the Court to be able to rule in some fashion on the constitutionality of federal or state statutes. Beginning about 1801, the Supreme
Court would assert successfully its power to decide whether or not an
act of Congress should conform to the Constitution of the United
States. President Jefferson, infuriated at this, hoped at the time of the
trial of Aaron Burr for treason that he might succeed in having Chief
Justice Marshall impeached and convicted of failing to maintain "good
Behaviour"—for Article III of the Constitution permits impeachment
of a judge on grounds far less serious than the "Treason, Bribery, or
other high Crimes and Misdemeanors" required for the impeachment
of president, vice president, and all civil officers of the United States.
But Marshall, a shrewd and humorous man, foiled the President.

Until the second administration of Jefferson, it had been thought
by many leading Americans that the power of impeachment might
serve to confine federal judges to the limits of original intent. Alexander
Hamilton, in Number 81 of *The Federalist*, had assured New Yorkers
that the judiciary could not conceivably usurp any powers, a principle
"greatly fortified by the consideration of the important constitutional
check which the power of instituting impeachments in one part of the
legislative body, and of determining upon them in the other, would
give to that body [the legislature] upon the members of the judicial
department. This is alone a complete security."

But this fancied "complete security" was undone by the boldness
and strength of mind of Chief Justice John Marshall, who was con-
vinced that the Constitution conveyed to the Supreme Court the
implied power of judicial review of legislation and of executive orders.
Chief Justice Marshall had his own concept of original intent. He
had known many of the Framers and was the biographer of George
Washington, who had been the Constitutional Convention's presiding
officer. A Supreme Court dominated by Federalists interpreted the
Constitution throughout the control of the executive branch by the
Virginia dynasty of Democratic Republicans.

Liberal construction of the Constitution during those years, however, and for long thereafter, did not signify repudiation of the doctrine
of original intent. After the death of Chief Justice Marshall, and the

death of his learned colleague Justice Joseph Story, still the Supreme Court adhered, by and large, to the concept that there could be discerned an original intent, in most matters, of the Framers and the ratifiers of the Constitution.

In federal and state courts, throughout most of the nineteenth century, the analyses of Story and Kent of constitutional points were cited with high respect, and both writers on jurisprudence were studied in American law schools. The dispassionate writings of these two scholars in the law strongly affected interpretation of the Constitution for decade upon decade, imparting an attachment to the intentions of the Framers. Story's *Commentaries* were carefully edited and enlarged by Professor Thomas Cooley in 1873, and the revised version of Story went through various large printings, remaining a major influence in courts and law schools down to the early years of the twentieth century.

I lack space to touch upon the rise of the schools of jurisprudence known as legal positivism and legal realism here in the United States. Gradually those innovating doctrines of law carried the day in American courts and law schools, despite stubborn resistance. Yet until just over half a century ago, the Supreme Court continued conservative in its decisions, for the most part exercised judicial restraint and, whatever the eccentricity of particular decisions, did not advance the theory that the Court is entitled to do as it likes with the text of the Constitution— although Justice Holmes and some others broadly hinted at that notion.

The doctrine of original intent did not perish utterly when Story and Kent went out of fashion; and today there is being carried on a strong endeavor to restore an understanding of the Constitution in the light of what the Framers and their generation were trying to achieve. Perhaps the best argument in favor of such a restoration is the bleak prospect of what is liable to occur if recent tendencies of the federal judiciary are much prolonged.

IF A REASONABLE ATTACHMENT to the written text of the Constitution— which does not mean a blinkered literalism at all times—is not retained or restored as the standard for interpretation of the basic law of the

United States, we will be left with a most unpromising alternative: the domination of American public policy, and much of American private life, by the impulses, prejudices, and ideological dogmata of the nine justices of the Supreme Court. Their power to do mischief would become almost infinite; their ability to rule prudently would be improbable. In any event, such a scheme would abolish American democracy and enfeeble both Congress and the presidency—if the justices were permitted to perpetuate their assumption of haughty authority, power that courts of law never were intended to exercise. But presumably the Supreme Court would not be permitted to continue in this usurping of power. The Congress and the executive branch, if pushed to the wall, have means for repelling judicial insolence.

The executive branch, given a strong-willed president, could undo the Supreme Court simply by refusing to enforce its writs: extreme medicine, that, but it has been swallowed down as a bitter dose in other countries and times, for good or ill.

The Congress could much curb and chasten the Supreme Court, should it decide to do so, in two ways: first, by greatly reducing the categories of cases over which the Supreme Court exercises appellate jurisdiction, as is authorized in Article III of the Constitution. (Senator Sam Ervin of North Carolina, a considerable constitutional authority, urged Congress to do just this with respect to compulsory "busing" of school pupils.) Such contraction of appellate jurisdiction, in effect leaving whole classes of actions at law within the jurisdiction of state courts only, or at least outside the sphere of federal courts, has happened before in the history of American law.[3]

Second, the Congress could resort to its power of impeaching justices, whose tenure of office depends on "good behavior." Deliberately ignoring constitutional texts and confessedly substituting one's own juridical notions is not good behavior in a justice of the Supreme Court; it might be called subversive of the spirit of the laws.

It would be a melancholy day if either of these remedies had to be applied, for it would mean some interruption of the usual rule of law, or at least of accustomed processes. But what if the Court should be thoroughly dominated by a majority of justices who do not think themselves confined in the least by respect for the terms of the Constitution itself?

The temper of public opinion nowadays will not abide much more eccentricity or perversity of Supreme Court decisions. The odder or more arbitrary those rulings become, the more swiftly does the public's respect for the federal judiciary decline. The Court's decisions in recent years have invaded some of the more intimate concerns and interests of American democracy, and resentments have accumulated. As Edmund Burke said of the notion that the people ought to accept a rational explanation of why their interests are being damaged by public policy, "No man will be argued into slavery."

The original intent of the Framers of the Constitution was to give the American people a Republic of elevated views and hopes. They desired to establish an independent judiciary; they did not mean to create a new form of government, unknown to Plato or Aristotle, that might be termed an *archonocracy*—a national domination of judges. As John Randolph of Roanoke observed, with reference to tendencies of the federal courts in his own time, "I can never forget that the Book of Judges is followed by the Book of Kings."

3

The Rights of Man or the Bill of Rights?

TWO CENTURIES AGO, the United States settled into a permanent political order, after fourteen years of violence and heated debate. Two centuries ago, France fell into ruinous disorder that ran its course for twenty-four years. In both countries there resounded much ardent talk of rights—rights natural, rights prescriptive. Yet the rights proclaimed by the National Assembly in France never took on flesh during a quarter of a century of ferocious social disruption, while the rights expressed in the American Bill of Rights, the first amendments to the Constitution, never have been seriously threatened. It may, therefore, be worthwhile to inquire why the French rights turned out to be such stuff as dreams are made of, and why the civil rights appended to the Constitution of the United States have been so peacefully maintained.

On August 26, 1789 at Versailles, the National Assembly adopted the Declaration of the Rights of Man and of the Citizen, and the tricky phrase "human rights" entered political discourse, so it seems, by its appearance in the first paragraph. The King, on October 5, would be compelled to assent to this Declaration.

On September 25, 1789 at New York, the First Congress of the United States approved and sent to the several states for ratification the first ten amendments to the Constitution, along with two other proposed amendments which, rejected by some states, would fail of incorporation into the Constitution. These ten ratified amendments— of which, strictly speaking, the first eight constitute the Bill of Rights— would take effect in December 1791.

Long before the middle of December 1791, fanatic ideology had begun to rage within France, so that not one of the liberties guaranteed by the Declaration of the Rights of Man could be enjoyed by France's citizens. One thinks of the words of Dostoievski: "To begin with un- limited liberty is to end with unlimited despotism." Declarations on parchment do not implement themselves: if they conflict with harsh reality, they still may work mischief, but they cannot then achieve their intended ends.

To almost anyone glancing for the first time at this French prologue or preamble to a new constitution and at this American appendix to a newly-framed constitution, it may seem that the two documents are similar. Some resemblances between the Declaration of Independence and the Declaration of the Rights of Man are noted readily. Among the seventeen articles of the French Declaration are prohibitions of arbitrary arrest and unusual punishments. Other articles provide for freedom of religious opinions, protection of rights of speech and publi- cation, and a guarantee of respect for private property. Parallels with provisions of the American Bill of Rights are obvious. Moreover, Article XVI of the French Declaration exalts the doctrine of the separa- tion of powers in government—a cardinal principle of the United States Constitution. So can there exist major differences between these American and French documents intended to secure the liberties of the citizen?

Since 1789, France has suffered from successive revolutions and has swept aside constitution after constitution. Since 1789, the United

States of America has experienced only one fierce period of disunity, 1861 to 1865, and America's Constitution of 1787 remains the Union's fundamental law. From the Left Bank of the Seine, revolutionary doctrines have been exported to Cambodia, to Ethiopia, to Latin America; from the city of Washington, conservative preachments issue and are disseminated throughout the world. French political theories and American political practices, during the last quarter of the eighteenth century, produced opposed consequences which still ferment around the globe.

So it may be profitable to examine the expectations, the intellectual sources, and the conflicting theories that shaped the judgments of most deputies to the National Assembly, on the one hand, and of the senators and representatives in the First Congress, on the other. But first, some remarks concerning the conduct of those two very different assemblies which argued constitutional questions during that summer two centuries ago.

THE NATIONAL ASSEMBLY was a tumultuous gathering of some 1,700 persons of widely different origins and backgrounds, shouting at one another. They were painfully aware of the menace of the mob, the Bastille having fallen only a month before their debates on the Declaration. Nevertheless, most of the deputies entertained extravagant notions of social perfectibility, being quite unacquainted with representative government. Intellectually, they deferred to speculative philosophers, among them Condorcet—who would himself fall victim to the Revolution—and the Abbé Siéyès, who edited the Declaration of the Rights of Man. The most earnest advocate of such a Declaration was Lafayette, then commanding the new National Guard, a nobleman of high courage but no great prudence. He sought advice from Thomas Jefferson, then minister to France—another seeming connection between the Declaration and the Bill of Rights—who, among other things, recommended that the French constitution should contain a provision for amending conventions periodically. In the National Assembly were a number of deputies conservative in their views, who inclined toward establishing in France an English form of government, but they were overwhelmed by what Burke was to call "a parcel of hack attorneys."

In striking contrast, the twenty-two senators and fifty-nine representatives who during the summer of 1789 debated the proposed seventeen amendments to the Constitution were men of much experience in representative government, experience acquired within the governments of their several states or, before 1776, in colonial assemblies and in practice of the law. Many had served in the army during the Revolution. They decidedly were political realists, aware of how difficult it is to govern men's passions and self-interest. Their debates at Federal Hall, in New York City, were earnest but civil. They stood in no danger of being intimidated by urban mobs, although disbanded soldiery had to be kept in mind. Agrarian dissidents of the sort who had made up Daniel Shays's following. The French Enlightenment had made little progress among them. Where amendments to the Constitution were in question, the dominant mind among them was that of James Madison—temperate, learned, prudent. Among most of them, the term *democracy* was suspect. The War of Independence had sufficed them by way of revolution.

The contrast of the expectations entertained at Versailles with the expectations in the Congress at New York is striking. Most of the deputies to the National Assembly were bent upon creating a Brave New World, from which rank and pomp, oppression, the remnants of feudalism, Christian orthodoxy, and a multitude of miseries would have been cleared away. Such Enlightenment notions had seduced the minds of even the highest classes in France—or perhaps especially the highest classes. I need not labor this point, which has been made repeatedly by such eminent historians as Tocqueville and Taine, and more recently by Simon Schama in his notable and popular book *Citizens: A Chronicle of the French Revolution.* The French reformers of 1789, with some honorable exceptions, demanded the establishing of an earthly paradise; many of them soon perished in an earthly hell. Mirabeau and a few others were bold enough to declare that a Declaration of the Duties of Man was more needed than a Declaration of

Rights. As in Hawthorne's tale "Earth's Holocaust," the revolutionary politicians flung into the fire every vestige of the old order but for one thing: the human proclivity to sin. Thus the sentimentality and the fantastic aspirations of 1789 brought on the Terror of 1793.

Across the Atlantic, the sober and practical gentlemen who had been elected to the First Congress of the United States knew politics to be the art of the possible. The purpose of law, they knew, is to keep the peace. To that end, compromises must be made among interests and among states. Both Federalists and Anti-Federalists ranked historical experience higher than novel theory. They suffered from no itch to alter American society radically; they went for sound security. The amendments constituting what is called the Bill of Rights were not innovations, but rather restatements of principles at law long observed in Britain and in the thirteen colonies. Freedom of worship, of speech, of the press, and of assembly already prevailed in British North America. The men of all the thirteen states were accustomed to bearing arms in a militia. And so might one run through the Third, Fourth, Fifth, Sixth, Seventh, and Eighth Amendments, pointing out that these, too, were merely protections of rights and usages that already existed in the several states. In short, the Framers of the Constitution, and the Congress that approved the first ten amendments, were concerned more with the preservation of an existing order than with marching to Zion. So amended, the Constitution of the United States kept the peace for seven decades.

We turn to the ideas or assumptions that lay behind the proceedings at Versailles and the ideas or assumptions behind the proceedings at New York. Obviously the Declaration of the Rights of Man is a document of the Enlightenment—that is, contemptuous of the Christian and medieval past, though often adulatory of things Roman or Hellenic, fascinated by scientific discoveries, proud of modernity. But in the National Assembly, the Enlightenment's rationalism and skepticism, derived from Voltaire, D'Alembert, Diderot, and other Enlighteners, were curiously intertwined with Jean-Jacques Rousseau's sentimental egalitarianism and primitivism. As Friedrich Heer observes in his *Intellectual History of Europe*, "Rousseau's importance was, perhaps, greater than Voltaire's. Virtually all the various streams of mystical and sectarian stamp came to expression in his capacious ego. There is hardly a false tone of feeling, joy in nature, self-intoxication, intuition, gush or enthusiasm in the nineteenth century which cannot be found somewhere in Rousseau. . . . He was revered as a prophet and a saint."[1]

The cynical Voltaire, enemy of absolutism and of religion; the sentimental Rousseau, who would sweep away state, church, property, and moral convention—these two, so different in mentality, were the ghosts haunting but inspiring the National Assembly, and later the Convention. Man, naturally virtuous and great-souled, had been corrupted by institutions, especially by private property: so Rousseau had preached. Wipe away the old order of things; set man free to follow his impulses, preferably on some tropic isle; follow nature. This vision is what Irving Babbitt called the idyllic imagination, as opposed to the moral imagination. As applied by enthusiastic revolutionaries, this idyllic imagination soon would be transformed into what T. S. Eliot called the diabolic imagination, with the Marquis de Sade, Terrorist, as its notorious champion in letters.

The perfection of human nature and society: that was the aspiration of the men who, amidst great confusion, patched together the Declaration of the Rights of Man and of the Citizen. To accomplish this, they fancied, the shackles of the past must be struck off. In that cause, Rousseau's "General Will" became, in the words of De Maistre, "a battering ram with twenty million men behind it." And the doctrine of the General Will crushed the liberty so ardently sought by the French enthusiasts.

Out of the Napoleonic era would come the word *ideologue*, previously unknown to the French and English languages. The Americans who approved the first ten amendments to their Constitution were no ideologues. Neither Voltaire nor Rousseau had any substantial following among them. Their political ideas, with few exceptions, were those of English Whigs. The typical textbook in American history used to inform us that Americans of the colonial years and the Revolutionary and Constitutional eras were ardent disciples of John Locke. This notion was the work of Charles A. Beard and Vernon L. Parrington, chiefly. It fitted well enough their liberal convictions, but—as I will point out later—it has the disadvantage of being erroneous.

The American politicians of the country's formative years did not shape their policies according to books. As Patrick Henry had declared at the beginning of the Revolution, "I have but one lamp by which my feet are guided, and that is the lamp of experience." Their political inheritance from Britain, and their social development during the colonial era: these were the principal sources of their political ideas. They had no set of *philosophes* inflicted upon them. Their morals they took, most of them, from the King James Bible and the Book of Common Prayer. Their Bill of Rights made no reference whatever to political abstractions; the Constitution itself is perfectly innocent of speculative or theoretical political arguments, so far as its text is concerned. John Dickinson, James Madison, James Wilson, Alexander Hamilton, George Mason, and other thoughtful delegates to the Convention in 1787 knew something of political theory, but they did not put political abstractions into the text of the Constitution.

The mentality of the American leaders, in short, differed greatly from the mentality of most deputies to the National Assembly. An historical consciousness was possessed by the Americans, but political and moral speculation obsessed the French of 1789, as becomes clear when one examines the text of the Declaration of the Rights of Man.

"MEN ARE BORN and always continue free and equal in respect of their rights," proclaims the first article of the Declaration of the Rights of Man. "Civil distinctions, therefore, can only be founded on utility." Those phrases seem to have the ring of the Declaration of Independence. But Carl Becker, in his study of that document, remarks that "it does not appear that the Declaration of Independence suggested to the French the idea of a declaration of rights, or that it served as a model for the Declaration of Rights which they in fact adopted. It was the event itself, the American Revolution rather than the symbol of the event, which exerted a profound influence upon the course of French history."[2]

The second article of the Declaration of the Rights of Man specifies the "natural and imprescriptible" rights of liberty, property, security, and resistance to oppression. These expressions seem to have been drawn from French and English political writers earlier in the century—not from the Declaration of Independence. Among reformers in Europe, such terms were the common currency of the age.

We ought not to assume that the Declaration of the Rights of Man was derived from American ideas and institutions. The American Constitution, written only two years earlier, makes no reference to natural and imprescriptible rights, not indeed to any body of political thought: it is not a philosophical discourse. It would be erroneous to analyze the Declaration of the Rights of Man as if Frenchmen had fancied *ex America lux*. Rather, the French Declaration reflects, as we observed, the politics and morals of Rousseau, as well as elements derived from Voltaire and from the Physiocrats. We glance here at certain articles of that Declaration.

Articles IV and V are concerned with the liberty of the individual, as Rousseau perceived it. The sort of liberty favored by Rousseau would become the creed of nineteenth-century liberals, notably of John Stuart Mill. "The exercise of the natural rights of every man has no other limits than those which are necessary to secure to every other man the free exercise of the same rights; and those limits are determinable only by the law."

And Article V instructs French citizens, "The law ought to prohibit only actions hurtful to society. What is not prohibited by the law, should not be hindered; nor should anyone be compelled to that which the law does not require."

Probably most members of the First Congress, being Christian communicants of one persuasion or another, would have been dubious about the doctrine that every man should freely indulge himself in whatever is not specifically prohibited by positive law and that the state should restrain only those actions patently "hurtful to society." Nor did Congress then find it necessary or desirable to justify civil liberties by an appeal to a rather vague concept of natural law—for a reason I will touch upon presently.

Article VI of the Declaration is an enactment of Rousseau's General Will. "The law is an expression of the will of the community. All citizens have a right to concur, either personally, or by their representatives, in its formation. It should be the same to all, whether it protects or punishes; and all being equal in its sight, are equally eligible to all honors, places, and employments, according to their different abilities, without any other distinction than that created by their virtues and talents."

A "right to concur" is guaranteed here, but no right to dissent from the General Will. (One thinks of the old Jewish doctrine of "compulsory consent.") "Natural law" abruptly vanishes from sight in this article, supplanted by the "will of the community." The phrases of the Declaration of Independence notwithstanding, the assertion of egalitarianism here would not have been relished by many of the delegates to the Philadelphia Convention in 1787; nor would President Washington have embraced this Article VI. (Washington did not reply to Lafayette's request for fatherly advice concerning the new frame of government in France.)

The final article in the Declaration of the Rights of Man, nevertheless, is not derived from Rousseau: "XVII. The right to property being inviolable and sacred, no one ought to be deprived of it, except in cases of evident public necessity legally ascertained, and on condition of a previous just indemnity." The Americans had not thought it necessary to insert in their Constitution a protection for property so emphatic: Article I, Section 10, forbade states to impair the obligation of contracts, and Amendment VI would forbid the taking of property without due process of law, or the taking of private property for public use without just compensation; but there was no solemn pronouncement of inviolability.

Nor did the Americans declare that property is sacred. As Christians, most of them would have said that only the things of God are sacred. This emphasis on the sacred, occurring repeatedly through the Declaration, seems somewhat amusing, when one recalls that the leaders of the successive revolutionary movements in France between 1789 and 1795 commonly were Deists, skeptics, or atheists. Yet the power of the dead Rousseau compelled the insertion into the nascent Declaration, on August 20, 1789, by amendment, of a reluctant acknowledgment of the existence of the Supreme Being.

That formidable and eccentric orator Mirabeau thought that this Declaration, unveiled so soon by the National Assembly, would tempt the common people to abuse their new powers. He regarded the Rights of Man as "a secret which should be concealed until a good Constitution had placed the people in a position to hear it without danger." But few other deputies supported him in this argument. Indeed the Declaration of the Rights of Man and of the Citizen was to the people of France an intoxicating novelty, its provisions to be realized immediately, while the American Bill of Rights was no surprise at all to American citizens, well accustomed to such provisions in their several state constitutions.

I PROCEED TO INQUIRE now concerning the chief line of demarcation between the primary assumptions of the French reformers and the primary assumptions of the Framers of the first eight amendments to the Constitution of the United States. The French deputies in 1789, seeking some sanction for the "sacred" rights of man, turned to natural right doctrines, although not really the tradition of natural law that runs from Cicero through the Schoolmen to Richard Hooker. This natural right argument not always sufficing them, also they turned to the abstractions and the visions of such speculative minds as Rousseau's.

Why did they not turn to precedent, prescription, custom, as did the British? Because the French reformers of 1789 held precedent, prescription, and custom in contempt, as if such influences were the dead hand of the past. Mounier, Lally-Tollendal, and some others did contend for the British understanding of social continuity, but they were a small minority. Moreover, France had lost long before any vestige of genuine representative government that might have been emulated in 1789.

Therefore the French "Rights of Man" were amorphous, and lacked legal precedents. From the moment of their declaration, they were flouted—and often by the very neophyte politicians who had promulgated them so vociferously as "a Declaration for all men, for all times, for every country, that will be an example to the whole world!" To apprehend how a professed zealot for the Rights of Man might condemn thousands of men and women to the guillotine, after trials in which the accused had been denied legal counsel or witnesses on their behalf, one need merely recollect the rhetoric of various Third World despots and recollect also the frightfulness of their rule. The Universal Declaration of Human Rights promulgated by the United Nations was inspired by the Declaration of the Rights of Man—and has been no more efficacious.

The Bill of Rights drawn up by the Congress in 1789, to the contrary, did not refer at all to natural rights or to utopian speculations. Its sanctions were ancient statute and charter, the common law, precedent, British usage, colonial custom. Freedom of religious belief and practice had been more fully experienced in British North America than anywhere else in the world. From the planting of British colonies in Virginia and Massachusetts onward, every American settlement had drilled its own "well regulated militia." The colonial governments never had quartered troops in private houses in time of peace, except "in a manner to be prescribed by law." Unreasonable searches and seizures had been prohibited by British statutes since the middle of the seventeenth century. Due process in criminal cases was another inheritance from English law, as was trial by jury. Excessive bail, excessive fines, and cruel and unusual punishments already were forbidden in English law and in the laws of the several states. In effect, the guarantees and protections of the first eight amendments were principally reaffirmations, binding the federal government, of rights and immunities already established and accepted as a matter of course in the thirteen states. Those rights were what Edmund Burke, in 1790, would call the "chartered rights" of Englishmen—and of Americans. Unlike the French reformers, such American statesmen as James Madison and Fisher Ames did not proclaim the Bill of Rights they had written as applicable throughout the world at all times. The first eight amendments were an inheritance, not a novel creation. Their genealogy might be traced back by Americans to the Bill of Rights, in England, of 1689; to the Petition of Right of 1628; all the way back, indeed, to the Magna Carta in 1215.

It was otherwise among the French of 1789, with their relish for grandiose abstraction. The judgment of Lord Acton upon the Declaration of the Rights of Man and of the Citizen summarizes the matter. Acton said, in 1896:

> The Declaration passed, by August 26, after a hurried debate, and with no further resistance. The Assembly, which had abolished the past at the beginning of the month, attempted, at its end, to institute and regulate the future. These are its abiding works, and the perpetual heritage of the Revolution. With them a new era dawned upon mankind.
>
> And yet this single page of print, which outweighs libraries, and is stronger than all the armies of Napoleon, is not the work of superior minds, and bears no mark of the lion's claw. The stamp of Cartesian clearness is upon it, but without the logic, the precision, the thoroughness of French thought. There is no indication in it that Liberty is the goal, and not the starting-point, that it is a faculty to be acquired, not a capital to invest, or that it depends on the union of innumerable conditions, which embrace the entire life of man. Therefore it is justly arraigned by those who say that it is defective, and that its defects have been a peril and a snare. [3]

Two centuries later, the provisions of the Bill of Rights endure—if sometimes strangely interpreted. Americans have known liberty under law, ordered liberty, for more than two centuries, while states that have embraced the Declaration of the Rights of Man and of the Citizen, with its pompous abstractions, have paid the penalty in blood.

PART II

REVOLUTIONARIES AND FRAMERS

4

A Revolution Not Made, but Prevented

F OR RIGHTLY APPREHENDING the purpose and the
character of the written Constitution of the United States,
one needs knowledge of that Revolution, or War of Independence, which had parted the original thirteen colonies from
their old source of order and authority, the Crown in Parliament. For
in essence the Constitution was drawn up to re-establish a civil social
order.

Was the American War of Independence a revolution? In the
view of Edmund Burke and the English Whig factions generally, it
was not the sort of political and social overturn that the word *revolution* has come to signify nowadays. Rather, it paralleled that alteration
of government in Britain which accompanied the accession of William
and Mary to the throne, and which is styled, somewhat confusingly,
"The Glorious Revolution of 1688."

Burke's learned editor E. J. Payne summarizes Burke's account of
the events of 1688 and 1689 as (in the phrase of Sir Joseph Jekyll) "in

truth and in substance, a revolution not made, but prevented."[1] Let us see how that theory may be applicable to North American events nine decades later.

We need first to examine definitions of that ambiguous word *revolution*. The signification of the word was altered greatly by the catastrophic events of the French Revolution, commencing only two years after the Constitutional Convention of the United States. Before the French explosion of 1789 and 1790, *revolution* commonly was employed to describe a round of periodic or recurrent changes or events— that is, the process of coming full cycle, or the act of rolling back or moving back, a return to a point previously occupied.

Not until the French radicals utterly overturned the old political and social order in their country did the word *revolution* acquire its present general meaning of a truly radical change in social and governmental institutions, a tremendous convulsion in society, producing huge alterations that might never be undone. When the eighteenth-century Whigs praised the Revolution of 1688, which established their party's domination, they did not mean that William and Mary, the Act of Settlement, and the Bill of Rights had produced a radically new English political and social order. On the contrary, they argued that the English Revolution had restored tried and true constitutional practices, preservative of immemorial ways. It was James II, they contended, who had been perverting the English constitution. His overthrow had been a return to the old constitutional order. The Revolution of 1688, in short, had been a healthy reaction, not a bold innovation.

But what of the events in North America from 1775 to 1781? Was the War of Independence no revolution?

That war, with the events immediately preceding and following it, constituted a series of movements that produced separation from Britain and the establishment of a different political order in most of British North America. Yet the Republic of the United States was an order new only in some aspects, founded upon a century and a half of colonial experience and upon institutions, customs, and beliefs mainly of British origin. The American Revolution did not result promptly in the creation of a new social order, nor did the leaders in that series of movements intend that the new nation should break with the conventions, the moral convictions, and the major institutions (except monarchy) out of which America had arisen. As John C. Calhoun expressed this three-quarters of a century later, "The revolution, as it is called, produced no other changes than those which were necessarily caused by the declaration of independence."

To apprehend how the leading Americans of the last quarter of the eighteenth century thought of their own revolution, it is valuable to turn to the arguments of Edmund Burke, which exercised so strong an influence in America—an influence more telling, indeed, after the adoption of the Constitution than earlier. (Until my own generation, Burke's *Speech on Conciliation with the American Colonies* was studied closely in most American high schools.)

In his *Reflections on the Revolution in France*, as earlier, Burke strongly approves the Revolution of 1688. "The Revolution was made to preserve our *antient* indisputable laws and liberties, and that *antient* constitution of government which is our only security for law and liberty," Burke declares.

> The very idea of the fabrication of a new government is enough to fill us with disgust and horror. We wished at the period of the Revolution, and do now wish, to derive all we possess as *an inheritance from our forefathers*. Upon that body and stock of inheritance we have taken care not to inoculate any cyon alien to the nature of the original plant. All the reformations we have hitherto made, have proceeded upon the principle of reference to antiquity; and I hope, nay I am persuaded, that all those which possibly may be made hereafter, will be carefully formed upon analogical precedent, authority, and example. [2]

The Whig apology for the expulsion of James II, then—here so succinctly expressed by Burke—was that James had begun to alter for the worse the old Constitution of England: James was an innovator. As Burke writes elsewhere in his *Reflections*, "To have made a revolution is a measure which, *prima fronte*, requires an apology." A very similar apology, we shall see, was made by the American leaders in their quarrel with King and Parliament, and for their act of separation. The Whig magnates had prevented James II from working a revolution; the American Patriots had prevented George III from working a revolution. If the events of 1688 and 1776 were revolutions at all, they were counter-revolutions, intended to restore the old constitutions of government. So, at any rate, runs the Whig interpretation of history.

By 1790, Burke and the Old Whigs were already involved in difficulty by this troublous word *revolution*. For the same word was coming to signify two very different phenomena. On the one hand, it meant a healthy return to old ways; on the other hand, it meant, with reference to what was happening in France, a violent destruction of the old order. The English Revolution and the French Revolution were contrary impulses—although for a brief while, with the summoning of the long-dormant Three Estates, it had appeared that the French movement might be in part a turning back to old political ways as well.

In America, the dominant Federalists—and soon not the Federalists only—were similarly perplexed by that word. Here they stood, the victors of the American Revolution—Washington and Hamilton and Adams and Madison and Morris and all that breed—aghast at the revolution running its course in France. They had fought to secure the "chartered rights of Englishmen" in America, those rights of the Bill of Rights of 1689; and now they were horrified by the consequences of the Declaration of the Rights of Man. The same revulsion soon spread to many of the Jeffersonian faction—to such early egalitarians as Randolph of Roanoke, Republican leader of the House of Representatives. It spread in England to the New Whigs, so that even Charles James Fox, by 1794, would declare, "I can hardly frame to myself the condition of a people, in which I would not rather desire that they should continue, than fly to arms, and seek redress through the unknown miseries of a revolution." In short, Whig revolution meant recovery of what was being lost; Jacobin revolution meant destruction of the fabric of society. The confounding of those two quite inconsonant interpretations of the word *revolution* troubles us still.

The Whig interpretation of history has been most seriously criticized, and perhaps confuted, by such recent historians as Sir Herbert Butterfield. No longer do most historians believe that James II could have worked fundamental constitutional alterations, nor that he intended to; and James was more tolerant than were his adversaries. What ruined him with the English people, indeed, was his Declaration for Liberty of Conscience, indulging Catholics and Dissenters; and what impelled William of Orange to supplant James was William's dread of a popular rising that might overthrow the monarchy altogether and establish another Commonwealth. William, too, preferred preventing a revolution to making one. For a convincing, brief study of the period, I commend Maurice Ashley's book *The Glorious Revolution of 1688*, published in 1966. Ashley doubts whether the overturn of 1688 did indeed constitute a "Glorious Revolution"; but he concludes that the event "undoubtedly contributed to the evolution of parliamentary democracy in England and of a balanced constitution in the United States of America." [3]

However that may be, Edmund Burke repeatedly and emphatically approved what had occurred in 1688 and 1689. The Whig interpretation was the creed of his party; it was the premise of his *Thoughts on the Present Discontents* and of his American speeches. It would not do for Burke, so eminent in Whig councils, to be found wanting in zeal for the Glorious Revolution that had dethroned a papist. For Irish Tories had been among his ancestors (his mother, sister, and wife were Catholics, although that fact appears not to have been widely known), and Burke was the agent at Westminster for the Irish Catholic interest. Early in his career he had been accused by the old Duke of Newcastle of being "a Jesuit in disguise," and a caricaturist had represented him in a Jesuit soutane. It was prudent for Burke to subscribe conspicuously to the Whig doctrines of 1688 and 1689.

Certainly Burke in part founded his vehement denunciation of the French Revolution upon his approbation of the English Revolution—of that *revolution* which had been a return, in Whig doctrine, to established political modes of yesteryear. Upon the same ground, Burke had attacked mordantly the American policies of George III, advocating a "salutary neglect" of the American colonies because it was to Britain's interest, as to the colonies' interest, that the old autonomy of the colonies should be preserved. It was King George, with his stubborn insistence upon taxing the Americans directly, who was the innovator, the revolutionary, in Burke's argument. Burke, with the Rockingham Whigs, sought to achieve compromise and conciliation.

But it does not follow that Burke approved what came to be called the American Revolution. The notion that Burke rightly supported the American Revolution but inconsistently opposed the French Revolution is a vulgar error often refuted—by Woodrow Wilson, for one.[4] Burke advocated redress of American grievances, or at least tacit acceptance of certain American claims of prescriptive right; he never countenanced ambitions for total separation from the authority of the Crown in Parliament. Burke's stand is ably summed up by Ross Hoffman in his *Edmund Burke, New York Agent*:

> Burke had no natural sympathy for America except as a part of the British Empire, and if, when the war came, he did not wish success to British arms, neither did he desire the Americans to triumph. Peace and Anglo-American reconciliation within the empire were his objects. After Americans won their independence, he seems to have lost all interest in their country.[5]

During the decade before the shot heard round the world, Burke seemed a champion of the claims of Americans. That sympathy, nevertheless, was incidental to his championing of the rights of Englishmen. It was for English liberties that the Rockingham Whigs were earnestly concerned. If the king should succeed in dragooning Americans, might he not then turn to dragooning Englishmen? It was the belief of the Whigs that George III intended to resurrect royal prerogatives of Stuart and Tudor times, that he would make himself a despot. That peril the Whigs—and Burke in particular—considerably exaggerated; but it is easy to be wise by hindsight. George III was a more formidable adversary than ever James II had been. Where James had been timid and indecisive, George was courageous and tenacious; and often George was clever, if obdurate, in his aspiration to rule as a Patriot King. At the end, Burke came to understand that in the heat of partisan passion he had reviled his king unjustly, and in his *Letter to a Noble Lord* (1796) he called George "a mild and benevolent sovereign."

Yet neither to the American Patriots nor to Burke, in 1774 and 1775, had George III seemed either mild or benevolent. Upon the assumption that King George meant to root up the liberties of Englishmen—to trample upon the British Constitution—the dominant faction of Whigs in America determined to raise armies and risk hanging. They declared that they were resisting pernicious innovations and defending ancient rights. They appealed to the Bill of Rights of 1689. They offered for their violent resistance to royal authority the very apology offered by the Whigs of 1688. In the older sense of that uneasy word *revolution*, they were endeavoring to prevent, rather than to make, a revolution. Or such was the case they made until a French alliance became indispensable.

THE THESIS that the Patriots of 1776 intended no radical break with the past—that they thought of themselves as conservators rather than as innovators—is now dominant among leading historians of American politics. It is most succinctly stated by Daniel Boorstin in *The Genius of American Politics*:

> The most obvious peculiarity of our American Revolution is that, in the modern European sense of the word, it was hardly a revolution at all. The Daughters of the American Revolution, who have been understandably sensitive on this subject, have always insisted in their literature that the American Revolution was no revolution but merely a colonial rebellion. The more I have looked into the subject, the more convinced I have become of the wisdom of their naïveté. "The social condition and the Constitution of the Americans are democratic," De Tocqueville observed about a hundred years ago. "But they have not had a democratic revolution." This fact is surely one of the more important of our history. [6]

The attainment of America's independence, Boorstin makes clear in his writings, was not the work of what Burke called "theoretic dogma." What most moved the Americans of that time was their own colonial experience: they were defending their right to go on living in the future much as they had lived in the past; they were not marching to Zion. To quote Boorstin directly again, "The American Revolution was in a very special way conceived as both a vindication of the British past and an affirmation of an American future. The British past was contained in ancient and living institutions rather than in doctrines; and the American future was never to be contained in a theory."[7]

This point is made with equal force by Clinton Rossiter in his *Seedtime of the Republic: The Origin of the American Tradition of Political Liberty*. In the course of his discussion of the thought of Richard Bland, Rossiter remarks, "Throughout the colonial period and right down to the last months before the Declaration of Independence, politically conscious Americans looked upon the British Constitution rather than natural law as the bulwark of their cherished liberties. Practical political thinking in eighteenth century America was dominated by two assumptions: that the British Constitution was the best and happiest of all possible forms of government, and that the colonists, descendants of freeborn Englishmen, enjoyed the blessings of this constitution to the fullest extent consistent with a wilderness environment." Men like Bland—and those, too, like Patrick Henry, more radical than Bland—regarded themselves as the defenders of a venerable constitution, not as marchers in the dawn of a Brave New World. As Rossiter continues in his chapter on the Rights of Man, "Virginians made excellent practical use of this distinction. When their last royal Governor, Lord Dunmore, proclaimed them to be in rebellion, they retorted immediately in print that he was the rebel and they the saviors of the constitution."[8] It was the case of James II and arbitrary power all over again.

Or turn to H. Trevor Colbourn's study *The Lamp of Experience: Whig History and the Intellectual Origins of the American Revolution*: "In insisting upon rights which their history showed were deeply embedded in antiquity," Colbourn writes, "American Revolutionaries argued that their stand was essentially conservative; it was the corrupted mother country which was pursuing a radical course of action, pressing innovations and encroachments upon her long-suffering colonies. Independence was in large measure the product of the historical concepts of the men who made it, men who furnished intellectual as well as political leadership to a new nation."[9] The appeal of even the more passionate leaders of the American rising against royal innovation was to precedent and old usage, not to utopian visions.

The men who made the American Revolution, in fine, had little intention of making a revolution in the sense of a reconstitution of society. Until little choice remained to them, they were anything but enthusiasts even for separation from Britain. This is brought out in an interesting conversation between Burke and Benjamin Franklin on the eve of Franklin's departure from London for America. Burke relates this in his *Appeal from the New to the Old Whigs*:

> In this discourse Dr. Franklin lamented, and with apparent sincerity, the separation which he feared was inevitable between Great Britain and her colonies. He certainly spoke of it as an event which gave him the greatest concern. America, he said, would never again see such happy days as she had passed under the protection of England. He observed, that ours was the only instance of a great empire, in which the most distant parts and members had been as well governed as the metropolis and its vicinage: but that the Americans were going to lose the means which secured to them this rare and precious advantage. The question with them was not whether they were to remain as they had been before the troubles, for better, he allowed, they could not hope to be; but whether they were to give up so happy a situation without a struggle? Mr. Burke had several other conversations with him about that time, in none of which, soured and exasperated as his mind certainly was, did he discover any other wish in favour of America than for a security to its ancient condition. Mr. Burke's conversation with other Americans was large indeed, and his inquiries extensive and diligent. Trusting to the result of all these means of information, but trusting much more in the public presumptive indications I have just referred to, and to the reiterated, solemn declarations of their assemblies, he always firmly believed that they were purely on the defensive in that rebellion. He considered the Americans as standing at that time, and in that controversy, in the same relation to England, as England did to King James the Second, in 1688. He believed,

that they had taken up arms from one motive only; that is, our attempting to tax them without their consent; to tax them for the purposes of maintaining civil and military establishments. If this attempt of ours could have been practically established, he thought, with them, that their assemblies would become totally useless; that, under the system of policy which was then pursued, the Americans could have no sort of security for their laws or liberties, or for any part of them; and that the very circumstance of our freedom would have augmented the weight of their slavery.[10]

Such were the language and the convictions of the American patriots, as Rossiter puts it, "right down to the last months before the Declaration of Independence." Then what account do we make of the highly theoretical and abstract language of the first part of the Declaration of Independence, with its appeal to "the laws of Nature and of Nature's God," to self-evident truths, to a right to abolish any form of government? Why is Parliament not even mentioned in the Declaration? What has become of the English constitution, the rights of Englishmen, the citing of English precedents, and the references to James II and the Glorious Revolution?

These startling inclusions and omissions are discussed penetratingly by Carl Becker in *The Declaration of Independence: A Study in the History of Political Ideas.* The language of much of the Declaration is the language of the French Enlightenment, and more immediately, the language of the Thomas Jefferson of 1776, rather than the tone and temper of the typical member of the Continental Congress.

> Not without reason was Jefferson most at home in Paris. By the qualities of his mind and temperament he really belonged to the philosophical school, to the Encyclopaedists, those generous souls who loved mankind by virtue of not knowing too much about men, who worshipped reason with unreasoning faith, who made a study of Nature while cultivating a studied aversion for "enthusiasm," and strong religious emotion. Like them, Jefferson, in his earlier years especially, impresses one as being a radical by profession. We often feel that he defends certain practices and ideas, that he denounces certain customs or institutions, not so

much from independent reflection or deep-seated conviction on the particular matter in hand as because in general these are the things that a philosopher and a man of virtue ought naturally to defend or denounce. It belonged to the eighteenth-century philosopher, as a matter of course, to apostrophize Nature, to defend Liberty, to denounce Tyranny, perchance to shed tears at the thought of a virtuous action.[11]

The Francophile Jefferson, in other words, was atypical of the men, steeped in Blackstone and constitutional history, who sat in the Continental Congress. Why, then, did the Congress accept Jefferson's Declaration unprotestingly?

Aid from France had become an urgent necessity for the Patriot cause. The phrases of the Declaration, congenial to the *philosophes*, were calculated to wake strong sympathy in France's climate of opinion; and as Becker emphasizes, those phrases achieved with high success precisely that result. It would have been not merely pointless, but counter-productive, to appeal for French assistance on the ground of the ancient rights of Englishmen; the French did not wish Englishmen well.

Here we turn again to Daniel Boorstin (who differs somewhat with Becker). It is not to the Declaration we should look, Boorstin suggests, if we seek to understand the motives of the men who accomplished the American Revolution: not, at least, to the Declaration's first two paragraphs. "People have grasped at 'life, liberty, and the pursuit of happiness,' forgetting that it was two-thirds borrowed and, altogether, only part of a preamble," Boorstin writes. "We have repeated that 'all men are created equal,' without daring to discover what it meant and without realizing that probably to none of the men who spoke it did it mean what we would like it to mean." Really, he tells us, the Revolution was about taxation without representation. "It is my view that the major issue of the American Revolution was the true constitution of the British Empire, which is a pretty technical legal problem."[12]

Burke declared, looking upon the ghastly spectacle of the French Revolution, that it is not merely mistaken, but evil, to attempt to govern a nation by utopian designs, regardless of prudence, historical experience, convention, custom, the complexities of political compromise, and long-received principles of morality. The men who made the American Revolution were not abstract visionaries. Suffering practical grievances, they sought practical redress; not obtaining that, they settled upon separation from the Crown in Parliament as a hard necessity. That act was meant not as a repudiation of their past, but as a means for preventing the destruction of their pattern of politics by King George's presumed intended revolution of arbitrary power, after which, in Burke's phrase, "the Americans could have no sort of security for their laws or liberties." That is not the cast of mind which is encountered among the revolutionaries of the twentieth century.

THE CAREFUL STUDY of history is of high value—among other reasons because it may instruct us, sometimes, concerning ways to deal with our present discontents. I do not mean simply that history repeats itself, or repeats itself with variations—although there is something in that, and particularly in the history of revolutions on the French model, which devour their own children.[13] I am suggesting, rather, that deficiency in historical perspective leads to the ruinous blunders of ideologues, whom Burckhardt calls "the terrible simplifiers," while sound historical knowledge may diminish the force of Hegel's aphorism that "we learn from history that we learn nothing from history."

The history of this slippery word *revolution* is a case in point. Political terms have historical origins. If one is ignorant of those historical origins—if even powerful statesmen are ignorant of them—great errors become possible. It is as if one were to confound the word *law* as a term of jurisprudence with the word *law* as a term of natural science. If one assumes that the word *revolution* signifies always the same phenomenon, regardless of historical background, one may make miscalculations with grave consequences—perhaps fatal consequences.

The American Revolution, or War of Independence, was a preventive movement, intended to preserve an old constitutional structure. Its limited objectives attained, order was restored. It arose from causes intimately bound up with the colonial experience and the British Constitution, and little connected with the causes of the French Revolution. In intention, at least, it was a revolution in the meaning of that term generally accepted during the seventeenth century and the first half of the eighteenth century.

The French Revolution was a very different phenomenon, as was its successor the Russian Revolution. These were philosophical revolutions—or, as we say nowadays with greater precision, ideological revolutions. Their objectives were unlimited in the sense of being utopian. Their consequences were quite the contrary of what their original authors had hoped for.

A considerable element of the population of these United States has tended to fancy, almost from the inception of the Republic, that all revolutions everywhere somehow are emulatory of the American War of Independence and ought to lead to similar democratic institutions. Revolutionary ideologues in many lands have played successfully enough upon this American naïveté. This widespread American illusion, or confusion about the word *revolution*, has led not merely to sentimentality in policy regarding virulent Marxist or nationalistic movements in their earlier stages, but also to unfounded expectations that by some magic, overnight "democratic reforms"—free elections especially—can suffice to restrain what Burke called "an armed doctrine." How many Americans forget, or never knew, that in time of civil war Abraham Lincoln found it necessary to suspend writs of habeas corpus?

Knowledge of history is no perfect safeguard against such blunders. It did not save Woodrow Wilson, who had read a great deal of history, from miscalculations about the consequences of "self-determination" in central Europe. It did not save his advisor Herbert Hoover, who knew some history, from fancying that an improbable "restoration of the Habsburg tyranny" in central Europe was a more imminent menace than live and kicking Bolshevism or the recrudescence of German ambitions. Nevertheless, knowledge of history generally, and knowledge of the historical origin of political terms, are some insurance against ideological infatuation or sentimental sloganizing.

There come to my mind certain remarks by John Randolph of Roanoke at the Virginia Convention in 1829: "Dr. Franklin, who, in shrewdness, especially in all that related to domestic life, was never excelled, used to say, that two movings were equal to one fire. So to any people, two constitutions are worse than a fire. . . . I am willing to lend my aid to any very small and moderate reforms, which I can be made to believe that this our ancient government requires. But, far better would it be that they were never made, and that our constitution remained unchangeable like that of Lycurgus, than that we should break in upon the main pillars of the edifice."[14]

Like much else that Randolph told his contemporaries, those sentences regain significance in our age, when the crying need is to avert revolutions, not to multiply them. Twentieth-century revolutions have reduced half the world to servitude of body and mind, and to extreme poverty. What we call the American Revolution had fortunate consequences because, in some sense, it was a revolution not made, but prevented. Folk who fancy the phrase "permanent revolution" are advocating, if unwittingly, permanent misery. The first step toward recovery from this confusion is to apprehend that the word *revolution* has a variety of meanings, that not all revolutions are cut from the same cloth, that politics cannot be divorced from history, and that *revolution*, in its common twentieth-century signification, is no highroad to life, liberty, and the pursuit of happiness. The Constitution's Framers, in 1787, wanted no more revolutions; and President Washington, in 1789 and after, set his face against the French revolutionaries.

5

A Natural Aristocracy

I F THE LEADING PATRIOTS of 1776 were no flaming radicals when they signed the Declaration of Independence, the delegates who framed the Constitution in 1787 were pillars of order. To understand that Constitution, it is well to know something of the minds and the manners of the fifty-five politicians who gathered at Philadelphia to "form a more perfect Union."

Three years after the Constitutional Convention had concluded its deliberations, Edmund Burke wrote that nothing was more consummately wicked than the heart of an abstract metaphysician who should attempt to govern nations by speculative political dogmas. He had in mind the Parisian *philosophes* who had brought on the French Revolution. The men of Philadelphia—some of Burke's admirers among them—did not at all resemble those *philosophes*.

Now and again one encounters allusions to "the philosophy of the Framers of the Constitution," but it will not do to attribute to them some peculiar "philosophy." With only three or four exceptions, they were Christians of one profession or another: that is, they took their primary assumptions about the human condition, consciously or unconsciously, from the Bible. Probably nearly all of them had been affected early by *The Pilgrim's Progress*. They were not political theorists, but men of much experience of the world, assembled not in hope of creating the Terrestrial Paradise, but rather to contrive a tolerable practical plan of general government: a plan for survival.

Those Framers of 1787 were not bent upon grand alterations in morals and manners. Perhaps the most extraordinary thing ever uttered about them was a sentence from Rexford Guy Tugwell in 1970. In Tugwell's judgment, the delegates at Philadelphia had assembled at the Convention to undo the existing religion and the established mores of the United States. In Tugwell's words, "The framers, meeting in Philadelphia in the summer of 1787, were there because neither the Ten Commandments nor the going rules for social behavior were any longer adequate."

Not one word was uttered, during the Convention's four months, about the Decalogue; and in the seven articles adopted, nothing whatever was said about religion except that no religious test should be required for holding federal office. This does not signify that the delegates aspired to establish some civil religion as an alternative to Judaism and Christianity. It is simply that their Constitution was to be a practical instrument of government, not a work of politico-religious dogmata. As for the subversion of "going rules of social behavior," those fifty-five gentlemen politicians were themselves the arbiters of behavior, if not of morals, in their generation. Being no Jacobins, they and their class entertained not the slightest notion of undoing the received mores and manners.

The Framers were not abstract metaphysicians. It was the most speculative man among them, Benjamin Franklin, who suggested that their crucial sessions should be opened with prayer. The names of Diderot, Helvetius, Voltaire, Rousseau, were not heard at the Convention. Only Montesquieu was mentioned repeatedly, and he chiefly because of his praise for the old Constitution of England.

Any tolerable order in politics necessarily is a bundle of compromises among interests and classes, and a principal merit of the Framers was their ready recognition of this ineluctable fact. As Burke said of government generally, it is a contrivance of human wisdom to supply human wants. Sometimes the Constitution of the United States is commended as if it had been created out of whole cloth, overnight, from the glowing imagination of the Framers. Sometimes the Framers themselves are spoken of with a veneration like that accorded to the Hebrew prophets or the mythical founders of Greek cities. Yet the politicians who framed the Constitution were not an elite of theorists, but an assembly of governors, in the old signification of that word *governor*. They were representatives of a class, in every former colony, that had exercised authority almost from the very early years of British settlement in North America; they were drawn from a natural aristocracy. Experience, education, and wealth, passed on from generation to generation of Americans, tended to develop a continuity of public influence within leading families; while the relatively broad franchises that came to pass in most colonies nevertheless gave provincial and local government a democratic cast.

Broadly speaking, it was the body of men familiar with America's provincial and local governments who made both the Revolution and the Constitution. Long participation in provincial and local public affairs shaped this American natural aristocracy; while the French Revolutionaries, for the most part, were men previously excluded from any effective exercise of power, and so naive in great questions of public policy. The Americans were men of political experience; the French, men of political theory, and that theory untested. The French Revolutionaries rejected the historical and political inheritance of their country, while the Americans declared that their revolution was fought to preserve their British heritage. Members of this natural aristocracy, which governed the Republic of the United States for almost precisely half a century, 1775 to 1825, thought of themselves as restorers of what was being lost—not as adversaries of the past. Let us have a look at the breed.

FOUR YEARS AFTER the Constitutional Convention, in the course of opposing the sentiments of "the insane Socrates of the National Assembly," Edmund Burke would describe the natural aristocracy that makes possible the existence of a nation; his sentences applied nearly as well to the leading class in America, at that hour, as to the gentry of England, Scotland, and Ireland. Burke wrote, in his *Appeal from the New to the Old Whigs*,

> A true natural aristocracy is not a separate interest in the state, or separable from it. It is an essential integrant part of any large body rightly constituted. It is formed out of a class of legitimate presumptions, which, taken as generalities, must be admitted for actual truths. To be bred in a place of estimation; to see nothing low and sordid from one's infancy; to be taught to respect one's self; to be habituated to the censorial inspection of the public eye; to look early to public opinion; to stand upon such elevated ground as to be enabled to take a large view of the wide-spread and infinitely diversified combinations of men and affairs in a large society; to have leisure to read, to reflect, to converse; to be enabled to draw the court and attention of the wise and learned wherever they are to be found;—to be habituated in armies to command and to obey; to be taught to despise danger in the pursuit of honour and duty; to be formed to the highest degree of vigilance, foresight, and circumspection, in a state of things in which no fault is committed with impunity, and the slightest mistakes draw on the most ruinous consequences—to be led to a guarded and regulated conduct, from a sense that you are considered as an instructor of your fellow-citizens in their highest concerns, and that you act as a reconciler between God and man— to be employed as an administrator of law and justice, and to be thereby amongst the first benefactors to mankind—to be a professor of high science, or of liberal and ingenuous art—to be amongst rich traders, who from their success are presumed to have sharp and vigorous understandings, and to possess the virtues of diligence, order, constancy, and regularity, and to have cultivated an habitual regard to commutative justice—these are the circumstances of men, that form what I should call a natural aristocracy, without which there is no nation.[1]

This description comprehends both the men of presumptive virtue and the men of actual virtue. Every delegate to the Constitutional Convention rightfully might have claimed to be numbered among the American natural aristocracy, according to Burke's categories of qualification.

John Adams, in his correspondence with John Taylor of Caroline, defined an aristocrat as any person who could command two or more votes—his own, and at least one other person's. But in employing the phrase "natural aristocracy" I signify something more coherent and demanding than Adams's simple test. From Maine to Georgia, along the Atlantic seaboard especially, there flourished a mode of breeding, schooling, and involvement in public affairs that produced what Edmund Burke would call a natural aristocracy. Many of the members of that body were men who rose to ascendancy principally through their own talents: such leading men Burke referred to as "the men of actual virtue." Other members of that natural aristocracy, in Burke's description, were the men of presumptive virtue—those endowed by birth with the unbought grace of life, the heirs to old families and broad lands.

No peer of the United Kingdom ever took up permanent residence in North America, and very few Americans were knighted during the colonial era. No bishops were consecrated for North America by the Church of England. Nevertheless, a ruling class, an aristocracy, had grown up quite naturally in the thirteen colonies. That class had fought and won the War of Independence and afterwards framed the Constitution of the United States.

Four decades after the Constitutional Convention, Fenimore Cooper upheld the premises upon which the concept of a gentleman rested. "The word 'gentleman' has a positive and limited signification," Cooper wrote in *The American Democrat*. "It means one elevated above the mass of society by his birth, manners, attainments, character, and social condition. As no civilized society can exist without these social differences, nothing is gained by denying the use of the term." [2] Fifty-five men so elevated, in one fashion or another, made up the body of delegates of 1787: gentlemen politicians.

Several of the more influential Framers indeed had been "bred in a place of estimation," some great family house and estate; had been taught "to respect one's self "; had enjoyed "leisure to read, to reflect, to converse." These gentlemen were at once persons of presumptive virtue and of actual virtue. Consider John Dickinson, heir to a property six miles square, in Maryland; George Mason, of Gunston Hall, one of northern Virginia's great planters, the fourth proprietor bearing the name of George Mason; John Rutledge, of the old Charleston family, who had been dictator of South Carolina during the Revolution; Gouverneur Morris, of Morrisiana, a man of means from New York; and, of course, George Washington.

As for being "habituated in armies to command and to obey" or taught "to despise danger in the pursuit of honour and duty", a good many of the Framers had been under arms during the War of Independence, supplying that "cheap defense of nations" of which Burke was to write in 1790: the martial obligation of gentlemen, rooted in the chivalric tradition. Alexander Hamilton, Charles Cotesworth Pinckney, John Dickinson, John Francis Mercer, Alexander Martin, John Langdon, David Brearly, William Few, Thomas Mifflin, and Richard Dobbs Spaight had commanded regiments; some Framers had held still higher commissions, and the Convention was presided over by the gentleman who had been commander in chief.

Administrators of law and justice may be said to have dominated the Convention, for more than half the Framers had been lawyers or judges: George Wythe of Williamsburg had been the most eminent of them. Rufus King and Gouverneur Morris, immensely successful lawyers, were perhaps the most conservative of all the Framers. James Wilson was to write the first American work on jurisprudence; Luther Martin was the energetic and almost perpetual attorney general of Maryland.

Men of "high science, or of liberal and ingenuous art" were not absent from the Convention, Benjamin Franklin the most famous among them. A good many Framers had been teachers at one time or another. James Madison seemed to be the most scholarly of the delegates, but many of them had studied profitably at the American colleges, at Oxford or Cambridge, or at the Scottish and Irish universities. Several—Hamilton in particular—wrote admirable prose; and rhetoric, "the art of persuasion, beautiful and just," was a discipline most of them had acquired systematically. Madison's mind, more than any other man's, gave shape to the Constitution, and Madison cited great writers more frequently than did any other delegate. He was more a man of theory than were most of the Framers; but Madison too, like David Hume, usually was empirical. With Burke, the well-read Framers who had been liberally educated were averse, most of them, to political metaphysics.

"Rich traders" possessing "the virtues of diligence, order, constancy, and regularity" had their considerable part in the convention, from Robert Morris, the Revolution's financier, to Elbridge Gerry, of Marblehead's "codfish aristocracy." No great differences of manners, schooling, or dress distinguished the men of commerce at the Convention from the landed men.

Thus the elements of natural aristocracy which Burke discerned in English society existed also in the United States; and from that aristocracy of nature every delegate to the Convention came. Factions, sectional and economic, developed to some extent at the Convention; the advocates of a strong general government and the defenders of states' powers had much to dispute about; yet the civility of the debates and the reasonable acceptance of compromises set off the Convention from nearly all other endeavors, ancient or modern, to establish a fundamental political compact. In an era of duelling, no delegate at Philadelphia called out any other delegate. Formal manners happily prevailed; gentlemen most civilly spoke with gentlemen; no marked class rivalries could be discerned in the proceedings; the four months of discussion passed as if friends engaged in an enterprise of common benefit, friends reared in a common culture who understood one another very well, were settling amicably the details of their venture. That, in fact, on a grand scale, was what the Convention amounted to. Although the beginning of the Deluge, the French Revolution, lay only two years in the future, in the United States the men of prescriptive virtue and the men of actual virtue had no falling out: they settled for security

and good order, but set limits to the power of the general government—
so effecting a very high achievement in the history of politics, the
maintaining of a healthy tension between the claims of authority and
the claims of liberty.

The spirit of religion and the spirit of a gentleman, Burke would
write in 1790, had sustained European manners and civilization. What
was the religion of the American natural aristocracy that drew up the
Constitution? One might call it the gentleman's religion. At least
fifty of the Framers would have subscribed to the Apostles' Creed; no
atheist raised his voice at the Convention; but neither was religious
enthusiasm (in the eighteenth-century sense of the term) much in
evidence. By 1787, Deism had nearly trickled away in North America,
but the natural aristocracy was tolerant and temperate in faith. Sectarian
distinctions often were blurred: one might be half Quaker and half
Episcopalian; half Presbyterian, half Methodist. It would have been
politically imprudent, and ungentlemanly besides, to raise questions
of religious differences when political consensus was being sought.[3]

Such were the common elements among the fifty-five Framers—
who, all things considered, got on uncommonly well one with another.
Despite their differences upon this or that prudential question, the
Framers formed almost a club of gentlemen united to secure an
enduring social order. It remains to inquire how this natural aristocracy
of the Convention was shaped, and why it differed so strikingly from
the circle of revolutionary victors who would seize power in France
only a few years later, and by what means those Framers were able to
construct a Constitution that would endure for two centuries, during
which era nearly all other national constitutions would be overthrown.

EXCEPT FOR THE EXPULSION or subjugation of what had been the "Tory"
interest in the thirteen colonies, a class of "gentlemen freeholders"
effectively had remained dominant from 1775 to 1787, preventing or
modifying any large radical alterations of the social structure and the
customary ways of life in what had been the thirteen colonies. The
American revolution and restoration of order was accomplished by

experienced public men who were steeped in knowledge of British constitutionalism, law, and history, and whose interest lay in maintaining a political and social continuity. That is one reason why the Constitutional Convention may be called a gathering of friends.

Another reason why it was possible for the delegates to work out a political consensus was their sharing of an inherited literary culture. American schooling and college education in the latter half of the eighteenth century had helped to prepare this natural aristocracy for high public responsibilities. Theirs had been the schooling of English gentlemen of their age, deliberately contrived to rear the rising generation in piety and manliness.

Most of the Framers, twenty or thirty years earlier, had been required to study certain enduring books that were intended to develop a sense of order in the person and in the commonwealth. Among the ancients, they studied Cicero, Plutarch, and Vergil especially. They had memorized Cicero's praise of Roman mores, the high old Roman virtue; their imagination had been roused by the lives of Plutarch's heroes; they had come to understand Vergil's *labor, pietas, fatum*.[4]

Instruction in classical history and humane letters did not necessarily incline the rising generation toward respecting the wisdom of their own national ancestors: a classical education did not have that salutary effect upon the Jacobins of France. But in America the classical models were reconciled with, and supplemented by, instruction in British political history and the wealth of English literature. The schooled American was aware of participating in a long continuity and essence of culture, even though he dwelt on the western extremity of that civilization. Unlike the French visionary, the schooled American did not presume to draw up a new calendar in which the Year One would record his own accession to power.

But as is true in most eras, books published in their own time, and pamphlet literature, influenced the American natural aristocracy more than did writings of an earlier age. The Framers had read attentively Montesquieu, David Hume, Samuel Johnson, Adam Smith, Edmund Burke (whose *Annual Register* had been for them a principal reliable source of knowledge of events). Few of them had been much affected by French thought published during their own formative years; indeed, for that matter, even Thomas Jefferson did not read Rousseau, Gilbert Chinard has shown, until well after 1776. Thus to their common heritage of practical political experience was joined a common literary culture. And in the English language, those important writers of their own time whom most of the Framers admired certainly were no social revolutionaries. Of course they had read Thomas Paine, too; but Paine went back to England in 1787, his influence upon American opinion already much diminished.

A third influence that made the Constitutional Convention a gathering of friends, rather than an assembly of political fanatics, was the concept of a gentleman. The first article of the Constitution would provide that the United States might grant no title of nobility, and that no office-holder should accept a foreign title without the consent of the Congress; but the delegates at Philadelphia, quite unlike the French constitution-makers a few years later, had no intention of putting down gentlemen. Presumably every Framer thought of himself as a gentleman, and desired to be so regarded. Gentility, by the eighteenth century, did not require that a man or a woman be high-born; rather, it signified outwardly manners and dress and speech; inwardly, a sense of honor and duty.

The English model of a gentleman did not cease to influence Americans with the British defeat at Yorktown. In 1787, Sansculotism, "many-headed, fire-breathing," had not yet inquired, "What think ye of me?" There were ragged men in America, true, and Shays had led some of them against courts of justice; but it was not partisans of Daniel Shays who deliberated at Philadelphia. Under the influence of the canons of gentle manners, the Convention was conducted with a decorum not since encountered in these United States, and Framers of divergent views observed with one another the old traditions of civility. Temperate speech led to temperate agreement and to permanence of the Convention's product.

Some of the Framers, especially the Episcopalians among them, had read Thomas Fuller's essays on the True Gentleman and on the Degenerous Gentleman, published in Fuller's quarto *The Holy State and the Profane State* (1642). "He is courteous and affable to his neighbors," Fuller wrote of the True Gentleman. "As the sword of the best tempered metal is most flexible, so the truly generous are the most pliant and courteous in their behavior to their inferiors."[5]

The gentleman must be a man of good breeding; also he must be a man of honor who would not lie or cheat; a man of valor, who would not flee before enemies; a man of duty, who would serve the commonwealth as magistrate or member of an assembly; a man of charity, spiritual and material. Undoubtedly some of the Founders were what Fuller called Degenerous Gentlemen, selfish and cunning opportunists; but most lived as best they might by gentlemen's rules. And some of them—Washington, Dickinson, Mason, Rutledge, Gouverneur Morris, others—had fulfilled all their lives the gentleman's obligations of manners, honor, valor, duty, and charity; and so would live to the end.

Politics, we cannot too often remind ourselves, is the art of the possible. The Framers were not a club of speculative *philosophes*. They had a remarkably clear understanding of what might be possible and of what was improbable; perhaps some of them had too keen an eye to the main chance, but they did not err in any visionary fashion. Their aristocratic realism made possible the survival of the American democracy. Near the close of the twentieth century, in most of the world, natural aristocracy has been destroyed, suppressed, or perverted to ideological servitude. Therefore nations, particularly emergent ones, are governed by squalid oligarchs or else are reduced to anarchy.

6

The Marriage of Rights and Duties

WHILE I WAS WRITING my book *John Randolph of Roanoke*, I first became acquainted with George Mason, author of the Virginia Declaration of Rights and the Bill of Rights, a wise opponent of centralizing power, and a member of the American natural aristocracy. Mason was one of the three Virginia statesmen most admired by Randolph. Under the wings of the federal butterfly, said Randolph, Mason had perceived the poison—that is, potency for the future growth of arbitrary political power.

The Declaration of Independence and the Bill of Rights in the Constitution of the United States owe much to Mason, who feared that the powers of the several states might be swallowed up by a central administration, and that personal liberties inherited from the English political experience might be broken in upon by an innovating regime. No sooner had the federal Constitution been drawn up than Mason published his "Objections to This Constitution of Government," in which he declares, "When we reflect upon the insidious art of wicked and designing men, the various and plausible pretenses for continuing and increasing the inordinate lust of power in the few, we shall no longer be surprised that freeborn man hath been enslaved, and that those very means which were contrived for his preservation have been perverted to his ruin." During the past two centuries, matters have not gone all that far under the Constitution of the United States. Yet one thinks of a prescient book, published in the 1950s, entitled *The Coming American Caesars*, and of the character and administration of President Lyndon Johnson.

IN HOPE OF FORESTALLING such usurpation of power, George Mason specified in the Virginia Declaration of Rights, in 1776, some sixteen provisions, some of which reappeared fifteen years later among the first eight amendments to the United States Constitution. (It might have been well if certain other articles of the Virginia Declaration had been included in the federal Bill of Rights, particularly the seventh article, on the suspending of laws, and the fifteenth article, on the need to adhere to virtues.) More than Jefferson, more even than Madison (who, a young man then, was Mason's coadjutor in this matter, at Williamsburg in 1776), George Mason institutionalized America's civil liberties.

Mason knew that individuals' liberties can exist only within a civil social order—that is, in community. Commendation of true community runs through Mason's writings; he champions the powers of the several states and the volition of communities within those states against a central political administration. He certainly held no anarchistic notion of liberty.

It is interesting to note a denunciation of the idea of community, in the pages of the *Wall Street Journal*, by Ira Glasser, executive director of the American Civil Liberties Union. Mr. Glasser replied in that newspaper, on November 1, 1991, to an earlier *Journal* article by Professor Amitai Etzioni, in which Professor Etzioni had written of "A New

Community of Thinkers, Both Liberal and Conservative," who seek the restoration of true community as an alternative to state coercion and a means of regaining civic and moral order, for the sake of the common good. To such a proposal, the director of the American Civil Liberties Union replied in part as follows: "It is ironic indeed that at a time when the early American idea of individual rights as the highest purpose of government is reasserting itself all over the world—in the Soviet Union and elsewhere—Prof. Etzioni would choose to revive in this country the profoundly dangerous and statist notion that individual rights and the common good occupy distinct and oppositional spheres."

If the fundamental purpose of government is to keep the peace, then government defends a country against external enemies, and endeavors to repress violence and fraud at home. The rights of individuals are found and maintained within a community—not against a community. As Professor Etzioni replied to Mr. Glasser, "It seems necessary to reiterate that those who care about individual rights should be sure that legitimate community needs will be attended to." Among those needs are "at least a modicum of public safety and public health and civility."

The present point is that apparently the American Civil Liberties Union has quite forgotten George Mason's emphasis upon community as the source of civil liberties. When community begins to collapse altogether, the most fundamental civil liberties, including even the right to life, cannot be secured. If, as Professor Etzioni points out, organizations such as the American Civil Liberties Union endeavor to obstruct moral education and persuasion, to protest against even the intervention of public authorities, as a last resort, against gross misconduct, in desperation the public may turn to force and a master. As a justice of the Supreme Court remarked once, the Bill of Rights is not a suicide pact.

GEORGE MASON did not fancy that rights are an individual's defiance of law and convention. As Robert Rutland, editor of George Mason's papers, remarks in his short biography of that great Virginian, "He wrote as an English-American, working on behalf of rights that arose from natural law and were assumed to be the birthrights of every free American. Those rights were also anchored deep in English common law and in the history of the American colonies."

Nor did George Mason think of rights as commandments that the federal judiciary would thrust upon unwilling states and communities. He had from the first a deep uneasiness with the federal judiciary, fearing that federal judges would overrule state judges (which, of course, has come to pass, even to an extreme degree). He would have been astounded that the majority of the Supreme Court of the United States should conjure up a constitutional "right of privacy" not mentioned even in statute, and deduce from that conjectural right the further right of mothers to slay their progeny in the womb.

Nowadays, new alleged rights and entitlements spring up mushroom-like. Zealots for "animal rights" burst into departments of zoology and public zoological gardens to rescue their oppressed brethren of the animal kingdom. Or there are discovered global rights: everybody in the world should enjoy the right to shift to the United States, should he so choose, to partake of the American cornucopia. Belligerent and malignant "minorities" can claim rights not possessed by the common man.

One reason why extravagant claims of civil rights are made, and even sustained by courts of law, is that few people today enunciate the ancient doctrine that every right is wedded to some duty. If one claims a right to a vacation with pay, then some employer or public agency has the duty of sustaining the cost of that vacation, the claimant has the duty of performing the work for which the vacation is a reward; and, ordinarily, the right and the obligation have been previously expressed in a contract. If one claims the right to address a public meeting, one has the duty of refraining from inciting to riot; and the organizers of the public meeting have the duty of endeavoring to avert the stoning of the speaker if he grows boring. If one claims the right to bear arms, expressed in the Virginia Declaration of Rights and in the Second Amendment of the federal Constitution, he must be prepared to serve in the well-regulated militia, as both the Virginia Declaration and

Constitution specify. In short, the exercise of rights is justified only if the claimant of rights stands ready to fulfill the corresponding duties.

Once upon a time I published in the weekly magazine *Commonweal* an essay on this theme of the marriage of rights and duties, in morals and in civic concerns. The editors of *Commonweal* printed my article, but in the same number published an editorial declaring that although I was right in theory, my doctrine ought to be ignored in practice. Such a course, indeed, is precisely what too many folk follow with respect to their professed religion, but it cannot be sustained in logic.

The rising generation in these United States have heard a great deal about rights; not much about duties. In many schools, classes are offered in "Your Rights" and how to obtain them to the full—rights to payments from public funds, often. On television, public service announcements forcefully remind viewers that very possibly they have claims upon the public purse. Employers are required to post notices in conspicuous places, instructing their staffs about every right and prerogative, and the means of complaint should they feel deprived. As for duties, who is so impolite as to mention oppression of that sort?

GEORGE MASON, who asserted the rights of Americans against the ministry at Westminster, was a man of many duties. He did not desire to become a public man; he would have preferred to reside always at his home, Gunston Hall, managing his own plantation, a very substantial paterfamilias with a wife, nine children, many grandchildren, and three hundred slaves. He suffered badly from the gout, "the affliction of genius," which made travel difficult; until he went to the Constitutional Convention at Philadelphia, he never had left his native Chesapeake region.

And yet, against his inclination, reluctantly he took upon himself large duties. For many years he was a gentleman justice of the Fairfax County Court—then a post of much influence; also a vestryman of Truro Parish, an office with large responsibilities; an overseer of the poor, too. He became Treasurer of the Ohio Company, which had vast interests in what was to become the Northwest Territory. Briefly, and only at George Washington's request, he served in the House of Burgesses; but, disgusted with the "babblers" on the committees, he resigned. In 1773, he wrote the first of his important state papers. In 1775, he wrote the Fairfax Resolves, a constitutional protest against British policy in North America, which was adopted by the Virginia Convention and by the Continental Congress. When Washington was appointed commander in chief, Mason took his place in the Virginia Convention that had become the provisional government of the province. He became a member of the Virginia Committee of Safety, planned the organization of troops, and formed a company of Fairfax volunteers. In 1776, he drew up the famous Virginia Declaration of Rights and wrote most of the new constitution of Virginia.

During the Revolution, Mason was busy with revision of the laws and implementing the Declaration of Rights and the Virginia Constitution. He collaborated with George Rogers Clark in gaining possession of the Northwest Territory and had much to do with carrying the boundary to the Great Lakes. Again, disgusted with the management of public affairs, during the early 1780s he retired to Gunston Hall. But he returned to the Virginia Assembly in 1786, intending to check inflation of the state's currency and to help develop a form of union better than the Articles of Confederation.

In 1787, he became a Virginian delegate to the Convention at Philadelphia, where he spoke frequently and always to the point; he did much to improve the document being drawn up there. Yet displeased with the degree of centralization settled upon near the Convention's end, he refused to sign the new Constitution, and opposed ratification by Virginia. Also he objected to the compromise in the Constitution regarding slavery. He had sought prompt abolition of the importing of slaves. "Every master of slaves is a petty tyrant," he had said. Until a Bill of Rights should be included, he continued to insist, the Constitution would be unsatisfactory. The first ten amendments, ratified two hundred years ago, resulted from Mason's arguments and influence. Mason, not Madison, brought about our Bill of Rights.

Such were the many works of a gentleman unambitious and desirous of rustic life, performed painfully out of a strong and nagging sense of duty. The gentleman who wrote most convincingly about Americans' rights was among the most zealous Americans in the performance of high duties. Americans should endeavor to emulate him as best they may.

7

Men of Property

THE SCIENCE OF POLITICAL ECONOMY was merely one generation old when, in 1787, the Constitution of the United States was drawn up. Both theoretically and practically, the relationships between America's Constitution and matters economic are intricate and interesting.

Were it not for certain provisions of the Constitution and certain judicial interpretations of those provisions, presumably the American economy would be less productive than it is nowadays. On the other hand, a constitution less congenial to entrepreneurs might have diminished certain causes of our present discontents.

Having said something in the preceding chapters about the manners and political attitudes of the Framers, we turn now to their economic opinions and interests. Economic concerns loom gigantic in most people's minds—even when people are under no pressing necessity to secure their daily bread. The principal immediate motives of the Framers in writing a new constitution were economic. Probably not one of the fifty-five delegates to the Convention would have denied the primacy of economic concerns in their deliberations. It is not sinful for a statesman to pay serious attention to a country's economy; to the contrary, it would be a sin for a statesman to ignore economic realities at the public's peril. Indeed, neglect of economic reforms would bring on the Revolution in France.

Charles A. Beard, in 1913, ruffled the dovecotes of complacent Americanism by pointing out, in *An Economic Interpretation of the Constitution of the United States,* that the Framers, almost without exception, were men of property desirous of obtaining more property. At the time, there came an outcry against this alleged defamation. I remain surprised at anyone's fancying that the Framers were innocent of public and private economic motives: property and power are wedded eternally, and if the one is transferred to new hands, the other will follow. It was family possession of property—in land, chiefly—that had given a fair number of the Framers their early advantages in life: private property, as everybody in the colonies knew, makes possible independence of action.

Of course, most of the Framers were men who had a care for the economic interests of their state and their region. Yet it should be added that with a few exceptions, notably that of James Wilson, the Framers were not notorious for avarice: that grasping appetite for the world's goods, that democratic materialism reproached by Tocqueville in the 1830s. It does not follow, therefore, that the Framers subordinated the national interest to private, state, and regional interests. As Samuel Johnson put it, "A man is seldom more innocently occupied than when he is engaged in making money." Even the most selfish and conniving delegate to that Convention at Philadelphia was preferable as a public man (and probably preferable in private conversation, too) to Robespierre, the Sea-Green Incorruptible, master of the National Convention in Paris five years later.

The Constitutional Convention in 1787 was convened because of economic necessities; so it is not at all strange that delegates to the Convention represented economic interests, as well as other interests.

The American economy had been stagnating under the Articles of Confederation. At Annapolis, the trade convention which had met in September 1786, had been the forerunner to the Consitutional Convention of 1787. What the commissioners at Annapolis had discussed, exclusively, had been the possibility of "a uniform system in their commercial relations," removing internal and external barriers to trade. In 1786 and 1787, commerce was a more important issue than common defense in every state.

In short, economic laments and economic hopes, chiefly, moved twelve of the thirteen state legislatures to send delegates to the Convention at Philadelphia. There may be discerned six major reasons for this economic concern.

First, the general government of the Confederation could not pay its bills. By 1786, the annual income of that general government (which in effect was the Congress, there being no real executive) amounted to merely the equivalent of one third of the year's interest on the national debt.

Second, the country lacked "hard money": gold or silver coin. The paper money then issued by the thirteen states fluctuated badly in value, and credit of any sort was insecure. A sound general government should be able to coin money, and perhaps to encourage reliable banking.

Third, the several states' barriers to interstate trade and other impediments to commerce within the boundaries of the United States needed to be swept away. This had been the great concern of the Annapolis Convention. Only an effective general government might accomplish that desirable end.

Fourth, on separating themselves from the British Empire, the thirteen states had cut themselves off from the advantages and protections of the British Navigation Acts, as well as from the limitations of that system. Trade barriers against American goods, erected by Britain, France, and other powers since the attaining of independence, amounted to a major cause of what we now call economic recession in Virginia and some other states. A strong general government might negotiate satisfactory trade agreements with foreign powers.

Fifth, the vast western territories acquired from Britain needed to be organized and states' conflicting claims to those territories reconciled. Only when that had been accomplished might systematic settlement be achieved and the economic resources of the West be drawn upon. The government of the Confederation seemed incapable of that undertaking.

Sixth, it was feared by many that the state governments might be unable to maintain order, unless assisted or supervised by a strong general government with military forces at its command. This reason too had economic circumstances behind it: for Shays's Rebellion, so alarming to George Washington and others, had been a militant protest against foreclosures of farm mortgages during an economic recession. Commercial contracts must be enforced, if the nation were to prosper.

So let us not be surprised that the gentlemen at the Constitutional Convention, most of them affluent, talked much of commerce, debts, and economic advantages: precisely that was expected of them by the state governments which had sent them to Philadelphia. But what were the delegates' motives and hopes? Were they concerned for the common good, or for their privy purses? Might they have sat as models for the Marxist image of the exploiting capitalist in politics? Was the Constitutional Convention a contest between creditors and debtors, city folk and rural folk? For an answer, one must look at the men.

CERTAIN OF THE FRAMERS had an eye to the main chance—too keen an eye, some. Of the number of these was James Wilson, whom Max Farrand calls second only to Madison at the Convention. Undeniably, Wilson was a man of remarkable talents. Having been well educated at St. Andrews University, Wilson rapidly bettered himself in Pennsylvania, being strong of mind and will. In short order, Wilson had made an enviable reputation at the law, and money, too, lectured famously at the recently founded College of Philadelphia, soon published a pamphlet denying the authority of Parliament over Americans, became a delegate to the Second Continental Congress, and with some hesitation signed the Declaration of Independence.

Closely associated during the Revolution with Robert Morris, the richest man in America, Wilson prospered through land speculation and investments in privateering and commerce, but his arrogance and avarice made him detested. Yet he continued to rise in wealth and power.

At the Constitutional Convention he was clever and successful; Lord Bryce writes that Wilson was one of the deepest thinkers and most exact reasoners there.[1] He dominated Pennsylvania's ratifying convention, and wrote his state's new constitution of 1790. Aspiring to undo Sir William Blackstone by becoming "the American Blackstone," Wilson wrote his *Lectures on Law*; but the book, published posthumously, never attained the authority of Story's or Kent's. For nine years he was an associate justice of the United States Supreme Court—though not daring to venture on circuit into certain states, lest he be arrested for debt, for he had borrowed immense sums for land speculation on a grandiose scale.

"Let no man call himself happy until the hour of his death," said Solon to Croesus. Grasping, proud, and unscrupulous, Justice Wilson fell to his ruin at the age of fifty-six. Overreaching himself in speculations, he lost everything, and fled to North Carolina, where he died penniless and raving.

Are we to set down Wilson, then, as a specimen of those reactionaries who, writers of the Marxist persuasion instruct us, dominated the Constitutional Convention—an oligarch bent upon repressing the People? Not at all. In his doctrines, James Wilson was the most democratic of all the delegates there. It was he who worked into the Constitution the principle that sovereignty belongs to the whole American people, not to the several states. He desired that the president of the United States and the members of both Senate and House be elected by popular vote. Frequently expressing his faith in the common people, he opposed all property qualifications for the franchise. "It is the glorious destiny of man to be always progressive," he declared. Even nowadays his political principles would be regarded as decidedly liberal. The central government, he argued, has "the right of acquiring everything without which its perfection cannot be promoted or obtained."[2]

So it will not do to rest content with stereotypes of the Framers: they conform to no simple pattern of economic interests. One might contrast with the self-seeking Wilson the gentleman, also a delegate, from whom Wilson learned law: John Dickinson, a leader from the Stamp Act Congress through all great events in America down to constitutional ratification, heroically public-spirited, generous, tolerant, "the penman of the Revolution," sacrificing much for the common good. In short, the motives and characters of the delegates to the Constitutional Convention, like the motives and characters of any representative American body of persons, varied widely from man to man.

Moreover, Beard's bold attempt to make an economic interpretation of the framing and ratification of the Constitution, a pioneering work of American historiography influential for several decades, has been undone by Forrest McDonald, who followed Beard's own methods, but with much greater thoroughness. McDonald concludes, in *We the People: The Economic Origins of the Constitution*, that "It is impossible to justify Beard's interpretation of the Constitution as an 'economic document' drawn by a 'consolidated economic group whose property interests were immediately at stake.'"[3] Factors other than economic interests strongly influenced the delegates, and their votes at the Convention do not follow the patterns Beard thought he had discerned. Nor did ratification of the Constitution in the several states actually follow the lines of Beard's economic interpretation.

A fatal flaw in Beard's thesis is the hard fact that mercantile, manufacturing, and public security investments were not the more important property holdings of the Convention's delegates, although Beard had so believed. Actually, their agricultural property, particularly in the case of the richer delegates (with few exceptions), bulked far larger in value. There occurred no contest at the Convention between capitalist and farmer, nor any other discernible class conflict along economic lines. As McDonald concludes, "Beard's thesis—that the line of cleavage as regards the Constitution was between substantial personalty increases on the one hand and small farming and debtor interests on the other—is entirely incompatible with the facts."[4]

Important though economic concerns are, it does not follow that men and women are concerned only with economic gain. Most of the delegates to the Constitutional Convention seem to have disregarded the question of their own personal advantage when voting or speaking on economic issues at Philadelphia: the public interest transcended private gain in their motives. The New England delegates were the exception: Gerry, King, Sherman, and Ellsworth clearly endeavored to bring about decisions at the Convention that would advance their private investments in personal property.

In short, interest in economic questions does not of itself warp the character in the direction of selfishness. In such matters, most of the delegates to the Constitutional Convention made their decisions on the basis of what they took to be the general welfare of America, rather than their private ephemeral advantage.

The religious and moral convictions of the Framers had something to do with this probity in prudential decisions. So the church connections of the delegates to the Convention seem worth noting. In his study of the subject, M. E. Bradford finds that "with no more than five exceptions (and perhaps no more than three), they were orthodox members of one of the established Christian communions: approximately twenty-nine Anglicans, sixteen to eighteen Calvinists (of various churches), two Methodists, two Lutherans, two Roman Catholics, one lapsed Quaker and sometime-Anglican, and one open Deist—Dr. Franklin, who attended every kind of Christian worship, called for public prayer, and contributed to all denominations."[5] Nearly half a century later, Tocqueville would write that the success of the American democracy was produced by Americans' mores, derived from Christian teaching.

DESPITE THE URGENT INTEREST of the delegates to the Constitutional Convention in economic questions, there were no political economists in their number—with the partial exception of Alexander Hamilton, who was present at Philadelphia only briefly. With political theory many of the delegates were well acquainted, and some few of them made their own contributions to that discipline. But economic theory was another matter: it was too new a field of thought to have taken root in the United States.

The Wealth of Nations had been published in 1776, and such eminent Americans as John Adams and Alexander Hamilton had been strongly impressed by it. But it cannot be said that Adam Smith's innovating book much influenced American economic policy for a great while to come. Hamilton, the one American statesman possessed of economic imagination of a high order during the early years of the Republic, understood Smith and also Smith's countryman Sir James Steuart, but did not make himself altogether their disciple. He had far more experience of the world than Adam Smith had acquired.

A great financier, Hamilton might have become a political economist of enduring repute, had he not been engrossed in public affairs and perished before his time. His famous "Report on Manufactures," when he was the first Secretary of the Treasury, gives evidence of real originality in economic concepts. And in the long run, his economic views would triumph in the United States—though more by historical accident and by certain decisions of the Supreme Court than by any design of the Congress.

Yet it ought not to be thought that Hamilton either intended or desired the industrializing of the United States on the scale which was achieved after the Civil War and has been much intensified since then. He argued that much manufacturing could be done in farm households, or by farmers working part of the time in small factories of neighboring towns—the early pattern of the New England shoe industry. He did not anticipate the growth of industrial cities with a population of millions, believing mechanized industry a liberation from monotonous drudgery. He began writing on economic subjects when the Industrial Revolution was but thirty years old, and neither he nor any other public man wholly foresaw the consequences, demographic and social, of increasing mechanization, specialization, and division of labor—though Smith had misgivings, and Burke soon would express some.

Hamilton's designs for the strong stimulation of the American economy, through measures of governmental encouragement and

direction including protective tariffs, were unpopular with most Sou-
therners and most New Englanders. For in the eighteenth century
neither of those regions engaged in even simple manufactures for
export, and they required low prices for the goods they imported from
abroad. Only the Middle States enjoyed the prospect, in 1787 and
1788, of gaining fairly promptly from Hamilton's economic measures.
Yet the new Constitution, as drafted and ratified, contained provisions
that in the fullness of time would transform the United States into the
greatest and most successful of industrial lands.

Article I, Section 8, empowered the Congress to "lay and collect
Taxes, Duties, Imposts and Excises, to pay the Debts and provide for
the common Defence and general Welfare of the United States; but
all Duties, Imposts and Excises shall be uniform throughout the United
States." The same section authorized the Congress to borrow money,
to regulate commerce foreign and domestic, to establish uniform bankruptcy laws, to coin money and regulate the value thereof, to establish
post offices and post roads, to secure patents and copyrights. Thus
were the nationalists or federalists of the Hamiltonian persuasion given
the instruments with which to industrialize America, increase its
prosperity, and create an urban civilization—even though most of the
delegates who subscribed their names to the new Constitution in 1787
could not have fancied how far these powers of Article I would be carried in years to come.

Had most of the delegates anticipated such sweeping economic
and social consequences, or had the subsequent state ratifying conventions been told by persuasive orators that such huge changes probably would come to pass, presumably we would have a different constitution and a different society today. Perhaps more than one country
would occupy what are now the territories of the United States. For
some leading Americans of that day thought such developments
impossible, and others found the prospect of such changes unendurable.

John Adams disbelieved in general economic growth: population
would catch up with food supply; mankind could make material
progress only by rigorously practicing frugality, hard work, temperance,
and sound judgment. James Madison hoped to arrest industrial growth

in America, through governmental measures, at a point where commerce and agriculture would predominate. Household manufactures would be carried on, but most manufactured products would be imported from Europe. The United States would expand westward on a grand scale, to provide land for more agriculture—thus averting the triumph of factories and cities. Hamilton's most formidable opponent, Thomas Jefferson, absent in Paris at the time of the Constitutional Convention, did not subscribe to the economic theories of David Hume and Adam Smith. For Jefferson was on cordial terms with the chief of the Physiocrats, Pierre Samuel du Pont de Nemours, the author of *Physiocracy* (1768). (*The Wealth of Nations* was intended in part to refute some errors of the Physiocrats.) All real wealth comes from the land, the Physiocrats taught, through agriculture and mining; large scale manufacturing is valueless at best; cities are abominations. (They are to the nation as sores are to the human body, Jefferson would say.) Thus Hamilton's vision of a populous and prosperous industrial America was anathema to Jefferson, and to Jefferson's allies and followers—at least in 1787 and 1788.

Jefferson's friendship with du Pont somewhat paradoxically resulted in the successful establishment of a major large scale industrial enterprise that endures prosperously to the present day: the great firm of DuPont. Samuel Pierre du Pont and his sons were courageous conservative reformers in revolutionary France; they could not prevail there. In 1799, encouraged by Jefferson, Pierre du Pont, with a dozen members of his family, would emigrate to the United States.

Irénée du Pont, better known as E. I. du Pont, Pierre's second son, made himself America's most imaginative entrepreneur. On a hunting expedition, he found his gunpowder unsatisfactory and undertook a "market survey" of American gunpowder. He had been the pupil of Lavoisier, the great chemist, chief of the royal powder works in France. E. I. du Pont calculated that even a small powder mill, run efficiently, could produce better gunpowder, at a lower price, than any available then in the United States—and make a profit of ten thousand dollars a year. By 1811, his year's profit was forty thousand dollars. That was the mere beginning of the DuPont industries. Both Jefferson and

Hamilton lent young du Pont their countenance and help: a rare case of collaboration. Thus a family of theorists became a family of industrialists, in American circumstances.

Yet the Jeffersonian interest set its face against public measures to industrialize America, despite this du Pont exception. New England, exporter of fish, naval stores, timber, and rum, opposed protective duties and subsidies to industrial manufacturing, and it took a good many years, as Hamilton had known it would, to persuade most Americans to give up a subsistence economy, rural and simple, in favor of division of labor and factory chimneys. Hamiltonian economic measures, protective tariffs especially, would drive the agrarian South into sectionalism and become one of the two principal causes of the Civil War. But in the year 1787 only the more militant opponents of the proposed Constitution, the dogmatic Anti-Federalists, hinted at such possibilities.

As for those delegates at Philadelphia who had hammered out the new Constitution, they are not to be either praised or blamed as creators of a brand new economy. They could claim to be the authors of a new political order, *Novus Ordo Seclorum*, but they expounded no novel economic doctrines. So far as most of them had a vision of America's social and economic future, they seem to have expected the United States to become a larger and somewhat more egalitarian England, agriculture and the extractive industries their economic mainstay, a flourishing countryside with a great many independent proprietors, much overseas commerce, only a reasonable proportion of manufactures. Even the most ardent speculators among them desired a country life of ease, not a hive of industry. Robert Morris, delegate from Pennsylvania, later United States Senator, had L'Enfant design for him, near Philadelphia, a splendid country house; in Louisiana, Morris would have made Orange Grove plantation a magnificent rural seat. Physiocratic tastes could be discovered readily in captains of commerce and finance.

Nor are we to regard the fifty-five Framers as hard-faced and hard-hearted men who had done well out of a revolution. My earlier account of James Wilson notwithstanding, few of them were concentered all in self; they did not much resemble the members of the Directory at Paris, eight years later. The Christian injunction to practice the theological virtue of charity is some restraint upon self-interest; it still so functioned among the natural aristocracy of the United States in the closing years of the eighteenth century. Jeremy Bentham's *Principles of Morals and Legislation* would not be published until 1789: systematic utilitarianism, with self-interest as its ruling principle, had no bold spokesman at the Constitutional Convention. The Framers were no dogmatic Manchesterian economists, because that school did not then exist. They took for granted, as natural, economic competition, security for private property, and ordered freedom.

RATIFICATION OF THE CONSTITUTION in 1787 produced no magical invigoration of the economy of the United States. In 1800, eleven years after Washington had been inaugurated as President, the young Republic remained economically underdeveloped. The total capital of the American people came to eighteen hundred million dollars, equal to $328 for each human being in the country. Agriculture was the only really important economic pursuit. Many things were manufactured in the Middle States, but nothing on a large scale. Total exports and imports of the country came to merely seventy-five million dollars.

The biggest city, Philadelphia, had seventy thousand inhabitants. In Washington, the half-finished Capitol and the half-finished White House stood amidst swamps. Wages averaged a dollar a day, but taxes were very low. Foreign visitors called the average American lazy and unenterprising. Travel was slow and difficult. Satisfactory goods, even important ones, were not easy to obtain. Few commercial companies existed. In short, the United States then seemed as unenterprising economically as it was enterprising politically. It was not that the new Constitution had failed, but Hamilton's economic designs had not yet come to fruition. Hamilton himself, in 1800, was about to experience bitter defeat in practical politics.

And yet a dozen years later American manufactures would be thriving, and the character of American society changing speedily.

What were the causes? Jefferson's embargo, the War of 1812, and as we shall discuss later, certain decisions of the Supreme Court.

We will not look again upon the like of the Framers of 1787. The discussion of their temperament, political and economic, leads us to the threshold of the great question of intellectual influences upon them: with the alleged ascendancy of John Locke over their minds, and with the way Edmund Burke's thought worked upon them.

It should be borne in mind that the Framers were not *philosophes*. Even the most bookish man among them, James Madison, praised experience over abstraction. When the Framers quoted dead philosophers, usually it was for ornament of their speeches and minor reinforcement of particular arguments. Nevertheless, the prevailing climate of intellectual opinion does exert some effect upon even the most empirical of politicians; so it is worthwhile to inquire what political writings the Framers read, and what use they made of those books and periodicals. We shall see that contemporary British thinkers moved them most: William Blackstone, David Hume, Edmund Burke.

PART III

SOURCES OF THE CONSTITUTION

8

John Locke and the Social Contract

I T IS A SAD ERROR, with unpleasant consequences, to fancy that the American Revolution and the Constitution broke with the British past and the American past; that the Republic of the United States was a radical undertaking, a repudiation of European civilization. It is no less an intellectual folly to argue that the Constitution of the United States was written in conformity to the ideas of John Locke, subjecting the American people to perpetual obedience to what are alleged to be Locke's political principles.

For decades, the typical American school textbook in history—supposing it to touch at all upon the intellectual background of the Constitution—has asserted that the great name of Locke commanded the minds both of the signers of the Declaration of Independence and of the Framers of the Constitution. This notion has been derived chiefly from the writings of Vernon Parrington, Charles Beard, and other egalitarian historians whose books were popular some sixty years ago.

Even Dr. Gottfried Dietze, who has written the best book about *The Federalist*, in which he expresses more perceptively than does any other commentator the strong influence of Hume upon its authors, suggests that "Locke is the philosopher to whom the authors of *The Federalist* are most indebted for an exposition of constitutionalism and free government."[1]

By the 1950s, however, other writers on American thought, although repeating the notion that John Locke was the great forerunner of American liberalism, were eager to repudiate or sweep away that alleged Lockean patrimony. Consider the late Dr. Louis Hartz, professor of government at Harvard University, in his book *The Liberal Tradition in America*. Practically everybody of any intellectual or political repute in the United States, from 1776 to the present, has been a disciple of Locke—so Hartz instructs us—much to the disadvantage of America. Hartz urges Americans to transcend Lockeanism: "Instead of recapturing our past, we have got to transcend it," he writes. "As a child who is leaving adolescence, there is no going home again for America. ...What is at stake is nothing less than a new level of consciousness, a transcending of irrational Lockeanism, in which an understanding of self and an understanding of others go hand in hand."[2]

As Daniel Boorstin wrote when Hartz's book was published, *The Liberal Tradition in America* is an illustration of what ails American liberalism today—abstract, bookish in the bad sense, insulated against reality. But a view of Locke's influence similarly exaggerated is held by a writer superior to Hartz—the late Richard Hofstadter, professor of history at Columbia University. In his widely-read book *The American Political Tradition and the Men Who Made It*, Hofstadter argues in effect that "the men who made it"—the Founding Fathers, Jefferson, Jackson, Calhoun, Lincoln, Phillips, Bryan, Theodore Roosevelt, Wilson, Hoover, F.D.R., and all the others—were captive in some degree to what Hartz calls "irrational Lockeanism." Hofstadter virtually identifies the influence of Locke with the economic doctrines of Manchester, and he regrets that we have not got rid of Lockean and Manchesterian notions: "Although it has been said repeatedly that we need a new conception of the world to replace the ideology of self-help, free enterprise, competition, and beneficent cupidity upon which Americans have been nourished since the foundations of the Republic," Hofstadter writes in his introduction, "no new conceptions of comparable strength have taken root and no statesman with a great mass following has arisen to propound them."[3]

Although Hartz and Hofstadter fall out on some questions, they hold to a common interpretation of the history of American politics, to the effect that all American leaders labored under a Lockean, or "conservative and Manchesterian," orthodoxy, whether they were called conservatives or liberals. Thus we have little to learn now from those leaders of yesteryear, although we may profit from a study of their deficiencies. Nevertheless, Hartz and Hofstadter seem unable to offer any clear alternative to this alleged Lockean ideology. They talk of centralization, planning, unification; they imply the need for some elite of centralizers and planners, presumably governed by the general aspirations of socialism, although emancipated from strict socialist ideology.

Since the 1950s, Locke has been apotheosized by disciples of Leo Strauss, who was strongly influenced by Greek philosophy. Many Straussians conform to a "Lockean interpretation" of the Constitution and of American history and politics generally. That interpretation, though sometimes called "conservative" (as indeed Professor Strauss was personally), is bound up with secularist and egalitarian assumptions. This adulation of Locke (or rather of a Locke who did not exist), erected into a dogma, is the more curious in view of Strauss's chapter "Modern Natural Right" in his book *Natural Right and History*, in which Strauss argues that Locke was powerfully influenced by the thought of Thomas Hobbes—that "presumptuous little upstart" (T. S. Eliot's phrase) whom Strauss did not love.[4]

We ought not to receive Locke's *Two Treatises of Civil Government*, or his other writings, as if they were immutable, inextricably woven into the fabric of American life and thought. Nevertheless an "irrational Lockeanism" does exist in certain American circles, even today—curiously enough, among persons who regard themselves as the leading lights of logicalism. Take, for examples, two writers on jurisprudence whose books received much solemn attention: John

Rawls, the author of *A Theory of Justice*, and Robert Nozick, the author of *Anarchy, State, and Utopia*.[5] These writers, although disagreeing in much, both take as the fundamental premise of their whole argument John Locke's hypothesis of a "state of nature" for mankind, out of which arose the social contract. Rawls and Nozick explicitly affirm that their whole concept of justice rests upon this footing. They do not trouble themselves to explain why, nor do they endeavor to answer the critics who, ever since the middle of the eighteenth century, have reduced Locke's social compact to dust. The social contract theory is patently absurd, if taken literally, and Locke's principal biographer, Maurice Cranston, writes that Locke himself did not mean it literally. Rawls and Nozick, however, accept unquestioningly Locke's notion that at some time all human beings lived without government, and then made a solemn compact so that property might be secure.

Although Locke was not easily moved to mirth, such an irony surely would have made him smile. The great rationalist Locke converted, three centuries later, into an icon of modern abstract liberalism. After this fashion, the imperial intellects of yesteryear sometimes suffer caricature at the hands of their latter-day devotees.

THE ACTUAL, HISTORICAL LOCKE was a political partisan deeply involved in the struggles of his age. Although his *Treatises*, published in 1690 (but probably written for the most part some years earlier) purport to be abstract discourses on the origin and character of society, in truth they amount to an explanation of the English political experience over several centuries.

The *Treatises* are a kind of apology for the Revolution of 1688. A Marxist might argue that they are ideological tracts: that is, a propaganda-veil for the advancement of certain economic interests, in this instance the interests of William III, the Whig magnates, and the landed classes generally. Locke's eagerness to protect "property" or "estate," and to establish it as one of three natural rights, seems to justify the application of the term ideology, as Marx defined that sinister word, to Locke's politics.

Locke's objectives in the closing years of the seventeenth century may be stated quite simply: to secure the Protestant ascendancy in Britain; to advance the interest of the commercial classes, which Locke identified with England's national economic interest; and to sustain what Disraeli long later would call a "Venetian constitution" for England, with the royal authority subordinated to the influence of the great Whig landed proprietors.

These objectives Locke—who was no democrat—shores up with a body of political theory. Political sovereignty belongs to the people, Locke argues—and not, by implication, to the king. The people delegate their power to a legislative body, Parliament, but they may withdraw that power. The executive authority, derived from the legislative, is dependent upon Parliament. That ought to be the constitution of England, Locke believed; and the Whig magnates with whom he was associated did establish such a constitution in 1688 and 1689.

Despite Locke's conformity to the Church of England, these ideas somewhat resemble the theories of certain Puritan writers and politicians, on either side of the Atlantic. In New England, between 1642 and 1660, the Puritan colonists had governed themselves on such principles—although they had found it necessary to submit to Stuart authority at the Restoration. The Massachusetts Declaration of Laws and Liberties, in 1649, obviously was not inspired by Locke; one may say that Locke, rather, was the inheritor of Puritan claims.

It is Locke's aspiration to prove that government is the product of free contract; that governors hold their authority only in trust; and that when trust is violated, a people rightfully may exercise their strength to undo tyranny—although only under unendurable provocation. These arguments explain and defend the Revolution of 1688, but also they purport to explain the nature of a long struggle for balanced government in England, from the thirteenth century onward. For the principle of parliamentary control of royal succession had been maintained successfully when Henry of Bolingbroke was crowned, and one finds the principle of resistance to tyranny in the pages of Hooker's *Laws of Ecclesiastical Polity*.

In most matters, Locke was not an original thinker, but rather a synthesizer or popularizer. In moral philosophy he endeavored to harmonize the findings of seventeenth-century science with Christian doctrine. Similarly, in politics he sought to work the opinions of earlier philosophers into a system consonant with the historical experience and the new needs of his country.

Society is the product of a voluntary contract, among men equal in a state of nature, Locke writes, to secure better the rights that are theirs by nature—life, liberty, property. Locke has much more to say about estate, or real property, than about life and liberty. Several times he declares that "the reason why men enter into society is the preservation of their property." This argument appealed strongly to colonial Americans, a very high proportion of the white inhabitants owning some sort of real property.

But can Locke's idea of the social compact be taken seriously in the twentieth century? Certainly no cultural anthropologist in the present day regards Locke's state of nature as ever having existed, nor subscribes to the notion of any formal social compact ever having been concluded by any primitive folk. For that matter, how much private property do primitive societies have to protect? Locke's social contract theory, intended as a reply to Hobbes, now seems insufficient.

Only sixty years later, David Hume would make mincemeat of Locke's theory that men, at any remote period, ever joined themselves into a formal concert for their common welfare. The historical origins of the state, Hume would point out, are nothing like Locke's primitive voluntary union: force and conquest, in England as elsewhere, have occurred recently or in some remote period, and have resulted in the forming of a state— although afterward most states are not held together by force alone.

So, too, Edmund Burke implied (though, like Locke, he stood for the Whig party) when, nearly a century after Locke, he advised his generation to "draw a sacred veil" over the remote origins of the state. Perhaps Locke's "law of nature" is not applicable to natural, primitive man, but rather to civilized Englishmen whose impulses and appetites have been chastened by Christian teaching.

In some of his other writings, Locke seems to contradict certain of his own assertions in the *Second Treatise*. He denies, for instance, the existence of innate ideas. This denial endangers his political postulate that men possess by nature an understanding of how life, liberty, and property are the equal rights of all. If no ideas are innate, how can there subsist the "self-evident truths" which the Declaration of Independence would proclaim?

The *Second Treatise*, then, cannot be accepted as a literal historical account of the origins of society. Nor is Locke's particular understanding of natural law tenable today. Despite Locke's frequent quoting of Richard Hooker, Locke did not really follow that acute divine in his theory of natural law, and still less did he follow Hooker back to Aquinas and other Schoolmen. As Maurice Cranston points out, Locke's notion of "natural law" was a Renaissance understanding, derived from Pufendorf and other secularists of the German school.[6]

A hundred years after Locke, Edmund Burke found it necessary to oppose the French Revolution on the very grounds that Locke had employed to justify the Revolution of 1688. But Burke did not turn to the "law of nature" in Locke's sense of that phrase; instead he affirmed the richer natural law tradition of Hooker, the Schoolmen of the fourteenth century, and Cicero. Replying to Rousseau's followers, Burke said that there exist genuine natural rights and a genuine contract that holds society together; but they are not the rights and the contract expounded by Rousseau. Had it not been politically awkward for him, because of his links with the Whigs, Burke might have added that neither were those rights and contract the ones expounded by Locke.

Society, Burke declared, is indeed in some sense a contract, a partnership; but it is no mere commercial contract to secure private profit, nor yet is it a contract comprehended in the General Will of Rousseau. Human beings do have rights by virtue of their human nature; but those rights are not bloodless abstractions, nor are they limited to mere guarantees against government. To narrow natural rights to such neat slogans as "liberty, equality, fraternity" or "life, liberty, property," Burke knew, was to ignore the complexity of public affairs and to leave out of consideration most moral relationships. One of the most important of the rights that men possess in society, Burke insisted, is the right to be restrained from actions that would destroy their neighbors and themselves—the right to have some control put upon their appetites.

Burke appealed back beyond Locke to an idea of community far warmer and richer than Locke's or Hobbes's aggregation of individuals. The true compact of society, Burke told his countrymen, is eternal: it joins the dead, the living, and the unborn. We all participate in this spiritual and social partnership, because it is ordained of God. In defense of social harmony, Burke appealed to what Locke had ignored: the love of neighbor and the sense of duty. By the time of the French Revolution, Locke's argument in the *Second Treatise* already had become insufficient to sustain a social order.

Locke's other principal work, his *Essay Concerning Human Understanding*, was taken in its time for a contribution to philosophy that never would die. In this famous book, the thesis of Locke is that the mind of every human individual, at birth, resembles a blank tablet, on which experience marks a series of impressions. These impressions gradually are formed into general ideas. No innate ideas exist, says Locke in the *Essay*, published in 1690: all that an infant inherits from his forefathers, or receives from God, is the means for giving significance to separate impressions.

As the *Treatises* were meant to demonstrate the sufficiency of individual interest and private judgment in politics, so the *Essay* was intended to establish an individualism of the mind. It opened the way for the rationalism of the eighteenth century: everything in heaven and earth must come under the critical scrutiny of private judgment. It would be easy for the deists, and for the skeptics who went beyond deism, to apply the theories of Locke to their own innovating impulses. Locke was neither deist nor thoroughgoing skeptic, but he did intend the *Essay* to be a weapon, especially against the Catholics, whose fortresses of authority and tradition would tremble before him.

Large though the influence of his chief philosophical work has been for nearly three centuries, there remain few people today who would defend the whole of his argument. Some would go beyond Locke, all the way to untrammeled materialism, denying that even the capabilities for comparing, distinguishing, judging, and willing are innate. Others, pointing to the wealth of inquiry into the mysteries of human nature since the end of the seventeenth century, would remark that Locke does not take into account those operations of the mind that lie below the level of consciousness; nor those that lift man, by mystical means or by poetic and mathematical insights, to a condition transcending the limits of pure reason. Yet other critics remark that Locke could know nothing about genetic inheritance, the science of genetics not having been dreamed of in Locke's age. Some such misgivings about Locke's first principles may be discerned among men of the Revolutionary and Constitutional eras in North America—that is, among those thoughtful Americans who had read Locke carefully, rather than receiving his concepts at second or third hand. It is worth noting that the *Treatises* were not printed in America until 1773.

AND YET ONE CONTINUES to encounter, even in works of reference, the delusion that somehow John Locke was the real author of the Constitution of the United States. Consider the following passage from the brief article on Locke in *The Columbia-Viking Desk Encyclopedia* (1953): "The state, he held, was formed by social contract and should be guided by belief in natural rights. This was in essence a plea for democracy, which bore fruit in the U. S. Constitution."

Now John Locke expressly denounced the notion of democracy in 1669; democracy is not mentioned in the Constitution of the United States, and indeed most of the Framers went to considerable pains to make sure that the general government would not be a democracy; there is not one word in the Constitution about social contracts and natural rights. The Constitution is not a theoretical document at all, and the influence of Locke upon it is negligible, although Locke's phrases, at least, crept into the Declaration of Independence, despite Jefferson's awkwardness about confessing the source of "life, liberty, and the pursuit of happiness."

If we turn to the books read and quoted by American leaders near the end of the eighteenth century, we discover that Locke was but one philosopher and political advocate among the many writers whose influence they acknowledged. The studies by Richard Gummere, Louis B. Wright, and other scholars of the reading of American leaders during the Revolutionary and Constitutional eras do not reveal any preoccupation with Locke.

Clinton Rossiter, in his *Seedtime of the Republic*, summarizes his painstaking research into Locke's influence upon American leaders of the decade 1765-1776:

> The unmistakable impression one gets from roaming through the entire range of Revolutionary literature is that he was definitely not so important a figure as we have hitherto assumed. There is no evidence that his treatise sold any better than a half-dozen other books that said pretty much the same thing, and until 1774 his name was mentioned only rarely in the columns of even the most radical newspapers. In hundreds of Whiggish pamphlets and letters he is not quoted at all; in other hundreds he appears as one of four or five English and Continental sources. Perhaps ninety percent of the quotations from *Civil Government* are limited to a few overworked passages about property and legislation. His discussion of "the dissolution of government" is hardly used at all. Many thoughtful colonists turned away from his confusions and omissions to summon other thinkers to testify about the origin of government and substance of natural law. [7]

Rossiter does not mean to deny that Locke nevertheless had his uses for the Patriots: "He was a famous, almost unassailable English philosopher who had glorified a rebellion of Englishmen against an English king. Despite his inconsistencies and omissions, despite his failure to give the ancient line any really new twist, he was therefore the most popular source of Revolutionary ideas. As such he was *primus inter pares*, not the lonely oracle of the American consensus." [8]

Yet by 1787, the American leaders required no apologist for rebellion. Quite the contrary, they did not desire to supply insurrectionary notions to such as Daniel Shays. It is no accident that Locke is not mentioned by the authors of *The Federalist*; while Shays is emphatically mentioned, by Publius (Hamilton), in Number 6.

Even Jefferson, though he had read Locke, cites in his Commonplace Book such juridical authorities as Coke and Kames much more frequently. As Gilbert Chinard puts it, "The Jeffersonian philosophy was born under the sign of Hengist and Horsa, not of the Goddess Reason"—that is, Jefferson was more strongly influenced by his understanding of British history, the Anglo-Saxon age particularly, than by the eighteenth-century rationalism of which Locke was a principal forerunner.[9]

Or consider John Adams. In the ten volumes of Adams's works, references to Locke are relatively few. Adams's *Thoughts on Government*, written in 1776, does contain praise of Locke; and in his *Novanglus*, written two years earlier, Adams quotes Locke at some length. Yet Adams treats Locke merely as one of several commendable English friends to liberty—"Sidney, Harrington, Locke, Milton, Neville, Burnet, Hoadley. . . ." Montesquieu appears to have made a far stronger impression upon the mind of Adams than did Locke.[10]

At bottom, the thinking Americans of the last quarter of the eighteenth century found their principles of order in no single political philosopher, but rather in their religion. When schooled Americans of that era approved a writer, commonly it was because his books confirmed their American experience and justified convictions they held already. So far as Locke served their needs, they employed Locke. But other men of ideas served them more immediately.

At the Constitutional Convention, no man was quoted more frequently than Montesquieu. Montesquieu rejects Hobbes's compact formed out of fear; but also, if less explicitly, he rejects Locke's version of the social contract. Actually Montesquieu disagrees with Locke more than he agrees; he learned as much at least from the Tory Bolingbroke, with whom he was personally acquainted. It is Montesquieu's conviction that political and civil institutions are not abstractly ordained or agreed upon at any one moment; instead, laws grow slowly out of people's experiences with one another, out of social customs and habits. "When a people have pure and regular manners, their laws become simple and natural," Montesquieu says. It was from Montesquieu, rather than from Locke, that the Framers obtained a theory of checks and balances and of the division of powers.

Hume, the "Tory by chance," was the most influential historian read by the Americans; and his interpretation of English history prevailed, despite Jefferson's endeavor to bring out a bowdlerized edition of Hume. It was the amusement of Hume, that amiable skeptic, to puncture balloons. The biggest balloon that came his way was John Locke, whom Hume thoroughly undoes in his *Enquiry Concerning Human Understanding* (1748). Reason with a capital "R," pure rationality as the guide to morals and politics, dominated the first half of the eighteenth century, and Locke was the grand champion of this system—though others carried it to extremes. Pure Reason never recovered from Hume's rapier thrust.

Intellectually, Hume refuted the contract theory in his *Treatise* and his *Morals*. The American Constitution would not be framed on the contract theory of Locke, and certainly not on that of Rousseau. Even among the states of eighteenth-century Europe, after centuries of civilization, Hume inquires, how many governments could be said to rest upon the consent of the governed, and so to require no domestic garrisons? Only the United Kingdom, the Dutch Republic, and some of the Swiss cantons, Hume replies.

Among Hume's more important American admirers were Hamilton and Madison. Through Madison, something of Hume went directly into the Constitution. As Irving Brant notes, "From David Hume, who saw that social conflicts were infinitely more complex than Aristotle thought them to be, came the idea that stability could be attained by balancing class against class, interest against interest, wherefore a large republic should be more stable than a small one, though harder to organize." [11]

What Madison and other Americans found convincing in Hume was his freedom from mystification, vulgar error, and fanatic conviction: Hume's powerful practical intellect, which settled for politics as the art of the possible. Although so mordant a critic of abstract Reason, David Hume was conspicuously rational. He shunned the narrow zealot in politics, and so did the Framers of the Constitution.

Blackstone, though a Tory, was in the minds of the Framers. His *Commentaries on the Laws of England*—published in 1765, the year of the Stamp Act—were sold so widely in the thirteen colonies that their total sale in North America nearly equaled their sale in Britain, despite the disparity in population. In Blackstone's account of English law there is something of Locke, and something of Montesquieu, but chiefly the inheritance of common law and equity. Especially in America, the *Commentaries* serve the highly useful purpose of making it possible (in Blackstone's phrase) for "the gentleman and the scholar," as well as the lawyer, to discern some order in the tremendous mass of precedents accumulated over seven centuries.

Despite Blackstone's own confusion as to the sources of natural law, clearly Blackstone teaches that good order results from precedent and prescription. Blackstone did declare three "absolute rights": the natural liberty of mankind, consisting of three articles, "the right of personal security, the right of personal liberty, and the right of private property." Yet these rights were not absolute in the sense of having no limits: as Blackstone wrote, "But every man, when he enters into society . . . obliges himself to conform to these laws which the community has thought proper to establish." In that sentence, more than in Locke's phrases, may be found a fundamental doctrine of American politics. The men of the Constitutional Convention had read their Blackstone more attentively than their Locke, both because Blackstone was a contemporary of some of them, and because the livelihood of many of them depended upon understanding Blackstone.

As for Edmund Burke, already we have touched upon some of his differences from Locke; and he will be discussed in detail in the next chapter. Appeal though he might to the Old Whigs, Burke was no pupil of Locke: he set himself against Locke's notion of the social compact (inherited by Rousseau, Burke's adversary) and against Locke's psychology.

My point is this: Americans of the Republic's formative years did not take their politics from closet philosophers, nor yet from philosophers who dabbled in practical politics, after Locke's fashion. Historical experience, practical considerations, religious convictions, established political usage: these were the foundations of the Constitution of the United States.

Ideas take root only if the soil of society has been prepared for them by circumstances. Locke's ideas in some degree influenced American leaders, but did not dominate their minds; his arguments took on flesh in America only so far as they accorded with social arrangements and customs already flourishing there. Even well-schooled Americans of those years did not study political theory systematically, and Locke's *Treatises* were not to be found in the classroom.

Since the Second World War, as William Lee Miller points out, there has grown up a school of reflective American historians who refute the "progressive" views of Beard, Parrington, and other writers concerning the founders of the American Republic. The intellectual triumph of this recent school, as Miller puts it, "means the comparative subordination, as a source and symbol of those ideas about society, human nature, and the moral requirements of citizenship, of John Locke—compared, that is, to the day when Locke's intellectual role would be seen in such exaggerated terms as to describe him as the 'Marx of the American Revolution', or the mind of the American nation as 'John Locke writ large'. . . . And with reference to ideas it [this new history-writing] has demoted John Locke, reducing him simply to one among a number of influences on American republic-making."[12]

Dr. Ellis Sandoz, in a learned study of the American Founding, points out that the Founders did not embrace the more subtle doctrines to be found in Locke's writings, and that such influence upon them as Locke exerted was interwoven with many other and stronger strands:

> The American founders did not dream (as they reflected on the hierarchical structure of reality) that the protection of property and the erection of an extended commercial republic contradicted their dedication to individual liberty or to the continuation of a Christian commonwealth moored in toleration of a denominational diversity and disestablishment. They were quite capable of reconciling Locke, the Italian republic tradition, Montesquieu's interpretation of constitutionalism, and the teachings of Aristotle, Polybius, and Cicero in devising their plan of government. Any doctrinaire interpretation of their thought is almost certainly misleading if not distorted, whether the factor is as fascinating and important as the place of Locke or of the Old Country Whig tradition or the influence of the Scottish Enlightenment.[13]

One last hard fact about all this: in *The Federalist*, there occurs no mention of the name of John Locke. In Madison's *Notes of Debates in the Federal Convention* there is to be found but one reference to Locke, and that incidental.[14] Do not these omissions seem significant to zealots for a "Lockean interpretation" of the Constitution?

John Locke did not make the Glorious Revolution of 1688 or fore-ordain the Constitution of the United States. The Revolution of 1776, like the Revolution of 1688, presumably would have occurred even if Locke, emulating his Cambridge friends, had devoted himself lifelong to the study of Plato, eschewing practical politics. And the Constitution of the United States would have been framed by the same sort of men with the same sort of result, and defended by Hamilton, Madison, and Jay, had Locke in 1689 lost the manuscripts of his *Two Treatises of Civil Government* while crossing the narrow seas with the Princess Mary.

9

Edmund Burke and the Chartered Rights of Englishmen

C ONSTITUTIONS ARE SOMETHING MORE than lines written upon parchment. When a written constitution endures—and most written constitutions have not been long for this world—that document has been derived successfully from long-established customs, beliefs, statutes, and interests. It has reflected a political order already accepted, tacitly at least, by the dominant classes or interests among a people.

True constitutions are not invented: they grow. The Constitution of the United States has endured for two centuries because it arose from the healthy roots of a century and a half of colonial experience and of several centuries of British experience. For the most part, the American Constitution expressed formally what already was accepted, practiced, and believed by the people of the new republic. A constitution lacking deep roots is no true constitution at all.

In a symposium at Kenyon College, I expressed such views. Clinton Rossiter dissented. A constitution can be created overnight, he said; just that had been done in several European countries shortly after the First and Second World Wars.

"Where are those constitutions now?" I inquired.

Today one might ask, with equal pertinence, "Where are the constitutions of the emergent African states, so grandly promulgated in the 1950s and 1960s?" The framers of a successful constitution must take into account the history, the moral order, the resources, the prospects of a country—and much else besides. Those framers must have some understanding of what Edmund Burke called "the contract of eternal society." Those framers must be endowed with political imagination—which is not at all the same thing as political utopianism—and with much practical knowledge of public affairs. Otherwise a constitution may live no longer than a butterfly.

Of leading Americans during the last quarter of the eighteenth century, none understood this hard truth better than did John Adams, reared in politically contentious Massachusetts. He ridiculed John Locke as a constitution-drafter. On the eve of the Constitutional Convention, Adams wrote, in *A Defence of the Constitutions*,

> A philosopher may be perfect master of Descartes and Leibnitz, may pursue his own inquiries into metaphysics to any length, may enter into the innermost recesses of the human mind, and make the noblest discoveries for the benefit of his species; nay, he may defend the principles of liberty and the rights of mankind with great abilities and success; and, after all, when called upon to produce a plan of legislation, he may astonish the world with a signal absurdity. Mr. Locke, in 1663, was employed to trace out a plan of legislation for Carolina; and he gave the whole authority, executive and legislative, to the eight proprietors, the Lords Berkley, Clarendon, Albemarle, Craven, and Ashley; and Messieurs Carteret, Berkley, and Colleton, and their heirs. This new oligarchical sovereignty created at once three orders of nobility . . . . Who did this legislator think would live under his government? He should have first created a new species of beings to govern, before he instituted such a government.[1]

Leading Americans had a very different opinion of their contemporary Edmund Burke, then engaged in struggles over the British Constitution which would end in establishing cabinet government and responsible parties. Burke was the most eloquent champion of the British Constitution (despite his reforming endeavors) and would become the most formidable adversary of the several French constitutions from 1789 onward. He touches upon constitutional questions from his earliest political speeches to his final publications. And yet Burke never said or wrote anything about the Constitution drawn up at Philadelphia in 1787.

Nevertheless, in this chapter I mean to describe the influence of Burke—experienced statesman, leader of party, and scholar in constitutional history—upon the American Constitution of 1787 and upon its interpretation in later years. This choice of theme may surprise some people. For Burke's name is not to be found in the recorded proceedings of that Convention at Philadelphia, nor is it mentioned in the pages of *The Federalist*. After the year 1782 and American independence, Burke scarcely mentions North American affairs in his speeches, his publications, or his correspondence. Why, then, assert that the great Whig politician, who never had visited the thirteen colonies, somehow may be associated with that highly successful political device the federal Constitution of the American Republic?

First, because the general frame and substance of the United States Constitution accords with the political principles of the Rockingham Whigs, whose manager and intellectual chief Burke was. The Framers of the American Constitution borrowed deliberately and liberally from the British Constitution. Sir Henry Maine remarks in his *Popular Government* that the American framers took for their model the British Constitution as it stood between 1760 and 1787—the years when Burke figured prominently in the House of Commons. The late M. E. Bradford suggests that Maine was inaccurate in his dating: what the Framers at Philadelphia took for their model constitution, rather, was the English Constitution as it had stood before passage of the Stamp Act in 1765—in effect, the Constitution of 1688. "It was a bond by way of inheritance," Bradford writes, "shaped more by corporate memory than by first principles: a legal bond, composed of a few texts, favored glosses upon those texts, and a disposition or habit of mind most easily identified with the Whig magnates of eighteenth century England—magnates whose spokesmen put text, gloss, and memory together." [2]

What certain writers on American history and politics mistake for the influence of John Locke on the Framers, in reality was rather the general Whig mentality and climate of opinion about the end of the seventeenth century and the beginning of the eighteenth: Americans did not need to open Locke's *Treatises*, or indeed ever to hear of that book, to acquire Whiggish constitutional opinions. It seems probable that most Americans with political inclinations, including the delegates to the Constitutional Convention, had more in mind the British Constitution as they had understood it in their youth, than the British Constitution under George III—whom they suspected of conspiring against their liberties.

The English constitution to which Burke appealed against George III and his ministers was that "minimal constitution" (Bradford's phrase) of the time before 1765 when the Crown's policy toward the thirteen colonies had been what Burke described as "salutary neglect." And it was to the memory of "the Whigs of the Revolution" (of 1688) that Burke turned for authority when, in 1791, he published his *Appeal from the New to the Old Whigs*. (He quoted from eminent Whigs testifying at the trial of Dr. Sacheverel, in 1710; he did not mention Locke.)

In short, the delegates to the Convention at Philadelphia thought of the British Constitution quite as Burke had thought of it. So whether or not Sir Henry Maine was accurate in his "1760 to 1787" contention, surely the British Constitution as expounded by Burke was the principal constitutional model in the mind's eye among the gentlemen politicians at Philadelphia.

I do not suggest that everything in the Constitution framed at Philadelphia would have been thoroughly approved by Burke; later I will discuss certain provisions of which he doubtless disapproved. Yet for the most part, the Constitution agreed upon in 1787 not only was derived from the eighteenth-century British Constitution, but was derived more precisely from the idea of that British Constitution which

Burke himself had enunciated so ringingly from his *Thoughts on the Present Discontents* (1770) to his *Speech on Moving Resolutions for Conciliation with the Colonies* (1775).

In substance, the Constitution of the United States was an amended version of what Burke called "the chartered rights of Englishmen." Burke had been the principal expositor of the Whig concept of the English Constitution held by John Dickinson and other Patriot leaders. Moreover, Burke, like the delegates sent to Philadelphia, was a practical public man of much experience—no coffee-house philosopher—and so was congenial to the Framers, whether or not they were well aware of Burke's influence upon them.

Also the Framers at Philadelphia, young men many of them (and only eight having been also signers of the Declaration of Independence), had grown up during the decade when the parliamentary addresses of Burke and Chatham had upheld the cause of the colonies against the Crown in Parliament; when Burke's Irish invective had been directed against George III's American policies and his ministers, and indeed against the King himself. Burke's famous American speeches from 1770 to 1775 had been read and discussed by every American of the rising generation who had taken any interest in politics—especially the *Speech on American Taxation* (1774) and the *Speech on Conciliation* (1775). Burke never had favored American separation from the British Empire; the Declaration of Independence struck him a sore blow; nevertheless, doubtless the large majority of delegates to the Convention at Philadelphia regarded Burke as a friend to America. Burke's constitutional doctrines, during those five years of vehement opposition to the King's Friends, had been intertwined with his denunciations of the folly of taxing Americans against their will. So it is not surprising that Burke's concept of a just constitution had come to be taken for granted by most of the delegates to Philadelphia.

Moreover, the Philadelphia delegates' understanding of the causes and course of the War of Independence had been formed by Burke himself through a medium quite distinct from his speeches. For also Burke was the editor of *The Annual Register*, the London publication that printed every year a detailed account of the Revolution—along with much else—in the thirteen colonies: the only such reporting available on either side of the Atlantic. Assuming the *Register*'s editorship when the publication was founded, Burke continued editorial supervision down to 1789. Much of the writing and editing of those articles was done by subordinates, from time to time; but those subordinates were Rockingham Whigs, Burke's friends and disciples. The whole political tone of the *Register* was Burke's.

Probably every delegate at Philadelphia in 1787 had read the *Register*, with its interpretations of American and British constitutional controversies, in its annual volumes from 1765 to 1785 (and perhaps the newly-published volume for 1786); indeed, they had available then no other systematic and tolerably impartial analysis of military and political events during those years. In this fashion, quite aside from his oratory in the House of Commons, Burke exercised through serious journalism an ascendancy over the minds of leading Americans of the Revo-lutionary and Constitutional eras, an influence greater than is obtained over the American people over two centuries later by the most famous or notorious publicists of our day.[3]

For an example of Burke's influence upon American political leaders of the 1780s and 1790s, take James Iredell, leader of the Federalists in North Carolina's convention to ratify the Constitution and later a justice of the Supreme Court of the United States. Iredell writes in 1783 to his brother, the Reverend Arthur Iredell, "You must know that I am particularly partial to Mr. Burke and I wish you could include in my little packet everything of his that has been published." Through the correspondence of the Iredell brothers, down to 1799 (when Arthur died), runs admiration for Burke, whose views of the British Constitution they shared. Burke's *Reflections* undid their early hopes for the French Revolution; they were won over to Burke's views.[4]

It was the reflective part of the public that the *Register* reached, of course; but then, as today, it is the reflective part of the public which tends to determine public policy. So powerful was the influence of Burke's *Annual Register* that the principal American historians of the early Republic not only accepted the *Register*'s information and judgments almost without question, but plagiarized shamelessly from its historical articles. David Ramsay, William Gordon, Charles Stedman, and Thomas Anburey—all well-reputed and much-read writers—were discovered, long later, to have borrowed many of their pages from Burke, without acknowledgment. But the most eminent of the plagiarists was John Marshall, Chief Justice of the United States, in his *Life of George Washington*, the first volume of which was published in 1804. (Marshall's heavy borrowings from the *Register* were not descried by American historical scholars until 1937.)[5] In effect, Burke's *Annual Register* established America's quasi-official version of the Revolutionary War—and so early as 1787, the authority of the historical articles in the *Register* for 1765 to 1783 stood almost unchallenged. The delegates to the Constitutional Convention at Philadelphia were unavoidably steeped in Burke.

Among the Framers with whom Burke appears to have had particular weight were John Dickinson of Delaware, Rufus King of Massachusetts, Alexander Hamilton of New York, William Samuel Johnson of Connecticut, Benjamin Franklin and Jared Ingersoll of Pennsylvania, James Blair and James McClung of Virginia, Hugh Williamson of North Carolina, and John Rutledge and the two Pinckneys of South Carolina. Some of these gentlemen had met Burke when they had visited England for commerce or schooling. Franklin often had conversed seriously with Burke in London, and had corresponded with him earlier. Hugh Williamson, in 1777, had published a pamphlet that drew heavily upon Burke; it appears that he and Burke had been personally acquainted in London.

Aside from delegates to the Constitutional Convention, other American leaders who exercised strong influence about 1787 had known Burke well. Samuel Chase of Maryland, for one, had been for a week a guest in Burke's house at Beaconsfield. Richard Champion of South Carolina had been Burke's close friend in Bristol and one of Burke's deputies when Burke had been paymaster-general to the forces.

Years later, some of the men who had been delegates to the Convention—James Wilson of Pennsylvania in particular—would come to disagree in theory with Edmund Burke. But in 1787, when Thomas Paine still fancied that his former patron Burke was a friend to revolutionary change, those distinctions did not exist, or at least were inconspicuous. Why then is Burke's name absent from Madison's *Notes of Debates*? Why do not the authors of *The Federalist* cite Burke?

Because the delegates at Philadelphia were too much occupied with urgent disputation over practical concerns to quote from living statists abroad. They did not mention, either, so far as reports of their debates go, the other two chief constitutional thinkers of the closing decades of the eighteenth century, Jean-Jacques Rousseau and Jeremy Bentham; nor even Sir William Blackstone, closely studied then by every American lawyer. Both the men of the Convention and the authors of *The Federalist* mention or quote Montesquieu several times; Hume, though a Tory, is commended; there occur references in *The Federalist* to Raynal, Delolme, and one or two other eighteenth-century writers. But the literary, historical, and philosophical allusions of Madison, Hamilton, and Jay are drawn chiefly from antiquity. Gentlemen having benefitted from a classical education, they turned naturally to familiar Greek and Latin authors, whose authority presumably would be recognized by many readers of *The Federalist*. Montesquieu was the principal exception to this predilection: *The Spirit of Laws* had been published in 1748, and the first English edition had appeared in 1750. Jay had been born in 1745, Madison in 1751, Hamilton in 1757. Montesquieu had been the grand political writer of their youth, his reputation unassailable. The elapse of nearly four decades sufficed to remove *The Spirit of Laws*, almost adulatory of the English constitution, from political partisanship.

Burke, on the other hand, in 1787 still was partisan and quick, a British party leader passionately committed to a reforming course in English politics. His indictment of Warren Hastings was of little immediate interest to the delegates at Philadelphia, even though Burke's disquisitions on the rule of law, in the course of Hastings's indictment and prosecution, had much to do with political constitutions. Burke's enduring reputation, unlike Montesquieu's, was yet to be determined. It was more prudent to cite, among recent writers, David Hume, also a friend to America. Hume having died in 1776, he could not demur from what might be said about him at the Convention.

There existed another reason why Burke was not acknowledged at the Convention or in *The Federalist*: Burke's presumed contempt for the Declaration of Independence. Although Burke's concerted assault upon *a priori* theories and fanciful claims of natural right would not commence until 1790, already it was clear enough in 1787 that Burke was the adversary both of Rousseau and of the *philosophes*. The Declaration of Independence, calculated to please Paris and Versailles, had broken with the constitutional argument of the Americans that had been advanced ever since passage of the Stamp Act. Until 1776, protesting Americans had pleaded that they were entitled to the rights of Englishmen, as expressed in the British Constitution, and particularly in the Bill of Rights of 1689. But Jefferson's Declaration of Independence had abandoned this tack and had carried the American cause into the misty debatable land of an abstract liberty, equality, and fraternity. Such reasoning was anathema to Burke the practical statesman. Once the Declaration of Independence was proclaimed, Burke ceased to interest himself in America. Why quote him at a Convention he might reproach?

Thus Burke's understanding of constitutions went formally unacknowledged at Philadelphia; nevertheless Burke's constitutionalism was pervasive there. Three years later, when *Reflections on the Revolution in France* would appear, Burke's arguments and aphorisms would be on the lips of every American politically literate—but it was not so in 1787. Nevertheless, the delegates of 1787 produced a constitution that conformed in large part to Burke's idea of what should be a good constitution for a nation that had arisen out of the British historical experience.

Reinhold Niebuhr expresses well Burke's superior understanding of English constitutional questions:

> English political sagacity is compounded of instinctive reactions to immediate situations and a wisdom, gained by cumulative experience, which guides instinct through the complexities, intricacies and imponderabilities of modern politics. The most typical social philosopher of England is not John Locke but Edmund Burke. Constitutional government may have found its

first justification in the rationally elaborated theories of "rights" in the philosophy of the former. But the actual history of constitutionalism in England has been dominated by the logic expressed in the philosophy of the latter. The Englishman trusts not in the abstract "natural rights" dictated by reason, but the "English rights" which are guaranteed to him by his own history.[6]

And such was the understanding of constitutions and rights which prevailed among the Framers at Philadelphia.

LET US DESCEND to particulars. In what respects would Burke have approved the new Constitution of the United States—if he had not been too busy in 1787 even to notice it in the pages of his own *Register*?

First, the Constitution did not break with the established institutions and customs of the American people: it was a healthy growth, an enlargement of a political structure of which the foundations had been laid early in the seventeenth century—or earlier still, in medieval England. As James Bryce would point out nearly a century later, the new federal constitution had for precedent and source the colonial charters or constitutions. These basic laws were altered somewhat with the coming of American independence, but some of them not changed greatly. The colonial constitution of Massachusetts was transmuted into the state constitution of 1780 without radical change, and as Bryce remarks, it "profoundly influenced the Convention that prepared the Federal Constitution in 1787."[7]

Second, the Constitution recognized and incorporated a body of historical experience far older than the North American colonies: the constitutional development of England, the country with the highest degree of both freedom and order during the eighteenth century. Many parallels between the old British Constitution and the new American Constitution are obvious enough. Sir Henry Maine points out somewhat wittily that the Convention's delegates conferred upon the President of the United States powers precisely of the sort which George III claimed for the kingly office—despite all their previous lamentations about royal usurpation of power.[8]

Third, the Constitution rejected *a priori* theories of government. As Sir William Holdsworth puts it in his *History of English Law*, "The political theory of the Declaration of Independence which dwelt upon the equality of men, their unalienable rights to life, liberty, and the pursuit of happiness, and their right to resist a tyrannical government, retired into the background. The founders of the American constitution recognized with Burke that such theories, however well they might be suited to a period of revolution, were of very little help in a period of reconstruction. They therefore abandoned the democratic theories of Paine and Rousseau, and went for inspiration to that eighteenth-century British constitution with which they were familiar."[9]

Fourth, the Constitution of the United States put strong constraints upon arbitrary power, distinctly limiting the operations of the general government. It preserved state powers for the most part, avoiding the curse of centralization for which Burke was to reproach the French revolutionaries; it recognized in the United States Senate a form of natural aristocracy; it established the Congress as a body of true *representatives*, not delegates, conforming to Burke's speech on declining the poll at Bristol.

Let us turn to provisions in the Constitution that ran contrary to Burke's principles. In the theory of checks and balances, Madison and the other principal Framers submitted to the authority of Montesquieu, endeavoring to establish through the Constitution a balance among three equal estates or powers. Yet this notion of an artificial balance, a kind of abstract triangle of powers, actually may end in anarchy or in impotence. So Stanley Pargellis reminds us in his essay "The Theory of Balanced Government" (1938). Burke did not subscribe to this ancient and almost sacrosanct concept, expressed by Madison in *The Federalist* as the principle "that the three powers, executive, legislative, and judicial, shall be forever separate and distinct." Burke did believe in the independence of the judiciary; but that is not the same thing as faith in "a delicate equipoise between equal powers," leading to stability through mutual jealousies. Pargellis summarizes Burke's quite different understanding of the arrangement of power within a constitutional order, beginning with his *Thoughts on the Present Discontents*:

In 1770 Burke recognized and rather vaguely defined a new convention of the constitution, the convention of cabinet government which a century later Bagehot was finally to popularize. As Burke read history, every sort of government, unless it was to fall into hideous disorder, must have its administration correspondent to its legislature. There are bound to be parties in a state, argued Burke. Set up, then, a party ministry in trust to the nation, with power to act efficiently, within limits defined by the law, responsible to the majority of the representatives of the people, and through them to the people themselves—that is Burke's great contribution to the art and practice of government.[10]

The presidential cabinet of the United States is not responsible to the Congress, of course; and the President of this country holds today the executive powers that George III longed for but could not obtain. The "balance" among the executive, legislative, and judicial branches of the federal government falls from time to time into confusion and hatred, working much mischief to the national interest—as during the second Nixon administration. The tremendous power conferred upon the President, in part through a plebiscitary elevation unintended by the Framers, may work at one time or another to the advantage of the nation; but also the misuse of that power may bring on ruinous consequences at home and abroad, as in the administration of Lyndon Johnson.

The Framers blundered in their design of the Electoral College, which very promptly malfunctioned. That College was meant, in effect, to choose an elective king of high rectitude and talent, the ablest conceivable chief magistrate. The Electoral College's early virtual collapse has given the country instead, much of the time, the sort of presidents described by James Bryce in 1893: "The only thing remarkable about them is that being so commonplace they should have climbed so high."[11] Conisdering the limited competence and imagination of many presidents, it is clear that great power falls into the hands of the executive branch generally, that is, into the hands of persons not responsible to Congress or to anyone else except an overworked and underendowed President.

Nor did the Framers foresee the necessity for responsible political parties—rather, they dreaded parties as "factions." Burke's Rockingham Whigs formed the first party of principle, as contrasted with parties of expedience and place-seeking. "Party is a body of men united, for promoting by their joint endeavours the national interest, upon some particular principle in which they are all agreed." This is Burke's definition in *Thoughts on the Present Discontents*. Parties lacking, representative government cannot be carried on.

The contest from year to year between the Congress on the one hand and the executive branch on the other—a rivalry well analyzed by Alfred de Grazia, James Burnham, and others—may yet undo America's security and prosperity, in some unguarded hour. Yet whatever might have been the advantages of cabinet government upon the pattern that developed in Britain (commencing there in Burke's day), two centuries later it seems inconceivable that the Constitution's theoretical division of the federal government into three branches should be discarded, or that presidential tenure should be made subject to a majority in the House of Representatives. *Quieta non movere*: for good or ill, two centuries' precedents cannot be undone, and prescription is the best of titles. If there is to occur some change in the relationships between the American legislative and executive branches, such a change must be effected only very gradually and with much caution. Edmund Burke himself instructs us that if an institution has functioned tolerably well for a great while, a legitimate presumption is established in its favor.

With every year that passed after 1787, the effectual power of the king of England would diminish, and the effectual power of the President of the United States would increase. Jefferson's professed deference to the Congress would not slow this drift. The two great constitutional systems moved in opposite directions. Montesquieu's doctrine of checks and balances quite overwhelmed Burke's concept of responsible cabinet and responsible party as constitutional agencies. Yet with this large exception, the Constitution framed at Philadelphia still conformed well enough to Burke's idea of a constitution in which the claims of order and the claims of freedom would be reconciled.

"When the American Constitution was framed," Maine concludes, in his *Popular Government*, "there was no such sacredness to be expected for it as before 1789 was supposed to attach to all parts of the British Constitution. There was every prospect of political mobility, if not of political disorder. The signal success of the Constitution of the United States in stemming these tendencies is, no doubt, owing in part to the great portion of the British institutions which were preserved in it. But it is also attributable to the sagacity with which the American statesmen filled up the interstices left by the inapplicability of certain of the then existing British institutions to the emancipated colonies." [12]

The wisdom and eloquence of Edmund Burke had something to do with that success of the Constitution of the United States—if more in subtle fashion than overtly.

IF BURKE'S VIEWS on constitutions obtained little public mention in 1787, by 1790 all was changed. Edmund Burke had commenced his denunciation of the French Revolution. From 1790 to 1797, everything Mr. Burke wrote about constitutions—the successively collapsing French constitutions, Poland's new constitution of 1791, the embattled British Constitution—was read eagerly on either side of the Atlantic.

In America, the leading Federalists, north and south, applauded Burke and adopted his arguments as their own; even John Adams and John Quincy Adams were won over, if grudgingly. Nor was it Federalists merely whom Burke persuaded: John Randolph of Roanoke, who had been the Republican speaker of the House, presently became Burke's hottest disciple; later, John C. Calhoun would find in Burke the foundation for his own constitutional reasoning. After his death, Burke came to exert a strong influence upon American jurisprudence. His thought helped to shape interpretation and application of America's federal constitution and of several state constitutions.

John Marshall, whose *Life of Washington* owed so much directly to Burke's *Annual Register*, was no great scholar: but he did know his Burke, and within certain of Marshall's important opinions the concepts and the phrases of Burke can be traced. Justice Joseph Story was yet more clearly an admirer of Burke; and in New York, Chancellor James Kent was of Burke's school. Story's *Commentaries on the Constitution* and Kent's *Commentaries on American Law* were of Burke's mode of thought. One might trace the influence of Burke upon this or that justice of the Supreme Court of the United States all the way down to the 1980s, when Chief Justice Burger quoted Burke.

Yet Burke's idea of a true constitution, so nobly expressed in his *Appeal from the New to the Old Whigs* (1792), was under assault in Britain even then. Holdsworth remarks "that Adam Smith, Bentham, and Paine were beginning to teach men to approach the law and constitution of England from a point of view which was the exact opposite to that of Blackstone and Burke."[13] The constitutionalism of Edmund Burke, together with his whole concept of law, ever since then has been battered by positivistic and utilitarian concepts of law and constitution on both sides of the ocean.

In the United States, Story's *Commentaries* disseminated Burke's views on law and politics everywhere; for Story's volumes quoted or cited Burke repeatedly. Out of Harvard Law School spread Story's jurisprudence, the mind of Burke woven into it. Story himself dominated American legal thought beyond the middle of the nineteenth century; and later editions of the *Commentaries*, edited by Thomas M. Cooley, a major scholar in the law, carried Burke right into the early decades of the twentieth century.[14]

Yet positivism, legal realism, and other schools of jurisprudence have prevailed in America's courts and schools of law. And gradually the American public, though not well understanding jurisprudential controversies, has grown bitterly resentful of many judicial decisions, far-reaching in their social effects, which have been the consequences of latter-day theories of law. Judges and professors of law would do well to repair to Burke, in an era of popular demand for conservative measures: for the alternative to a conservatism of reflection is a conservatism of mere impulse, or else of stagnation. And in an age of virulent ideology, an age of immensely quick, unthinking communication, old institutions everywhere require intelligent defense—even the Constitution of the United States.

Burke's unfinished *Fourth Letter on a Regicide Peace*, his last published work, terminates with the fragment of a sentence: "There is no such Euthanasia for the British Constitution. . . . " Here Burke refers to an early essay by Hume, in which the speculative Scot suggested that in the fullness of time the decaying British Constitution might die an easy death from inanition, a case of euthanasia, "gently expiring without a groan in the paternal arms of a mere Monarchy." The end of the British Constitution would not be painless, Burke protested, not if Jacobin France, or Jacobins within Britain, should gain the mastery. The end would be terrible, a destruction of Britain's civil social order by merciless fanatics.

Today we may say of the Constitution of the United States what Burke said of the British Constitution in 1791:

> It is no simple, no superficial thing, nor to be estimated by superficial understandings. An ignorant man, who is not fool enough to meddle with his clock, is however sufficiently confident to think he can safely take to pieces, and put together at his pleasure, a moral machine of another guise, importance, and complexity, composed of far other wheels, and springs, and balances, and counteracting and co-operating powers. Men little think how immorally they act in rashly meddling with what they do not understand. Their delusive good intention is no sort of excuse for their presumption. They who truly mean well must be fearful of acting ill. The British constitution may have its advantages pointed out to wise and reflecting minds; but it is of too high an order of excellence to be adapted to those which are common. It takes in too many views, it makes too many combinations, to be so much as comprehended by shallow and superficial understandings. Profound thinkers will know it in its reason and spirit. The less inquiring will recognize it in their feelings and their experience. They will thank God they have a standard which, in the most essential point of this great concern, will put them on a par with the most wise and knowing. . . . We ought to understand it according to our measure; and to venerate where we are not able presently to comprehend.[15]

IO

Natural Law
and the Constitution

T HE LITERATURE OF NATURAL LAW is complex, copious, and monthly growing vaster. All I aspire to accomplish is to offer some examination of the relationships between natural law doctrines and the Constitution of the United States. The present pressing question is how we are to restore a true understanding of natural law in the discussion of legislation and the decisions of the Supreme Court of the United States.

Clearly, a good many public men and women have but a vague notion of what is meant by the term *natural law*. It was objected to Judge Robert H. Bork's nomination to the Supreme Court that he did *not* believe in natural law. When Judge Clarence Thomas was interrogated for the same bench, the objection was raised that he *did* believe in natural law.

Notre Dame Law Review 69, no. 5, (1994): 1035-48. © *Notre Dame Law Review*, University of Notre Dame. Reprinted with permission. The editor of this volume bears responsibility for all errors.

During very recent years there have appeared serious studies of natural law, and its relationship to our present discontents, that deserve high praise. Among the more important books are Russell Hittinger's *A Critique of the New Natural Law Theory*, Graham Walker's *Moral Foundations of Constitutional Thought: Current Problems, Augustinian Prospects*, and Hadley Arkes's *Beyond the Constitution*. Also there has occurred a lively exchange of opinions on such themes in a good many periodicals, among them *Public Affairs Quarterly*, *The Wake Forest Law Review*, *The Review of Politics*, *Crisis*, *Modern Age*, and *First Things*.

Although since 1938 judicial positivism has prevailed conspicuously in decisions of the United States Supreme Court, in recent decades a number of important decisions seem to have been founded, somewhat surreptitiously, upon natural law or natural rights notions in consequence of the doctrine of *stare decisis*. Was not Justice Brennan given to appealing to judges' private understanding of concepts of natural justice? But that complex question is not directly before us.

Misunderstanding of natural law, or its misapplication, may work great mischief. Permit me to offer a succinct definition of the general term—a sweeping definition.

Objectively speaking, natural law, as a term of politics and jurisprudence, may be defined as a loosely-knit body of rules of action prescribed by an authority superior to the state. These rules variously (according to several different schools of natural law and natural rights speculation) are derived from divine commandment, from right reason with which man is endowed by his Creator, from the nature of mankind empirically regarded, from the abstract Reason of the Enlightenment, or from the long experience of humankind in community.

I am concerned not directly with distinguishing among several schools of thought, but rather with the ancient and central tradition of natural law, with its roots in Plato and Aristotle, later and more fully expounded by Cicero, Seneca, and the Roman jurisconsults; then passing from the Stoic sages to the Fathers of the Church, and presently amplified and defined by St. Thomas Aquinas. From the Schoolmen that understanding of natural law enters into English common law, and in the sixteenth century obtains fresh expression in Hooker's *Laws of Ecclesiastical Polity* and the later writings of other Anglican divines. This apprehension of natural law passes into America during colonial times, and in some degree survives, if often submerged, in twentieth-century America. We may call it the Catholic doctrine of natural law—supposing we are aware of its classical roots, and that communicants of the Catholic Church are not the only defenders and guardians of natural law. C.S. Lewis, in his Appendix, "Illustrations of the *Tao*," of his book *The Abolition of Man*, shows convincingly how a recognition of natural law may be encountered in many religions and philosophies.

On the one hand, natural law must be distinguished from positive or statutory law, decreed by the state; on the other, from "laws of nature" in a scientific sense—that is, from propositions expressing the regular order of certain material phenomena. Also natural law sometimes is confronted with assertions of "natural rights" which may or may not be founded upon classical and Christian concepts of natural law.

The legacy of the classical *ius naturalis*, as baptized by Schoolmen and canonists, endured with little challenge until the seventeenth century. During those centuries, in the Christian world, the natural law was received as a body of unwritten rules depending upon common sense and universal conscience, ascertained by right reason. But the stirrings of secularism and rationalism in the seventeenth century brought about first the Protestantizing of natural law by Grotius and others, and presently its secularization by Pufendorf, Vattel, Burlamaqui, and lesser thinkers. This latter secularized notion of natural law took on flesh in the latter part of the eighteenth century, vulgarized by Thomas Paine and ferocious in the French Revolution.

Yet the older understanding of natural law was not extinguished. It was ringingly asserted by Edmund Burke, in his distinction between the "real" and the "pretended" rights of men and in his prosecution of Warren Hastings. Through the disciples of Burke and the influence of the Catholic Church, classical and Catholic natural law has experienced a renewal of interest in the latter half of the twentieth century.

It should be understood that natural law does not pertain merely to states and courts of law. For it is a body of ethical perceptions or norms governing the life of the person and the life of people in community, quite aside from politics and jurisprudence. When many people flout or ignore this law for human beings, the consequences are ruinous—as with the unnatural vices that result in venereal diseases, or with the ideological passions, defying the norms of justice, that have so disastrously ravaged most nations since the beginning of the First World War.

LET US PASS from these general considerations to the relationship between natural law and American beliefs, and between natural law and the American Constitution framed in 1787. When Associate Justice Joseph Story adorned the Supreme Court from 1811 to 1845, much was said in judicial decisions about natural law. Until the defeat of President John Quincy Adams by General Andrew Jackson, the executive branch of the government of the United States from time to time acknowledged the suzerainty of natural law. But only occasionally, during the twentieth century, have justices and presidents forthrightly affirmed their reliance upon natural law.

The reality of natural law was taken for granted by Americans of the Revolutionary era and of the years in which the Constitution was framed and ratified. Generally speaking, theirs was what we may venture to call the Catholic apprehension of natural law, fundamentally. It should be remembered that the Church of England had been the church established by law in most of the thirteen colonies; so the natural law teachings of Richard Hooker and other Anglican divines were imparted from American pulpits. It should be remembered, also, that Hooker's *Laws of Ecclesiastical Polity*, with its exposition of natural law, had the endorsement of Pope Clement VIII: "There is no learning that this man hath not searched into," wrote Clement. "This man indeed deserves the name of an author; his books will get reverence by age, for there is in them such seeds of eternity that if the rest be like this, they shall last until the last fire shall consume all learning."

A more immediate influence upon Americans' understanding of natural law during the closing quarter of the eighteenth century was

Blackstone's *Commentaries*. Blackstone commenced his great work with an affirmation of the natural law. In Blackstone, two streams of natural law thought mingle: that of Cicero, the Schoolmen, and the Anglican divines; and that of the seventeenth-century scholars Grotius and Pufendorf and the Swiss jurist Burlamaqui.

"This law of nature," Blackstone wrote, "being coeval with mankind, and dictated by God himself, is of course superior in obligation to any other. It is binding over all the globe, and all countries, and at all times; no human laws are of any validity if contrary to this; and such of them as are valid derive all their force, and all their authority, mediately or immediately from this original."

American political leaders and lawyers and jurists at the time of the Constitutional Convention in 1787 were disciples of Blackstone. While in the formative years of the new Republic, Story and Kent, the two chief American writers on jurisprudence and authors of textbooks on American law, affirmed doctrines of natural law in the form presented by Blackstone. I need not labor the point that the Framers of the Constitution in 1787 accepted the concept of natural law presented by Blackstone.

Is the Constitution of the United States, then, a natural law document? No, it is not a philosophical treatise at all, but instead a practical instrument of government. We are safe in saying, nevertheless, that the Framers, with few conceivable exceptions, believed in the reality of natural law and had no intention of contravening natural law by the instrument they drew up at Philadelphia; nor did anyone suggest during the debates over ratification that the Constitution might in any way conflict with the old truths of the natural law.

Of course it is quite true, as Robert H. Bork puts it, that "if the Founders intended judges to apply natural law, they certainly kept quiet about it."[1] But also the Founders, as Bork next remarks, kept quiet in the Constitution about judicial review—and about much else, including relationships between the Constitution and common law (within which is much natural law doctrine), the existence of political parties, and commercial navigation by steamboats. John Marshall's Supreme Court subsequently supplied some of those deficiencies.

Nor does the Constitution make reference to Christianity; nevertheless, all but three or four delegates to the Constitutional Convention professed themselves Christians, and the old tradition of natural law comes down from Christian divines. Presumably the Founders did not doubt that judges—who would know the common law—like other public men in America, would be cognizant of the ethical principles called "natural law" although Congregationalists and some others preferred the term "Divine Law."

Champions of natural law doctrines as applied to the judiciary retort upon Mr. Bork that even though the Constitution itself does not mention natural law specifically, still natural rights are affirmed by the Declaration of Independence, which they take to be a preamble to the Constitution's Preamble. That particular argument will not stand. They are confused about the history of ideas, for the Declaration is not part and parcel of the Constitution. The eighteenth-century Enlightenment's doctrine of "natural rights" is not at all identical with the venerable Catholic and Anglican doctrine of natural law, nor with Blackstone's version of natural law. Moreover, as I discussed earlier, the Declaration and the Constitution were drawn up under different circumstances for quite different purposes: the first in the enthusiasm of revolution, the second in the restoration of order, and the men of 1787 were not the men of 1776.[2]

So to quote the Declaration as signifying the Constitution's recognition of natural law is to have confidence in a frail reed. Still, it does not follow that, Bork notwithstanding, natural law has no rightful place in the reasoning of federal courts.

As I have implied already, natural law is not primarily an instrument intended for use in common courts of law; rather, it is a body of precepts helping us to govern ourselves. Incidentally, rather than primarily, it is of help to magistrates. This natural law should not be taken for graven tables of governance, to be followed to jot and tittle; such moral law must be appealed to in different circumstances, and applied with prudence. We must remind ourselves that natural law is not a kind of inflexible code set up in deliberate opposition to the positive laws of every state. The natural law does offer magistrates guidance, especially when they sit in equity, as it offers guidance to all of us in our private lives. As A. P. D'Entreves writes, "the doctrine of natural law is simply in fact nothing but an assertion that law is a part of ethics. . . . The lesson of natural law . . . [is] simply to remind the jurist of his own limitations."[3]

THE QUESTION HAVING BEEN RAISED of natural law and its relationship to the American Constitution, we may turn to an historical example and to the judgment of a leading Catholic political and religious writer in these United States. He instructs us that public men ought to be guided always by respect for the natural law, but that magistrates, appointed or elected, are bound ordinarily by Constitution and statute, and ought not to set up their private interpretations of natural law in opposition to the positive laws they are supposed to enforce.

I refer to the "higher law" controversy of 1850 and to Orestes Brownson, the Catholic scholar and polemicist. In March 1850, on the floor of the United States Senate, William Henry Seward made his famous declaration that there exists "a higher law than the Constitution." He was referring to proposals for the emancipation of slaves. At once a heated controversy arose. In January 1851, Brownson published his review essay entitled "The Higher Law," in which he refuted the claim of Seward, the Abolitionists, and the Free Soilers to transcend the Constitution by appealing to a moral "higher law" during debate on the Fugitive Slave Bill. Brownson agreed with Seward that

> there is a higher law than the Constitution. The law of God is supreme, and overrides all human enactments, and every human enactment incompatible with it is null and void from the beginning, and cannot be obeyed with a good conscience, for "we must obey God rather than men." This is the great truth statesmen and lawyers are extremely prone to overlook, which the temporal authority not seldom practically denies, and on which the Church never fails to insist. . . .
>
> But the concession of the fact of a higher law than the Constitution does not of itself justify the appeal to it against the Con-

stitution, either by Mr. Seward or the opponents of the Fugitive Slave Law. Mr. Seward had no right, while holding his seat in the Senate under the Constitution, to appeal to the higher law against the Constitution, because that was to deny the very authority by which he held his seat. . . . After having taken his oath to support the Constitution, the Senator had, so far as he was concerned, settled the question, and it was no longer for him an open question. In calling God to witness his determination to support the Constitution, he had called God to witness his conviction of the comparability of the Constitution with the law of God, and therefore left himself no plea for appealing from it to a higher law.[4]

We cannot be bound, Brownson continued, to obey a law that is in contravention of the law of God:

This is the grand principle held by the old martyrs, and therefore they chose martyrdom rather than obedience to the state commanding them to act contrary to the Divine law. But who is to decide whether a special civil enactment be or be not repugnant to the law of God? Here is a grave and perplexing question for those who have no divinely authorized interpreter of the Divine law. The Abolitionists and Free Soilers, adopting the Protestant principle of private judgment, claim the right to decide each for himself. But this places the individual above the state . . . and is wholly incompatible with the simplest conception of civil government. No civil government can exist, none is conceivable even, where every individual is free to disobey its orders whenever they do not happen to square with his private convictions of what is the law of God.[5]

The Church, Brownson writes, is the authoritative interpreter of the Divine law. He reminds his readers that the state is ordained by God; but the state is not the supreme and infallible organ of God's will on earth.

Now it is clear that Mr. Seward and his friends, the Abolitionists and the Free Soilers, have nothing to which they can appeal from the action of government but their private interpretation of the law of God, that is to say, their own private judgment or opinion as individuals; for it is notorious that they are good Protestants, holding the pretended right of private judgment, and rejecting all authoritative interpretation of the Divine law. To appeal from government to private judgment is to place private judgment above public authority, the individual above the state, which, as we have seen, is incompatible with the very existence of government, and therefore, since government is a divine ordinance, absolutely forbidden by the law of God,—that very higher law invoked to justify resistance to civil enactments. . . . No man can ever be justifiable in resisting the civil law under the pretense that it is repugnant to the Divine law, when he has only his private judgment, or, what is the same thing, his private interpretation of the Sacred Scriptures, to tell him what the Divine law is on the point in question, because the principle on which he would act in doing so would be repugnant to the very existence of government, and therefore in contravention of the ordinance, therefore of the law, of God.[6]

Brownson's argument in substance is this, in his own words: "Mr. Seward and his friends asserted a great and glorious principle, but misapplied it."[7] It was not for them to utter commands in the name of God. Their claims, if carried far enough, would lead to anarchy. The arguments of some of their adversaries would lead to statolatry, the worship of the state. "The cry for liberty abolishes all loyalty, and destroys the principle and the spirit of obedience, while the usurpations of the state leave to conscience no freedom, to religion no independence. The state tramples on the spiritual prerogatives of the Church, assumes to itself the functions of schoolmaster and director of consciences, and the multitude clap their hands, and call it liberty and progress!"[8]

Brownson advocated compliance with the Fugitive Slave Law, which clearly was constitutional, indeed obligatory under Article IV, Section 2 of the Constitution. It was his hope to avert the Civil War which burst out ten years later. "Now there is a right and a wrong way of defending the truth, and it is always easier to defend the truth on sound than on unsound principles. If men were less blind and headstrong, they would see that the higher law can be asserted without any attack upon legitimate civil authority, and legitimate civil authority and the majesty of the law can be vindicated without asserting the absolute supremacy of the civil power, and failing into statolatry,—as absurd a species of idolatry as the worship of sticks and stones." [9]

IN BROWNSON'S ARGUMENT may be found much highly relevant to our own era of startling or contradictory interpretations of natural law. Professor Russell Hittinger, in a long and learned and illuminating article entitled "Liberalism and the American Natural Law Tradition," distinguishes three chief phases of recourse to natural law in America's history. The most recent of these is "the emergence in our day of a natural law of lifestyle choices." [10] Let me offer some desultory observations on the tendency of federal courts toward this socially destructive "lifestyle" perversion of natural law doctrine.

As Brownson remarks, the natural law (or law of God) and the American civil law are not ordinarily at swords' points. Large elements of natural law entered into the common law of England—and therefore into the common law of the United States—over the centuries; and the Roman law, so eminent in the science of jurisprudence, expresses the natural law enunciated by the Roman jurisconsults. No civilization ever has attempted to maintain the bed of justice by direct application of natural law doctrines by magistrates. Necessarily, it is by edict, rescript, and statute that any state keeps the peace through a system of courts. It simply will not do to maintain that private interpretation of natural law should be the means by which conflicting claims are settled.

Rather, natural law ought to help form the judgments of the persons who are lawmakers—whether emperors, kings, ecclesiastics, aristocratic republicans, or representatives of a democracy. The civil law should be shaped in conformity to the natural law—which originated, in Cicero's words, "before any written law existed or any state had been established."

It does not follow that judges should be permitted to push aside the Constitution or statutory laws and substitute their private interpretations of natural law. To give the judiciary such power would produce some curious decisions, sweeping away precedent, which might be highly distressing to friends of classical and Christian natural law.

Only the Catholic Church, Brownson reasoned, has authority to interpret the natural law, but the Supreme Court of the United States takes no cognizance of papal encyclicals. Left to their several private judgments of what is "natural," some judges indubitably would do mischief to the person and the republic.

The Supreme Court's majority decision in *Roe v. Wade*—in which, as in a few other recent cases, a deathly sort of "right to privacy" was discovered—amounted to a declaration of the "natural rights" of a mother to destroy her offspring. This is a fierce blow at the family, the most fundamental of human institutions. Such are the "lifestyle" individualistic natural rights being developed at law nowadays. This being done in the green tree, what shall be done in the dry, when the Supreme Court may be totally dominated by ideological secularism?

Such is the clear and present danger of turning to a radicalized concept of natural law, as determined by politicized judges. Today, as in the past, we ought to remind ourselves that the true natural law is not a mere congeries of appetites, and that it is not from the vagrant musings of the hour's judges that the natural law derives its high authority.

I repeat that we have recourse to natural law, as opposed to the letter of the Constitution, only as a last resort, ordinarily. My only service as a jurist occurred in Morton Township, Mecosta County, Michigan, some decades ago, when for two consecutive terms I was elected justice of the peace. When determining a boundary dispute between two farms, a justice of the peace does not repair to theories of natural law, meditating upon which of two claimants is the more worthy of judicial compassion. Instead, the justice of the peace, fulfilling his ancient and honorable office, turns to statute, common law, possibly to local custom, and initially to the files of the recorder of deeds at the county seat. So it is with the ordinary administration of law at every level. Statute, charter, and prescription ordinarily suffice to maintain the rule of law.

During the nineteenth century, natural law concepts were overshadowed by the powerful utilitarian system of Jeremy Bentham, by the theories of John Austin and the Analytical Jurists, by legal positivism, and later—especially in the United States—by legal pragmatism. Yet appeals to the "natural law" or a "higher law" have recurred often in American politics and jurisprudence; both radicals and conservatives, from time to time, have invoked this law of natural justice.

As Russell Hittinger remarks in his article "The Natural Law in the Positive Laws," "there is nothing contradictory in arguing, on the one hand, for a natural law basis of government, and indeed of positive law itself, while at the same time holding that judges ought, whenever possible, to be bound by written law." [11]

The Catholic tradition of natural law, to borrow a phrase from Sir Ernest Barker, holds that "law—in the sense of last resort—is somehow above lawmaking." This understanding, in effect, still prevails among many Americans, not all of them Catholics. They agree with Justice Frankfurter that natural law is "what sensible and right-minded men do every day."

Yet often the public's apprehension of the teachings of natural law is much decayed, in part because of the total secularization of instruction in public schools. Most judges—indeed most lawyers—are taught little about natural law in schools of law; for that matter, jurisprudence itself is a forgotten science in many such schools. The apprehension of natural law displayed by Robert H. Bork in his book, *The Tempting of America*, is confusing; the references thereto by Justice Thomas are timid and dubious.

The champion of natural law knows that there is law for man, and law for thing, and that our moral order is not the creation of coffee-house philosophers. Human nature is not vulpine nature, leonine nature, or serpentine nature. Natural law is bound up with the concept of the dignity of man, and with the experience of humankind ever since the beginning of social community.

Ordinarily, natural law is applied through positive law. Hittinger points out that we ought not to create a patchwork theory of natural law's meaning out of a congeries of Supreme Court decisions over the years. What natural law provides is the *authority* for positive law, not an alternative to positive law: "The business of a judge is litigation, and, on the whole, litigation is not the best context for taking stock of what the natural law requires.... [P]reoccupation with judicial uses of natural law provides not only a very narrow, and probably misleading theoretical picture of natural justice, but it also furnishes an unsteady practical approach to how a body of positive law is to be made congruent with the natural law." [12]

Belief in natural law underlies the Constitution, is in no way inconsonant with the Constitution, and ought to be accepted by everybody in public office. Yet the justices of the Supreme Court are not entitled to turn when they will to some "higher law" rather than to be bound by the text of the Constitution, by *stare decisis*, and by the original intent of the Framers. Were it otherwise, they might convert themselves into "a kind of *ius gentium* court in perpetual session," an infallible and omniscient body of moral authorities elevated to the Court in some nonpartisan fashion. It would be absurd to fancy that the American Republic would accept such a regime.

It will not do to substitute private interpretations of natural law for the rule of common law or civil law, any more than it would have been well for England, in Elizabeth's time, to have obeyed the "Geneva Men" by sweeping away common law and the whole inherited apparatus of parliamentary statutes, to substitute the laws of the ancient Jews. Positive law and customary law, in any country, grow out of a people's experience in community; natural law could not conceivably supplant judicial institutions. Yet were natural law concepts to be abandoned altogether, the world would find itself governed by the doctrine of survival of the fittest.

II

The Christian Postulates of English and American Law

TRUE LAW NECESSARILY is rooted in ethical assumptions or norms; and those ethical principles are derived, in the beginning at least, from religious convictions. When the religious understanding, from which a concept of law arose in a culture, has been discarded or denied, the laws may endure for some time, through what sociologists call "cultural lag"; but in the long run, the laws also will be discarded or denied.

With this hard truth in mind, I venture to suggest that the corpus of English and American laws—for the two arise for the most part from a common root of belief and experience—cannot endure forever unless it is animated by the spirit that moved it in the beginning: that is, by religion, and specifically by the Christian people. Certain moral postulates of Christian teaching have been taken for granted, in the past, as the ground of justice. When courts of law ignore those postulates, we grope in judicial darkness.

Nowadays those postulates are being ignored. We suffer from a strong movement to exclude such religious beliefs from the operation of courts of law, and to discriminate against those unenlightened who cling fondly to the superstitions of the childhood of the race.

Many moral beliefs, however, though sustained by religious convictions, may not be readily susceptible of "scientific" demonstration. After all, our abhorrence of murder, rape, and other crimes may be traced back to the Decalogue and other religious injunctions. If it can be shown that our opposition to such offenses is rooted in religion, then are restraints upon murder and rape unconstitutional?

We arrive at such absurdities if we attempt to erect a wall of separation between the operation of the laws and those Christian moral convictions that move most Americans. If we are to try to sustain some connection between Christian teaching and the laws of this land of ours, we must understand the character of that link. We must claim neither too much nor too little for the influence of Christian belief upon our structure of law. To those demarcations I now turn.

For the past two centuries, the tendency of writers upon the law has been to claim too little for Christian influence. The decline of these claims has been gradual. If we turn to that high juridical authority Sir Henry Maine, who was no Christian enthusiast, we find that in his *Early History of Institutions* he remarks many Christian influences upon law: how Christianity restrained the liberty of divorce; how it affected the Brehon laws; how it altered the character of contracts; how it worked in favor of women with respect to the laws; how it promoted donation; how "the Will, the Contract, and the Separate Ownership were in fact indispensable to the Church as the donee of pious gifts; and they were also essential and characteristic elements in the civilization amid which the Church had been reared to maturity."[1] Parallel treatment of Christian influence could be cited in various other important nineteenth-century writers on legal institutions and jurisprudence— although still more about Christian teaching will be found in the works of seventeenth- and eighteenth-century legal writers.

But twentieth-century commentators have been somewhat timid about referring to religious sources for law. Take that eminent scholar

Roscoe Pound, in his *Interpretations of Legal History*, written in 1922. Pound is by no means unfriendly to Christian concepts; indeed, he thinks their influence is held in too low esteem. Nevertheless, he grants them no broad sway:

> The prevailing view has been that, after the stage of primitive law is passed, religion has played relatively a small part in legal history. . . . Yet I venture to think that the influence of religious ideas in the formative period of American law was often decisive and that without taking account of Puritanism we shall fail to get an adequate picture of American legal history and shall not understand American law as it was in the last century. I suspect also that some day we shall count religious ideas as no mean factor in the making of what are now the doctrines of English equity. Undoubtedly such ideas played a substantial part in the history of the modern Continental law of obligations. So far as it directs attention to a factor which often may be of the first moment in shaping legal rules and doctrines and institutions the religious interpretation is by no means to be neglected. [2]

Let it be noted that here Pound is writing of law—both statutory law and common law—rather than of the sources of the law. "One of the main difficulties and causes of confusion in Jurisprudence," J. C. Gray writes in his *Nature and Sources of the Law*, "has been the failure to distinguish between Law and the sources of Law." A country's law is "composed of the rules for conduct that its courts follow and that it holds itself out as ready to enforce." [3] But these rules, Gray continues, though enforced regardless of abstract theories of justice, in part arise from ethical principles; and, I may be allowed to add to Gray, ethical principles ordinarily arise from religious perceptions.

Of course I am suggesting that Pound and Gray, though conceding something to Christian ethics as a source of law, still conceded too little. They wrote in a climate of opinion not cordial toward religious concepts, a climate in which flourished Justice Oliver Wendell Holmes's dicta. I am suggesting that Christian faith and reason have been underestimated in an age bestridden, successively, by the vulgarized notions of the rationalists, the Darwinians, and the Freudians. Yet I am not contending that the laws ever have been the Christian word made flesh nor that they can ever be.

My Puritan ancestors of Massachusetts Bay, like their fathers the "Geneva Men" of Elizabethan England, hoped to make the laws of the ancient Jews into a code for their own time—a foolish notion. My Scottish Covenanting ancestors, too, aspired nearly to that. Upon such misconceptions, my direct ancestor on the distaff side, Abraham Pierce, was tried at Plymouth, Massachusetts, in 1625 for indolence on the Sabbath. By a miscarriage of justice, doubtless, he was acquitted. This attempt at legal archaism was absurd, and failed before it began, because the particular laws of a people ineluctably mirror the circumstances of an age. Hebraic legal institutions would no more suit seventeenth-century England, say, than the English common law of the seventeenth century would have been possible for Jerusalem in the sixth century before Christ. What Christianity (or any other religion) confers is not a code of positive laws, but instead some general understanding of justice, the human condition being what it is.

As Gray reminds us humorously, the actual law of the hour cannot be administered by judges upon abstract speculative considerations.

> In many of the States, the question of the liability of the Pullman Car Company for the loss by theft from a sleeping car of a commercial traveler's bag containing samples of hat pins, is a novel one, and the judges are or will be called to make Law upon it. What question should a judge ask? Should it be, "What protection of a sample bag is desirable to secure the greatest happiness of the greatest number?" or should it be, "What is my intuitive moral sense on the subject of Pullman cars?" or again, should it be, "What is God's revealed or unrevealed will regarding bagmen?" or again, "What dealing with drummers is most in accordance with the Freedom of the Will?" or, "What protection to hat pins is most according to Nature," or is it a mixed affair to which two or more of these tests should be applied? It is conceivable that application of these different tests might lead to different results. [4]

In short, judges cannot well be metaphysicians—not in the execution of their duties upon the bench, at any rate, even though the majority upon the Supreme Court of this land, and judges in inferior courts, seem often to have mistaken themselves for original moral philosophers during the past quarter century. The law that judges mete out is the product of statute, convention, and precedent. Yet behind statute, convention, and precedent may be discerned, if mistily, the forms of Christian doctrines, by which statute and convention and precedent are much influenced—or once were so influenced. And the more judges ignore Christian assumptions about human nature and justice, the more they are thrown back upon their private resources as abstract meta-physicians—and the more the laws of the land fall into confusion and inconsistency.

Prophets and theologians and ministers and priests are not legis-lators, ordinarily; yet their pronouncements may be incorporated, if sometimes almost unrecognizably, in statute and convention and precedent. The Christian doctrine of natural law cannot be made to do duty for "the law of the land"; were this tried, positive justice would be delayed to the end of time. Nevertheless, if the Christian doctrine of natural law is cast aside utterly by magistrates, flouted and mocked, then positive law becomes patternless and arbitrary. Becoming aware of this, Ernst Troeltsch, in his *Social Teaching of the Christian Churches*, wrote concerning the Christian theory of natural law (even before it was reformulated by Aquinas), that "it is the real ecclesiastical doctrine of civilization, and as such it is at least as important as the doctrine of the Trinity, or other fundamental doctrines."[5]

Would it be preferable to have the law arise from the narrow and fanatic speculations of some ideologue? Just that disaster has befallen Russia, China, and other lands. I think of the words of T. S. Eliot: "If you will not have God—and he is a jealous God—you should pay your respects to Hitler or Stalin."

Christian doctrine, in the United States as in Britain, is not the law; yet it is a major source of the law, and in particular a major foundation of jurisprudence. This reality was understood by the two principal legal scholars of the formative era of American Law, Justice Joseph Story and Chancellor James Kent, and to them I turn once again.

SIR MATTHEW HALE, Justice of the King's Bench, ruled in *Taylor's Case* (1676) [6] that "the Christian religion is a part of the law itself." In *Woolston's Case* (1729),[7] King's Bench found that "Christianity in general is parcel of the common law of England; and therefore to be protected by it." (Both were cases concerned with blasphemy.) These precedents, cited by Blackstone in his *Commentaries*, were accepted by those American champions of common law, Justice Story and Chancellor Kent. There runs through Story's and Kent's respective commentaries the assumption that in America also the common law is bound up with Christian doctrine.

In important decisions in their courtrooms, Story and Kent sustained the special standing of the Christian religion in the common law. In *Terrett v. Taylor* [8] Story recognized that the Episcopal Church in Virginia derived its rights from the common law; in *Vidal v. Girard's Executors* [9] he accepted Daniel Webster's argument that the Christian religion was part of the common law of Pennsylvania. Kent, in *People v. Ruggles*, when Chief Justice of New York, found that the defaming of Christianity might be punished under common law. He wrote in his opinion:

> The people of this state, in common with the people of this country, profess the general doctrines of Christianity, as the rule of their faith and practice; and to scandalize the author of these doctrines is not only, in a religious point of view extremely impious, but even in respect of the obligations due to society, is a gross violation of decency and good order . . . things which corrupt moral sentiment . . . have been held indictable; or shall we form an exception in these particulars to the rest of the civilized world? No government among the polished nations of antiquity, and none of the institutions of modern Europe (a single and monitory case excepted) ever hazarded such a bold experiment upon the solidity of the public morals as to permit with impunity, and under the sanction of their tribunals, the general religion of the community to be openly insulted and defamed. The very idea of jurisprudence with the ancient law-givers and philosophers embraced the religion of the country: *Jurisprudentia est divinarum atque humanarum rerum notitia*.[10]

Story's and Kent's decisions, and their arguments in their commentaries, remained powerful influences upon later important federal and state decisions that touched upon questions of morals—for instance, the Supreme Court's stern ruling against bigamy and polygamy, written by Chief Justice Waite and Justice Field, who called these customs crimes against "the laws of all civilized and Christian countries." [11] Even though weakened by the ambiguity of a series of Supreme Court decisions during the past half-century, the opinions of Story and Kent continue in some degree to affect court rulings on public morality.

Did Story and Kent imply that an establishment of religion existed in the United States? Not so: both jurists strongly expressed their approval of the separation of church and state. In 1813, touching upon the practice of the New England Puritans, Story denounced (and somewhat misrepresented) the Puritan error of "the necessity of a union between church and state." In his *Commentaries*, he remarked that "Half the calamities with which the human race have been scourged have arisen from the union of Church and State." [12] And in *Vidal v. Girard's Executors*, Story noted in his decision that "although Christianity may be a part of the common law of the State, yet it is so in this qualified sense, that its divine origin and truth are admitted, therefore it is not to be maliciously and openly reviled and blasphemed against, to the annoyance of believers or the injury of the public." [13] In a letter to Story, Kent expressed his full concurrence in the *Vidal* decision.

In effect, Story and Kent tell us that Christianity is not the "law of the land" in the sense that Christian teachings might be enforced upon the general public as if they were articles in a code. Story and Kent had no intention of emulating in the nineteenth century the Geneva Men's ambition to resurrect the laws of the Jews. Rather, the two great American commentators point out that Christian moral postulates are intricately woven into the fabric of the common law, and cannot be dispensed with, there being no substitute for them in ethical matters. Furthermore, the Christian religion, as the generally recognized faith (in one profession or another) of the American people, is protected against abuse by defamers, that the peace may be kept and the common good advanced.

Story's and Kent's position is well summarized—in a passage referring to the general relationship between common law and Christian belief—by John C.H. Wu, who in his volume about the common law, *Fountain of Justice*, observes,

> The question has often been asked, if Christianity is a part of the common law. It depends on what you mean by Christianity. If you mean a revealed religion, a faith as defined by the Apostles' Creed, it is not a part of the common law in the sense that you are legally bound to believe in it. Christianity as a Faith comes into the courts, not as a law, but as a fact to be taken judicial notice of, on a par with other facts of common knowledge. On the other hand, if you mean by Christianity the fundamental moral precepts embodied in its teachings, it is part of the common law in the sense that all the universal principles of justice written in the heart of every man are a part thereof. [14]

Story and Kent affirmed their belief in the Christian connection with common law, and their belief in the need for separation of church and state, without lack of consistency.

WHAT WE CALL LAW does not exist in an intellectual and social vacuum. To cut off law from its ethical sources is to strike a terrible blow at the rule of law. Yet many such blows are inflicted upon the law today—and ordinarily in the names of liberation and modernity.

The wisest brief treatise on the present plights of the law with which I am acquainted is the Cardozo Lecture delivered in 1962 by Huntington Cairns entitled *Law and Its Premises*. Cairns emphasizes that the forces of order, symbolized in ancient times by the god Apollo, are attacked in every age by the forces of license, symbolized by the god Dionysius. In our time that struggle affects the whole of the Law. Cairns put the matter in this fashion:

> From the beginnings of Western thought law has been a field of knowledge derived from a larger whole, the understanding of which has been held to be indispensable to any effort to reach the

standards applicable to human affairs. At the same time, there has been a volitional element in the legal process stemming from the contrary view that law is not derived from a larger whole; man devises his own standards and law need not be understood in terms of any ultimate order. These two ways of seeing law are in conflict today, and the consequences of this conflict in the long run could be fatal.[15]

In this contest during the present century, the Dionysian powers are those influences that would sweep away altogether any influence of Christian postulates—along with classical wisdom—upon modern law; and the Apollonian powers set their faces against this emasculation of the law. Christian belief is not the only source of ethical principle behind law, but it is the most powerful and popular source. If all connection between the Christian religion and the verdicts of courts of law is severed in this country, the law will become erratic and unpredictable at best (when it is supposed to be regular in its operation), and tyrannical rather than protective.

Although the law stands independent of churches and of philosophies, committed formally to none of those, still whenever the law touches upon ethical questions, it must repair to the sources of law— whether those ethical judgments are expressed in statute, in precedent, or in equity. In a Christian nation, necessarily that nation's laws have an intricate connection with that nation's faith. And the people of the United States, though President Jefferson might instruct the Dey of Tunis that the United States was "not a Christian nation," form a nation predominantly Christian, perhaps more so now than a decade ago— even though, to employ strictly the definitions of politics, the United States is not a Christian state, having no one church by law established, or any prescribed creed.

Educated persons understand nowadays, better than before, that all culture arises out of the cult. We have been taught that by such sober historians of our time as Christopher Dawson, Eric Voegelin, and Arnold Toynbee. At the dawn of civilization, people unite in search of communion with a transcendent power, and from that religious community, all the other aspects of a culture flow—including, and indeed especially, a civilization's laws. So it is contrary to the character of civilization, and indeed contrary to human nature, that there should come to pass a great gulf yawning between a country's religion and its laws.

Some moral convictions must be the foundation of any system of law. In this country, were the Christian postulates swept away, by what moral principles might they be supplanted? Not by the amorphous notions labeled "liberalism," now thoroughly unpopular, called by Santayana "a mere adventitious phase." No, the Christian moral understanding presumably could give way, in the long run, only to the commandments of the Savage God—enforced by some Rough Beast, his hour come round at last.

Just this conceivable subjection of American law and American morals by a clever oppressive ideology is what Huntington Cairns warned his audience against in the concluding sentences of his Cardozo Lecture:

> Law is part of a larger whole, and the history of the common law is witness to the validity of this idea. At no time has legal thinking been able to dispense with principles derived from an estimate of the character of that larger whole. No subject which thinks deeply about its own premises can avoid formulating such principles; and it is the part of wisdom for law to return to those which can make it effective. Without such knowledge law is an art of blind conjecture. To the Greek thinkers it was a dangerous delusion that human affairs could be separated from, or worse, opposed to the world in which they function.[16]

Huntington Cairns emphasizes the patrimony of jurisprudence that we receive from the classical philosophers, and I emphasize our legacy of justice from the Christian fathers. Both these great sources of moral knowledge and legal philosophy stand in opposition to the latter-day positivism that would reduce law to administrative policy and human beings to producing and consuming units.

In the domain of the law today, as in all other realms of human endeavor, there is waged a battle between those who believe that we human creatures are made in the image of a Creator, and those who believe that we are not much more than fleshy computers. Even within the courts of law, created to help to keep the peace, this war is fought to the knife. How will this struggle over the nature of law, with the followers of Apollo on one side and the votaries of Dionysius on the other, be terminated? Will the Christian sources of the law be effaced in America—or will the Christian moral imagination and right reason rise up again in strength in our courts of law? In the chapters that follow, I inquire whether our Constitution demands of us that we accept "the inevitability of gradualism," the steady diminishing of religious remnants and the steady advance of the Dionysians.

PART IV

THE FIRST AMENDMENT AND THE MORAL FOUNDATIONS OF THE REPUBLIC

12

Politics and Religion

HIGH AMONG THE CONSERVATIVE PURPOSES
of the Constitution, as amended by the Bill of Rights, was
the preservation of Americans' accustomed freedom of religion. But what the amending Congress meant by the First
Amendment's first clause (or clauses, for some maintain that the comma
is a demarcation) often is badly misunderstood.

Original intent, that concept so much debated in recent years, is
easily determined in this case when the first clause of the First Amendment
is discussed. That provision is simply and directly expressed: "Congress
shall make no law respecting an establishment of religion, or prohibiting
the free exercise thereof."

This right to "freedom of religion" was so expressed by two eminent
congressmen who disagreed considerably about several other matters:
Fisher Ames, of Massachusetts, and James Madison, of Virginia. Their
motives in drawing up this guarantee of liberty of worship are readily

ascertained. And yet this first clause (or clauses) in recent decades has been interpreted extravagantly by some federal courts, so that some writers suggest a quite new signification for those few words: freedom *from* religion.

Such an inversion would have startled Congressman Madison, a rather liberal Episcopalian, and Congressman Ames, a Congregationalist, and later an Episcopalian as well. They were not advocating some radical new understanding of the old doctrine of church and state, and commentators on the Constitution who argue that the Congress affirmed a novel abstract principle concerning religion are wide of the mark.

The reasons for advocating and adopting the "religion clause" of the First Amendment were two. The first—which weighed heavily with Ames—was that Massachusetts and two other New England states still maintained in 1790 churches established by law: Congregationalist establishments. And in that year it still was conceivable that some other states, notably Virginia, might decide to restore their old church establishments. Should Congress decide to establish a national church, almost certainly that national church would not be Congregational. Therefore Ames and other New Englanders insisted on prohibiting federal legislation on such matters, lest their state churches be disestablished by act of Congress. It should be remembered that the provisions of the First Amendment were not regarded as binding upon the several states until the year 1940.

The second reason advanced in favor of the proposed first clause was a desire to avert disunity among the several states. The differences in theology and church structure between Congregationalist New England and Episcopalian Virginia were conspicuous enough. Still more formidable, in some ways, were the doctrinal disputes among Presbyterians, Quakers, Baptists, Methodists, Dutch Reformed, deists, and other denominations or religious and quasi-religious associations. Had any one of these churches been established nationally by Congress, the rage of other denominations would have been irrepressible. The only security lay in forbidding altogether the designating of a national church. Surely the Union was shaky enough in 1790 without risking hostilities to the tune of fife and drum ecclesiastic. The clause was in no way a disavowal

of the benefits of religious belief; it owed nothing to the atheistic preachments of Diderot, D'Alembert, and other free Gallic spirits of the Enlightenment. It was out of expediency, not from anti-religious principle,
that Congress accepted, and the states ratified, the first clause of the First
Amendment.

The first clause, in short, declared that the national government must
tolerate all religious beliefs—short of such fanatic beliefs as might undo
the civil social order; and that no particular church may be endowed by
Congress with privileges of collecting tithes and the like. The purpose of
the clause was placatory: America's "dissidence of dissent" was assured
that no orthodoxy would be imposed upon their chapels, bethels, con-
venticles, and churches. Roman Catholics, too, were satisfied with a
guarantee of freedom to worship in their way, as were the few Jews in
eighteenth-century America.

The general understanding of the Framers of the Constitution, and
of the Congress that approved the First Amendment, was this: Christian
teaching, like Jewish teaching, is intended to govern the soul, not to govern
the state. But also the leading Americans of the time believed that religious
convictions form the basis of any good society. They were aware that
both Christianity and Judaism have coexisted with imperial structures,
feudalism, national monarchies, aristocracies, republics, and democracies.
Religion, they assumed, is not a system of politics or of economic
management: it is an attempt, instead, to relate the human soul to divine
power and love.

Yet many people, judges among them, today maintain a very different
view of the meaning of the first clause of the First Amendment. They
persist in fancying that somehow or other the Constitution, or at least
the First Amendment, or perhaps the Declaration of Independence, speaks
of "a wall of separation" between church and state. But of course no such
phrase appears in any American state paper. Those words about the
hypothetical "wall," which have provoked so much controversy during
the latter half of the twentieth century, occur merely in a letter written
in 1802 by Thomas Jefferson, addressed to an assembly of Baptists.

Nevertheless, public officials are reproached by militant secularists
for having made incidental mention of the divine or even for having

attended a church in public. The same folk fret about the violation of
the alleged "wall of separation" by the retaining of chaplains in the armed
forces and are outraged that the sessions of Congress open with prayer.
Much confusion exists concerning the relationships between religion and
politics or between church and state. I offer you therefore the following
considerations on these grave concerns.

THERE EXISTS something worse even than the confounding of religion
and politics: I mean total separation of religion from the civil social order,
so that—in the phrase of Dr. Philip Phenix—church and state would rot
separately in separate tombs.

For the first clause of the First Amendment never was meant to signify
that the American government was indifferent to religion, or hostile toward
it. Justice Story, in his *Commentaries on the Constitution* (1833), gave a
clear explanation of the clause:

> It was impossible that there should not arise perpetual strife and
> perpetual jealousy on the subject of ecclesiastical ascendancy, if
> the national government were left free to create a religious estab-
> lishment. The only security was in extirpating the power . . .
> Probably at the time of the adoption of the Constitution and of
> the First Amendment . . . the general if not the universal sentiment
> in America was that Christianity ought to receive encouragement
> from the state so far as was not incompatible with the private
> rights of conscience and the freedom of religious worship. An
> attempt to level all religions, and to make it a matter of state
> policy to hold all in utter indifference, would have created uni-
> versal disapprobation, if not universal indignation. [1]

There is no national establishment of religion, but the American government acknowledges the benefits of religion and desires to encourage
religious faith.

Religion in America never has been a private concern merely. It is
religious faith, indeed, that has made American democracy successful;
lack of religious foundation has been the ruin of other democracies. Alexis
de Tocqueville expresses this strongly in *Democracy in America*: "I do not

know whether all Americans have a sincere faith in their religion," Tocqueville puts it, "—for who can search the human heart?—but I am certain that they hold it to be indispensable to the whole nation and to every rank of society. . . . While the law permits the Americans to do what they please, religion prevents them from conceiving, and forbids them to commit, what is rash or unjust."[2]

Those who would like to erase religious principles from political contests ought to be reminded of the opinion of that liberal justice William O. Douglas in *Zorach v. Clauson*:

> We are a religious people whose institutions presuppose a Supreme Being. We guarantee the freedom to worship as one chooses. We make room for as wide a variety of beliefs and creeds as the spiritual needs of man deem necessary. We sponsor an attitude on the part of government that shows no partiality to any one group and that lets each flourish according to the zeal of its adherents and the appeal of its dogma. . . . To hold that government may not encourage religious instruction would be to find in the Constitution a requirement that the government show a callous indifference to religious groups. That would be preferring those who believe in no religion over those who do believe. . . . We find no constitutional requirement which makes it necessary for government to be hostile to religion and to throw its weight against efforts to widen the effective scope of religious influence.[3]

It will be noted that Justice Douglas referred to religion in general, rather than (as Story did) to the Christian religion in particular; American pluralism had grown more diverse with the passage of more than a century. Yet as late as the *Zorach* case, even the more liberal justices of the Supreme Court did not interpret the "wall of separation" doctrine as a declaration of hostility against Christian churches. Story was heard, at least through echoes, until very recently.

Religious concepts about order and justice and freedom powerfully influence the political beliefs of the large majority of American citizens. Of course, religious belief is not confined to one party. It is to be expected that in the United States nearly all candidates for public office will declare that religious assumptions underlie their political programs. But neither party can claim to know the will of God. In the words of President Lincoln, "In great contests each party claims to act in accordance with the will of God. Both may be, and one must be, wrong. God cannot be for and against the same thing at the same time." Religious convictions do not confer political infallibility, but political action without religious restraints can bring on public ruin. Likewise, to try to govern a country by religious dogmata alone always has been a mistake; yet it is a mistake still worse to argue that politics comes first and that one's religion ought to be subordinate to political programs.

Was Hitler's neopaganism of no public concern? Was Stalin's hatred of all religion irrelevant to the welfare of the Russian people? Does anybody really think it desirable, for instance, to elect as president of the United States a person lacking religious convictions and moral principles? A public official who should fancy that he is not responsible to divine power—or that faith, hope, and charity are at best merely private eccentricities—would be a lion in the streets, seeking whom he might devour.

Nevertheless, there exists an evil substitute for religion in public affairs: fanatic ideology, which pretends to offer the people an earthly paradise, to be achieved through revolutionary politics. But all that ideology can create is an earthly hell. When such an ideology is intertwined with false religious notions, as in the "liberation theology" of Latin America, a country may experience the worst excesses of political fanaticism and religious fanaticism combined.

We Americans stand in no clear and present danger of such a ruinous combination of these two forms of religious intolerance. But those people—still happily a small minority—who would deny elected officials the right to let religious principles influence their public recommendations are no friends either to religious freedom or to the Constitution of the United States.

Nor are the people, some of them in high office, who would drive out of public instruction any remaining vestiges of religious teaching true friends to the Constitution of the United States. Aside from Communist-ruled lands, in recent years the United States has become the country most hostile toward religious studies in its system of public instruction.

In dread of any form of religious activity—even Bible-study before school or at lunch, even voluntary prayer or a moment of silence during which pupils *might* be praying, even (in many school districts) the mention of religious teachings in a course in history or literature—"neutrality" about religious beliefs has been carried beyond absurdity to positive prohibition.

Most textbook publishers thoughtfully omit from their manuals all but incidental references to religion, lest they lose school adoptions. Christianity and Judaism are becoming Forbidden Faiths, so far as public instruction is concerned, although there is more indulgence of "non-western" religions as part of "global education."

Formal schooling was commenced by churches. Ultimate questions cannot be answered except by religious doctrines—unless we are prepared to embrace the dialectical materialism of the Marxists. Congress has chaplains and engages in public prayer. The armed forces commission and pay chaplains and support religious services. Every president of the United States has professed his belief in divine wisdom and goodness. Yet certain judges deny the right of young Americans to pray in the public schools—even as an act of "commencement" concluding their twelve or thirteen years of school.

If our federal Constitution were hostile toward religion, it would be hostile toward our survival. Alexsandr Solzhenitsyn touched on this point memorably in his Templeton Address at London in 1983:

> Our life consists not in the pursuit of material success but in the quest of worthy spiritual growth. Our entire earthly existence is but a transition stage in the movement toward something higher, and we must not stumble or fall, nor must we linger fruitlessly on one rung of the ladder. ... The laws of physics and physiology will never reveal the indisputable manner in which The Creator constantly, day in and day out, participates in the life of each of us, unfailingly granting us the energy of existence; when this assistance leaves us, we die. In the life of our entire planet, the Divine Spirit moves with no less force: this we must grasp in our dark and terrible hour.[4]

So the great exile expresses the ineluctable need for religious understanding in the civil social order: the alternative is grinding servitude, soon or late, to the total state. So much, at the moment, for the second great error in current discussions of religion and politics: the notion that religion should be driven out of politics altogether.

POLITICS IS the art of the possible, not the reign of the saints upon earth. Religion is the means for an ordering of the soul, not for undertaking prudential political decisions. One cannot be surprised that certain pietist sects since the sixteenth century have sought to withdraw the religious community almost wholly from concerns of state. In Communist-ruled lands, religious communicants—supposing them to be tolerated at all— are compelled to renounce any participation in the political order.

Nevertheless, Christian faith surely must be concerned to some degree with political questions, and surely Christian belief has affected political forms from age to age, and will continue to influence political modes, in any tolerably free society. But to assume that Christian dogma, meant to order the soul, can be applied without qualification to the multitudinous prudential concerns of the civil social order leads to much confusion and violence. Christian faith may transform this world through working upon the minds and the hearts of many human beings, with healthy consequences in the body politic. But the Christian Church is no instrument for administering secular justice, conducting secular diplomacy, or waging war. The Kingdom of Heaven is taken by storm only in a personal and mystical sense.

We live in an era when the passions of ideology and the passions of religion become joined in certain zealots. Thus we hear intemperate talk, in many communions and denominations, of "Christian revolution." Doubtless most of the men and women who use such phrases mean a bloodless, if abrupt, transformation of social institutions. Yet some of them nowadays, as in past times, would not boggle at a fair quantity of bloodletting in their sacred cause. Whether bloodless or bloody, an upheaval justified by the immanentizing of Christian symbols of salvation defies the Beatitudes and devours its children. Soon the "Christian ideologues" find themselves saddled and ridden by some "great bad man," a Cromwell at best.

This "revolutionary Christianity" has been popularized by professors of theology tenured at handsome salaries in American universities, remote in place and time from the ultimate consequences of their doctrines. Consider the curious case of Dr. Harvey Cox at Harvard's divinity school. Professor Cox has been called the most influential Protestant theologian in America; that was nearly true, at any rate, during the 1960s. From Harvard, Cox has preached "liberation theology" in the name of a "politician-God" and a "servant-God" who through Jesus has shown his willingness "to become the *junior* partner in the asymmetric relationship" between God and man. This Zeitgeist deity, politician, servant, junior partner, nevertheless decrees a world in which people no longer will crave power and property. Doubtless Cox has in mind "revisionist" Marxism— the dreary prospect of a universal Secular City, utterly immanent, utterly boring. Cox is merely a well-known example of this mode of ideologized religiosity. His counterparts are present in every Protestant mainline denomination and among the Catholic clergy. But the views of such persons are not the teachings of the historic Christian Church.

The Church always has striven for liberty, justice, and peace; but throughout the centuries the Church has known that man and society are imperfect and imperfectible, here below. The only possible perfection is perfection through grace in death. Christian teaching has endured because of its realism; because it does not mistake the City of This Earth for the City of God. In upholding the theological virtues of faith, hope, and charity, the Church has not neglected the cardinal virtue of prudence. Most of the time the Church has not endeavored to usurp the powers of the State. "Two there are by whom this world is ruled," said Gelasius I, saint and pope, in the fifth century.

The Church cannot confer upon the world immediate, perfect secular liberty, justice, and peace—any more than could the zealots of the French or Russian Revolutions. But Christian truth does offer this: that perfect freedom which is the service of God, that justice which transcends time and circumstance, that peace which passeth all understanding. The Church has known that liberty, justice, and peace are preserved and extended only through patient and prudent striving; that Providence moves deliberately, while the devil always hurries.

Christian faith may work wonders if it moves the minds and hearts of an increasing number of men and women. But if professed Christians forsake Heaven as their destination, and come to fancy that the State (which nevertheless they denounce in its present form) may be converted into the Terrestrial Paradise, they are less wise even than Marx. Such distortions of Christian teaching rise again and again, through the centuries, among professing Christians. One such was the Lambeth Conference of 1930, which provoked T. S. Eliot to write one of his more enduring essays. All times are corrupt, Eliot declared then, and in our time Christianity is dispossessed and divided.

"The world is trying the experiment of attempting to form a civilized but non-Christian mentality," Eliot concluded. "The experiment will fail; but we must be very patient in awaiting its collapse; meanwhile redeeming the time; so that the Faith may be preserved alive through the dark ages before us; to renew and rebuild civilization, and save the world from suicide."[5]

ALTHOUGH CHURCH AND STATE stand separate, the political order cannot be renewed without theological virtues working upon it. This consideration brings us to a question frequently asked of me by people dismayed at social decadence: "Is there such a thing as a Christian polity? Does Christian doctrine prescribe some especial form of politics—and conformity by all communicants to that political model?"

If we know the history of the Christian Church, particularly in the West, we are aware that the Church does not prescribe some particular civil social order. When the Church has presumed to decree the prudential policies of the State, the Church has failed, falling into dismal confusion. The political successes of the Church have occurred rather in limiting the claims of the State than in dictating courses to the captains and the kings. All the same, it is conceivable that the Church may do a work of political regeneration in our bent age, rebuffing totalist dominations. Christian belief works upon the political order in three principal ways: faith's influence upon statesmen; faith's influence upon the mass of mankind; and faith's shaping of the norms of the social order.

People sustained by Christian faith, hope, and charity form a "colony of Heaven"—a social order in which it is possible to strive together for the preservation and the advancement of justice and freedom and peace. Without the bond of a shared faith, any society begins to disintegrate: even a society governed by soldiers and secret policemen. Religious sanctions lacking, it becomes difficult even for the total state to enforce the most essential laws.

During the Cambodian campaign, I talked for an hour, in the White House, with President Nixon, then disheartened. He spoke of a lack of purpose and public spirit in the United States, and then inquired of me, "Do we have any hope?" For emphasis he repeated the question: "Do we have any hope?"

I replied that it is all a matter of belief. If the people believe the prophets of despair, then indeed hope vanishes, for everybody seeks his private hidie-hole, contenting himself with petty ephemeral pleasures. But if the people, disbelieving the prophets of doom and their self-fulfilling prophecies, retain belief in what endures, then indeed hope for the social order has not departed, for it remains possible for men and women to brighten the corners where they are and to confront together the trials of the time. Given hope, great renewal is possible. The thinking Christian knows that here below the race is not necessarily to the swift, nor the battle to the strong. He is not easily beguiled by predictions of imminent dissolution. "The men signed of the cross of Christ go gaily in the dark," in Chesterton's brave line.

Although human beings live in time, there exists a timeless ground of being, with which our little lives and our mundane institutions are interwoven. This is a perception of Christian mystics and philosophers. Only very gradually and imperfectly does humankind become conscious of this transcendent reality. Yet only through such imperfect human consciousness, painfully acquired, does it become possible for human beings to live together in peace and justice; to know a mundane order, both the internal order of the soul and the external order of community.

The myths and symbols through which the truths about order are conveyed grow dim with the passage of world-time and many disrupting events. When those symbols have become opaque at best, restless men seek to erect new symbols of their own creation, and to establish a new order in which the revolutionaries exercise total power. But this denial and inversion of the symbols of transcendence does not bring forth a new heaven and a new earth: instead, the Four Horsemen of the Apocalypse bring fire and slaughter. So it has come to pass in most of the world in our time.

The fanatic political ideologies of the eighteenth, nineteenth, and twentieth centuries, falsely promising the perfection of man and society, on earth and in time, are the present form taken by revolt against Christian insights into the nature of reality. Among the victims of ideological heresy are those "Christian activists" who presume to give commands to armies and orders to nations, confounding Caesar's things and God's. Some declare that they speak with the tongues of angels, binding all others who profess their faith in Christ. With just such good intentions is the road to Hell paved.

Those fulminatory men and women who set themselves up as judges of the actions and convictions of our age, on the principles of a "liberation theology," may come to worship the Savage God, mistaking him for the Redeemer. But when the revolution is done, the world is ruled not by self-proclaimed saints. Those have been corrupted or extirpated in the process. The new masters are those hard-faced men who do well out of revolutions; gun and grenade have opened their path to power, and the spoils are theirs.

"Over half a century ago, while I was still a child," Solzhenitsyn began his Templeton Address, "I recall hearing a number of older people offer the following explanation for the great disasters that had befallen Russia: 'Men have forgotten God; that's why all this has happened.'"[6] And having forgotten God, one may add, such men embrace ideology, nature abhorring a vacuum. It is worse still when men pretend still to believe in the divine but in reality yield themselves slaves to ideology, so living a lie.

The first ideology, Jacobinism, arose in France during the years of Washington's presidency. The Constitutional Convention over which Washington had presided had been altogether innocent of ideological delusion and passion. In France, when Washington was president, the revolutionaries proscribed the clergy, sacked the churches, and enthroned a prostitute to represent the Goddess Reason. In America, during Washington's presidency, the several states ratified the First Amendment, meant to countenance and protect religious belief. It is sufficiently ironical that in recent years American courts have handed down certain decisions in questions of church and state which have a decidedly Jacobinical ring to them.[7]

13

A Christian College in the Secular City

TWO CASES WILL SERVE to illustrate the radically differing interpretations of the "establishment" and "free exercise" provisions of the First Amendment that have been debated in federal and state courts. The first, the interesting if depressing case of Shelton College, I discuss in this chapter. The second was the famous "Mobile textbook case," which I examine in the next chapter.

Years ago I was a witness in litigation concerning a little Christian college at Cape May, New Jersey. Shelton College was a Bible Presbyterian school for educating preachers and teachers—something of a seminary, something of a liberal arts college. The educational authorities of New Jersey determined to crush that college because it did not conform to state regulations. Eventually, after the case was fought in a series of state and federal courts, at huge expense to the little college and the small denomination supporting it, crush it the state did.

This interesting case raised long-debated questions of relationships between church and state in America, including the "entanglement test" announced for the "establishment clause" by the Supreme Court.[1] The principal issue in the Shelton College case was this: How far may state agencies regulate "pervasively religious" educational institutions? May a state forbid a college or school to exist unless it complies with state requirements and regulations repugnant to that educational institution's sponsoring religious body? Or, if such a college or school is permitted to continue to teach, may a state's agencies nevertheless prohibit the granting of degrees or certificates, and even the use of the term *college*?

Church-state relationships as they impinge on educational institutions have, of course, been scrutinized by courts outside New Jersey. Similar issues are involved, for instance, in attempts of the Internal Revenue Service to remove the tax exemptions of Christian schools not complying with "affirmative action" policies and the like.[2] Courts have protected the claims of religious groups against the claims of agencies of the federal and state governments, especially where free exercise has outweighed entanglement danger. Such decisions have exempted Amish children from having to attend public schools [3]; have relieved Christian schools in Ohio, Kentucky, and other states from much regulation by state departments of public instruction [4]; have prevented the National Labor Relations Board from ordering collective bargaining elections in Catholic schools [5]; and have found unconstitutional the imposition of federal-state unemployment compensation programs upon schools conducted by Christian denominations.[6] These decisions are neither conclusively nor uniformly protective. Some such cases have been appealed, and somewhat similar cases remain contested in various courts.

It does not necessarily follow that the cited instances of relative immunities for church-related institutions will be extended by American courts. Many of the sheltering decisions mentioned above followed naturally enough from the Supreme Court's entanglement test, introduced by Chief Justice Warren Burger, but soon taken up by some of his colleagues with a zeal far exceeding his own.[7] The Burger Court had also to harmonize its approach with two Supreme Court decisions on the permissibility of certain state allowances made for religion in the schools. In *Everson v. Board of Education*, the Court had upheld state reimbursements to parents of parochial-school children who used public buses.[8] A few years later, in *Zorach v. Clauson*, a state "released time" program was upheld, where the religious training of the students occurred off public premises.[9]

The Court, especially after 1970, found various state programs unconstitutional as too entangling: supplementation of teachers' salaries in religious schools for those teachers giving secular courses [10]; reimbursements for the costs of entire "packages" (salaries, textbooks, instructional materials) in secular subjects [11]; direct loans of instructional materials such as maps and equipment [12]; auxiliary educational state services provided on non-public campuses [13]; field trip transportation costs of parochial school students [14]; state testing services when the tests are prepared by the parochial school [15]; and maintenance and repair of sectarian schools, tuition costs paid to parents of parochial school students, and tuition tax credits for such parents. [16] These denials were based upon the principle that so to indulge "pervasively religious" schools would bring on the peril of entangling church affairs and political concerns—with the possible subordination of church to state.

Other types of state assistance to sectarian schools have been upheld on the basis that they did not involve excessive entanglement: loans of secular textbooks to parochial school children [17]; costs of administering mandatory tests prepared by the state [18]; diagnostic health services provided on religious campuses [19]; therapeutic health and education services provided to sectarian students off the religious campus [20]; possibly, all health services and public lunch programs for parochial school students on their campuses [21]; federal construction grants to church-related institutions of higher learning [22]; and state revenue bonds to finance construction on campuses of non-public colleges.[23]

The neutrality principle, if consistently applied, would touch benefits as well as burdens. It seems to follow logically that if religious schools are to be denied benefits from the state, then in justice they ought to be exempted from various forms of state control which are prescribed for state-financed, state-operated public schools. The logical converse of no entanglement in funding is no entanglement in direction.

Court entanglement decisions in recent years can be said, under this view, not to have *advanced* the cause of church-related schools so much its they have *halted* encroachments by the state. Converse restraints upon state government *control* over religious schools have seemed the fair counterpart—the logical reverse pole of the neutrality principle—to Court restraint upon state government assistance to religious schools. The present question is whether extension of the entanglement doctrine will lead to virtual immunity of religious schools from federal and state supervision.

To put the matter another way, does a "compelling state interest" justify state agencies in licensing, regulating, and taxing church-related educational institutions, notwithstanding the provisions of the establishment clause of the First Amendment and other constitutional guarantees? Or are "pervasively religious" institutions entitled constitutionally to determine their own standards and conduct their own studies, without intervention from the political state? Does the entanglement doctrine operate more as a restraint upon churches than as a restraint upon government? Will all types of schooling tend to be assimilated into uniform state-prescribed patterns? Will public policy come to override, generally, the exemptions, immunities, and autonomy of American church schools and churches? Shelton College's resistance to the New Jersey Board of Higher Education bears upon these large questions.

SHELTON COLLEGE did not seem outwardly an object calculated to incur the hostility of the state of New Jersey. It had fewer than thirty students (and all but one or two of those were members of the Bible Presbyterian Church), a mild-mannered and well-schooled president, and a faculty that served competently for very small pay. Through its preceding incarnations as the National Bible Institute and the Union Missionary Training Institute, Shelton College traced its continuity back to 1885. Undoubtedly Shelton was one of those educational institutions which are described as "pervasively religious." For the College's catalogue declares its attachment to "That theology . . . commonly known as the historic Reformed faith or Calvinistic doctrine . . . articulated in the Westminster Confession of Faith. . . . The purpose of the College was summarized in the motto proclaimed by the founder, 'Training Christian Warriors.'" [24]

The core curriculum at Shelton College consisted of three courses in the Bible, two in communication, two in humanities, two in mathematics and science, one in history, and one in political science. Majors were offered in Biblical literature, elementary education, English, history, music education, and business administration. The study of classical languages was also encouraged. It would have become clear to anyone who visited the Cape May campus that the professors and students were devout members of their denomination and were strongly attached to their College. Shelton did not seek to enroll young people from other denominations, although it accepted qualified applicants who subscribed to the Apostles' Creed and abided by the College's regulations and standards.

In fact, Shelton was not very different from the Harvard or Yale of an earlier time. Certainly Shelton conformed to the familiar pattern of the church-related denominational college in America, with its ministerial guidance and its rural setting. Shelton may have been old-fangled, but it was no fraud: it had the limitations and the virtues of its educational type. Why was it chosen by the New Jersey State Board of Higher Education for reduction? The formal charge was that Shelton had not obtained a license from the Board. Therefore, the Board sought and obtained in 1979 from the New Jersey Superior Court a preliminary injunction restraining Shelton College "from engaging, advertising, assisting in or causing the offering of any courses or classes of instruction, or engaging in any form of educational instruction . . . except for presently enrolled students until the conclusion of the academic semester on December 22, 1979, unless a license for same is issued by the New Jersey Department of Higher Education. . . ." [25]

Shelton would not seek a license because its directors and the Bible Presbyterian Church feared with reason that submission to licensing would bring state control over the College, and that such control would be exercised in ways repugnant, in the phrases of the College catalogue, to "a liberal arts college . . . operated in harmony with conservative American principles and the historical Christian conviction that the Bible is the Word of God. . . ."[26] Shelton College did not desire to be licensed by the Board, for submission to licensing would have brought permanent submission to state specifications and controls. Even had the College's directors applied for a license, it seemed improbable that such a license would have been issued.

Shelton College, on principle, accepted no public funds from local, state, or federal treasuries. It was recognized as an educational institution by the federal Veterans' Administration, the Immigration and Naturalization Service, and the Social Security Administration; it was licensed at Cape Canaveral by the Florida State Board of Independent Colleges and Universities; and it was affiliated with the International Council of Christian Churches, a fundamentalist association.

The state of New Jersey had probably the strictest statutes regulating "private" or "independent" colleges of any state in the Union. According to William Bentley Ball, attorney for Shelton College in the case,

> [t]he New Jersey statutes are remarkable, in that they vest *total* control of higher education in the State, and they even consider all private colleges to be part of a state "system" of higher education. Further, the regulations which the State Board of Higher Education has published implement the total control of the State. These are really absurd—but very dangerous. Throughout these regulations there appears repeatedly wording such as "staff shall be *sufficient*," "teaching backgrounds must be *adequate*," "the program of the college must be *appropriate* in terms of its stated purposes." While all of these sound innocuous, we then find that there is a definitional section in the regulations which states that the meaning of "sufficient," "adequate," "appropriate," etc., shall be determined by—guess who?—the State Board of Higher Education.[27]

New Jersey statutes provided that every private or independent college within the state must be licensed by that same State Board.[28] These licenses would be periodically reviewed and then renewed or revoked. (The older New Jersey universities and colleges, including

Princeton and Rutgers, were exempted from this inquisition under a
"grandfather" clause.[29]) In other respects as well, the power of the State
Board of Higher Education over non-public colleges appeared to be
arbitrary and in practice little limited.

Probably there was more to the state's repeated actions against
Shelton than the matter of this license. A question of personality was
perceptible in the background—the personality of Dr. Carl McIntire,
chancellor of Shelton College and chairman of its board. Dr. McIntire's
troubles with the state of New Jersey began in the 1950s when Shelton
College was situated at Ridgewood, New Jersey, across the Hudson
from New York City. Dr. McIntire relocated the College at Cape
May in 1965, and the state commenced action against Shelton for not
being licensed. In 1967, having lost in the courts,[30] Shelton College
retreated to Cape Canaveral, Florida. But in the autumn of 1979, the
Shelton campus at Cape May was reopened, prompting the New Jersey
Board of Higher Education, acting through the attorney general, to
institute suit to enjoin Shelton's operation.

What with its history of difficulties with the state of New Jersey,
and its chancellor's unpopularity in several quarters, it seemed in the
autumn of 1979 that Shelton College was in for a very thin time. The
Bible Presbyterian Church was a very small denomination indeed, and
far from rich; the costs of a legal contest with the state of New Jersey
were very large. But the College did not give way. So commenced the
complex *New Jersey State Board of Higher Education v. Shelton College*.
The College's response to the Board would lead to a series of court
actions which eventually carried the case to the Supreme Court.

THE 1979 STATE COURT INJUNCTION against Shelton College was based
on the New Jersey statutes, without regard to constitutional questions.
There was precedent for such a course: in 1967, during the earlier
litigation between the Board of Education and Shelton College, the
Supreme Court of New Jersey had ruled that the New Jersey licensing
scheme for colleges was constitutional.[31] But that earlier case had paid
little attention to the issue of religious liberty.

Had the Superior Court's preliminary injunction gone into full effect, the religious mission of Shelton would have been seriously interrupted, and the small student body of the College might have disappeared altogether after the Thanksgiving recess. At this point, Shelton College engaged William Bentley Ball to defend its interests. Ball, a specialist in church-state cases, had won the case of the Amish children, *Wisconsin v. Yoder*, before the Supreme Court.

Ball swiftly brought an action in the federal district court against the New Jersey State Board of Higher Education and related New Jersey officials responsible for the action against Shelton College.[32] In the complaint to the federal court, Ball objected to the delegation of "blanket authority" to the Board:

> The statutes leave wholly to the uncontrolled discretion of the Board of Higher Education, for its approval, the determination whether the College, as a religious organization, may recognize the attainment or proficiency of any student who has chosen to participate in its program through giving each student a "degree." The regulations and standards cover eight (8) categories and are 47 in number, including subparts, and they cover every conceivable aspect of the life and activity of a private institution. Some of these controls are stated in language that is unconstitutionally vague. The statutory grants of power are in violation of the rights of the plaintiff churches and the College protected by the Due Process Clause of the United States Constitution.[33]

On December 14, Judge Dickinson R. Debevoise granted an injunction in favor of the college. He found that the College was entirely religious in character and possessed the right to teach and to advertise. Yet, perhaps troubled by this federal intervention in what had been a state case, Judge Debevoise returned to the New Jersey Superior Court the determination of whether Shelton College might award degrees. More specifically, it was left to the state court to determine whether the state's interest in "the integrity of the bachelor's degree" outweighed the College's interest in protecting its religious and educational liberties.

Judge Debevoise's opinion appears to have been the first decision by a federal court to the effect that a college, if pervasively and genuinely religious, enjoys under the First Amendment a right to teach, solicit students, and advertise. His opinion called New Jersey's denial of the right to teach a violation of the religious liberty of Shelton College. It should be noted that this opinion was restricted to colleges still possessed of a dominant church relationship. It did not cover substantially secularized educational institutions. This was a heartening victory for Shelton; but it returned the case, in part, to the state court.

Both the Attorney General of New Jersey and Shelton College eventually appealed from Judge Debevoise's opinion to the U. S. Court of Appeals for the Third Circuit. The state appealed on the ground that New Jersey's "compelling interest" in public instruction must take precedence over the liberties of a church-related college. Shelton's lawyer, however (after a second adverse decision in state court, months later), appealed the Debevoise ruling on the ground that the judge had erred in returning to the state court the essential issue of the integrity of the bachelor's degree. Ball argued the point before the Third Circuit on October 16, 1980. On April 14, 1981, the Third Circuit sustained the correctness of the federal district court's decision to grant a preliminary injunction and to abstain from deciding the issue of whether Shelton College could grant degrees.

The question of degree-granting was thus referred back to the Superior Court of New Jersey—indeed to the very judge whose injunction against Shelton College had been overturned by the federal judge. As matters were to turn out, the state judge chose not to change his mind about Shelton.[34] Shelton College was thus set the task of proving in state court that the degrees it wished to grant to graduates, but had not yet begun to award—the degrees of bachelor of arts, bachelor of sacred music, bachelor of Christian education, bachelor of sacred Scripture—ought not to be subject to a state educationist bureaucracy, whatever New Jersey's public concern for "the integrity of the bachelor's degree."

The argument that the state's concern for the integrity of the bachelor's degree conceivably justifies a state agency in refusing to permit a religious school to grant degrees or to call itself a college, even though the school may continue to teach, has troubling practical implications. In present-day America, how could a little institution like Shelton attract students and therefore survive and do its work for the church, if it were not permitted to confer degrees or at least let its graduates say they had attended a real college? Again Shelton had to confront the unfriendly officials of the State Board of Higher Education.

THE SHELTON CASE shifted back to Judge Gruccio's courtroom at Atlantic City, where I participated in the presentation of the College's case as an expert witness. The dreary decayed streets around the courthouse seemed symbolic of a civilization already far gone toward centralization, secularism, and intellectual apathy. Within the courtroom a good many Bible Presbyterians gathered during the trial early in July 1980, prayerful, hopeful. Dr. McIntire did not appear.

The grand point at issue in this new trial was whether the state of New Jersey had a compelling interest in maintaining the integrity of the bachelor's degree, and if so, whether letting Shelton call itself a college and grant degrees would impair that vaunted integrity. Judge Gruccio, during the questioning, expressed his dissatisfaction with the standards of higher education.

My testimony on the stand was to the general effect that the bachelor's degree scarcely can be said to retain much integrity on the typical contemporary campus—it having been cheapened by the rapid quantitative expansion of student populations over the past quarter of a century. I offered examples of frivolous and meaningless degrees conferred by various colleges, including some in New Jersey. There is Centenary College, offering a degree in "equine science"—horseman-ship; there is Edison State College, for external degrees, with no regular curriculum at all. What common standard for the bachelor's degree may be discerned among such diverse institutions as St. Thomas Aquinas College in California, Embry-Riddle Aeronautical University, Goddard College in Vermont (with its Institute for Anthroposophical Studies, joining practical organic gardening to yoga exercises), and City College of New York? I suggested that the curriculum and the standards of little Shelton College, whatever its limitations, are sounder than those of many New Jersey institutions long licensed by the Board. What compelling interest could the Board have in overseeing the workings of a little church school?

I departed before the day on which the attorney general's expert witnesses testified; I am told that Judge Gruccio questioned them somewhat sharply. Ball filed a forty-nine page brief on August 1. This civil action between the Board and Shelton College produced a defendant's brief by Ball as telling, it seems to me, as his famous brief in *Wisconsin v. Yoder*. In his treatment of the subject, he summed up the more important Supreme Court decisions on this grave issue.[35] Then he swept into the pith of his argument:

> The imposition of the State's licensing system on Shelton College, as the condition precedent to its granting of the bachelor's degree, is an imposition of government-church entanglements prohibited under the First Amendment. The very justification for the statutes and regulations, as representing a compelling state interest, is found in their comprehensiveness and pervasiveness. The State's theory is that there is imminent and extraordinary public need for protection of the bachelor's degree; the licensing scheme, to meet so great a need, must be comprehensive—that is, in relation to any church entity, entangling. If the State now argues that its licensing scheme is really a mild affair, calling only for a little information-gathering, an occasional look-in, and some friendly advice, then the State destroys its argument of compelling state interest.
>
> In fact, the statutes and regulations are, as applied to Shelton, entanglement itself. They do not merely contain "some element of governmental evaluation and standards," they bristle with it . . . . the worst vice of entanglement—the thrusting of the State into the role of making, or influencing, religious determinations— is found in the New Jersey licensing-control system, whereby the State, as the State's witness, Suarez, frankly acknowledged, has the power to pass on whether a religious institution is achieving its religious purposes. Even that vice, however, is exceeded by New Jersey's statutory provision that would pave Shelton into the State's system of higher education. . . . This is not mere "entanglement"; it is envelopement.[36]

This powerful brief was of no immediate avail. Judge Gruccio did not hand down his opinion for more than two months; when it was finally announced, it went against Shelton College. Shelton appealed in the New Jersey federal courts against the Superior Court decision, and eventually appealed to the Supreme Court as well, but to no avail. The U. S. District Court for New Jersey affirmed the Superior Court ruling, and the Supreme Court denied review.[37]

WHAT IS THE SIGNIFICANCE of this prolonged litigation concerning a tiny, stubborn denominational college? The affair touches upon large concerns of freedom and diversity in higher learning and upon the conceivable subordination of things spiritual to things temporal. The Shelton College case is a microcosm of the difficulties in which church colleges, schools, and related religious institutions have become involved. Why are church-related colleges and schools seemingly in such a peck of troubles? Why are we hearing so much about "entanglement"? One reason for this flood of litigation is that church schools have offered increasing resistance to the irksome interference of state departments of public instruction and of various federal agencies.

Church-related colleges and schools have been willing in a good many instances to litigate against state agencies, despite heavy required expenditures of money and time—and they have not acted without provocation. A book might be written about the growth, in recent years, of hostility toward churches and church-related institutions among certain influential groups in the United States. It is not merely the militant atheistic mentality which may be discerned in this development. It is rather the attitude of John Dewey's "Religious Humanist Manifesto," reaffirmed a few years ago by eminent secularists.[38] Such secular hostility is bound up with what Max Picard called "the world of the Flight"[39]—that is, of the flight from God, who pursues.

This attitude may be called "ritualistic liberalism," of which one aspect is a dread and suspicion of institutional Christianity—a kind of latter-day discipleship to Diderot and D'Alembert. It leads, in courts especially, to an interpretation of "separation of church and state" that means indifference or prohibition on the state's part. Sometimes this interpretation lies behind decisions of the Supreme Court, at least implicitly—as illustrated by the Burger Court's ruling in late 1980 that the Kentucky superintendent of public instruction might not place copies of the Decalogue in that state's public school classrooms. [40]

As public schools become secularized by courts, Christian parents and parents of other religions naturally seek to maintain the doctrinal character of church-related schools: sanctuaries from crusading "humanists." On the one hand, "establishment clause" interpretation may be carrying entanglement to extremes, as in the Decalogue case. On the other hand, the "free exercise clause" and "non-entanglement" under the establishment clause serve to protect church-related colleges and schools, in a good many instances, against state agencies that aspire to regulate them. The paradox may be structural.

The present Supreme Court understanding of entanglement and separation of church and state bears small resemblance to the germ of the establishment and free exercise clauses, as we find it in George Mason's sentences in the *Virginia Declaration of Rights* (1776): "That religion or the duty we owe to our Creator, and the manner of discharging it, being under the direction of reason and conviction only, not of violence or compulsion, all men are equally entitled to the free exercise of religion, according to the dictates of conscience, unpunished, and unrestrained by the magistrate, unless the preservation of equal liberty and the existence of the state are manifestly endangered. And that it is the mutual duty of all to practice Christian forbearance, love and charity toward each other." [41]

For the time being, the current entanglement test, which might have seemed strange even to the tolerant George Mason, serves often as a shield to church-related institutions. The popularity of such colleges, schools, and other institutions has increased rapidly recent decades, especially among religious fundamentalists. As they grow stronger and more numerous, it becomes more difficult for militant secularists and other adversaries to undo them.

I write "and other adversaries" because the pressure groups working against religious schools consist of more than the people who look upon all religions as unfortunate vestigial survivals of the childhood of the human species. They are leagued with educational bureaucrats, dismayed at the rapid increase of enrollments in Christian schools, while public school enrollments tend to decline.

The foes of religious schools are various. But just as all important differences of opinion at bottom are theological, so at bottom the opposition to religious schools is founded upon dislike of religious orthodoxy—and often upon desire to substitute for religious dogmas those of some ideology. It is to just such a substitution that we turn in the next chapter.

14

An Establishment of Humanitarianism?

THE IMMEDIATE QUESTION at issue in the Mobile textbook case, *Douglas T. Smith, et. al. v. Board of School Commissioners of Mobile County*, tried in the U. S. District Court for the Southern District of Alabama, was whether a religion or anti-religion called "secular humanism" pervaded the public schools of Mobile—and, for that matter, the public schools of Alabama generally. And if so, was that domination constitutional? And if unconstitutional, what might be done about it? The arguments in the courtroom at Mobile could have been applied in some degree to every state in the Union. I was an expert witness for the court (not for plaintiff or defendant) in the Mobile trial.

For a century and more after the Constitution's ratification, the first clause of the First Amendment created no difficulties for churches or church-related schools; nor did the religion clause or clauses operate upon the state governments. Thomas Jefferson's assurance to the Dey of Tunis notwithstanding, nearly all Americans professed themselves Christians of one kind or another.

As Professor T. M. Cooley wrote in the 1896 edition of his textbook *General Principles of Constitutional Law* (used for decades at nearly every American law school), "It was never intended that the government should be prohibited from recognizing religion . . . where it might be done without causing any invidious distinctions between religious beliefs, organizations, or sects." Until well into the twentieth century, courts applied the First Amendment to the federal government only; it was understood that state governments were not intended to be subject to the restraints placed upon the Congress by the Bill of Rights.

Throughout the nineteenth century, American courts generally assumed that there subsisted a close connection between American public institutions and the Christian moral order. Take the ruling of the U.S. Supreme Court in the case of *The Late Corporation of the Church of Jesus Christ of the Latter-Day Saints v. United States* (1891). "The organization of a community for the spread and practice of polygamy is, in a measure, a return to barbarism," the Court's decision ran. "It is contrary to the spirit of Christianity and of the civilization which Christianity has produced in the Western world." [1]

But this old amicable relationship between the American political order and the Christian moral order has been changing. If often inconsistently, the Supreme Court has held that the provisions of the Bill of Rights now are binding upon the several states—or at least some of those Amendments, some of the time. In effect, the First Amendment's provisions, along with much of the rest of the Bill of Rights, have been thrust upon the states by the Supreme Court. Thus the federal courts, Congress, and the federal administrative apparatus increasingly have tended to intervene in questions of church-state relationships.

Ever since 1947, when the Supreme Court enunciated in the case of *Everson v. Board of Education* a doctrine of absolute separation of state and church, courts have tended to push religious knowledge and observance out of public schools and public affairs generally. The long series of decisions, beginning in the 1950s—against prayer in public schools,

Bible reading, quotation of certain religious passages from public documents, display of the Decalogue on school walls, even against a moment of silence (made possible by act of the state legislature) in classrooms of New Jersey and Alabama—to employ a phrase used by the courts about other concerns, have exerted a chilling effect. Any reference to the transcendent or even to prescriptive morals has been driven out of most public schools.[2]

In *obiter dicta*, true, the Supreme Court suggested that schools still might take up the history of religion, comparative religions, and similar subjects, short of imparting dogma. But school boards, school administrators, and nearly all teachers, shuddering at the possibility of lawsuits by militant atheist parents or the American Civil Liberties Union or other "separation" zealots, speedily purged themselves of any odor of sanctity. And the publishers of school textbooks willingly— nay, eagerly, often—cooperated in the elimination of even glancing references to religion in manuals on history, social science, natural science, psychology, government, home economics, and any other sensitive disciplines. Religion went down the Memory Hole.

The trouble with purging the school curriculum of religious knowledge is that ultimate questions cannot be answered without reference to religious beliefs or at least to philosophy. With religion expelled from the schools, a clear field was left for the entrance of the mode of belief called humanitarianism, or secular humanism—the latter a term employed by the cultural historian Christopher Dawson. During the past four decades and more, the place that religion used to hold in American schooling, always a rather modest and non-dogmatic place, has been filled by secular humanism. Its root principle is that human nature and society may be perfected without the operation of divine grace.

During the 1930s, John Dewey and his colleagues founded the American Humanist Association for purposes not altogether humane, in the old sense of the words "humanism" and "humanities." It was the aspiration of the subscribers to their Humanist Manifesto to sweep away the old order, spiritual and temporal, and to establish a Brave New World, rejecting the superstitions of traditional religion and establishing egalitarian social patterns.

This secular humanism of the school of Dewey (not to be confused with the Christian humanism of Erasmus or Sir Thomas More, nor yet with the New Humanism of Irving Babbitt and Paul Elmer More in the 1920s and 1930s) has amounted to what philosophers of religion call "a secular religion." The Humanist Manifesto of 1933 (sometimes called by Dewey himself the Religious Humanist Manifesto) declares that the universe is self-existing, not created; that science shows the unreality of supernatural sanctions for human values; that this earthly existence is the be-all and end-all; that religious emotions are best expressed in heightened personality and in efforts to advance social well-being; that man himself is maker and active power, unmoved by transcendent forces.

In his book *A Common Faith* (1934), Dewey advocated his brand of humanism as a religion. "Here are all the elements for a religious faith that shall not be confined to sect, class, or race," he wrote. "Such a faith has always been implicitly the common faith of mankind. It remains to make it explicit and militant."

Much more evidence exists to suggest that humanitarianism, or secular humanism, should be regarded in law as a religion, with respect to both establishment and free exercise in the First Amendment. It is this non-theistic religion, hostile to much of the established morality and many existing American institutions, that has come close to being established as a "civil religion" in American public schools.

WHAT OCCURRED in the federal courthouse at the old port of Mobile, late in 1986 and early in 1987, was a contest at law between Christian parents (the plaintiffs) and the state educational establishment of Alabama (the defendants). It was necessary for Chief Judge Brevard Hand to decide whether "secular humanism" amounts to a religion; whether, if those charges be true, use of textbooks advocating secular humanism constitutes an establishment of religion, in violation of the First Amendment; and if, indeed, the use of such textbooks is unconstitutional, what remedies might be found.

The Mobile case had roots extending back to 1982, when Ishmael Jaffree, a Mobile resident, brought suit against Mobile County's school commissioners, to require cessation of prayer or other religious services in the public schools. (An Alabama statute authorized moments of meditation or of voluntary prayer in public schools.) Judge Hand did not desire to have his federal court intervene at all in this matter; at first he inclined toward the plaintiff, but after study held that jurisdiction in religious questions lies with state governments, and that the Supreme Court of the United States had erred in its decisions construing the First Amendment's religion clauses. Judge Hand had written in his *Jaffree* opinion, "Because the Establishment Clause of the First Amendment to the United States Constitution does not prohibit the state from establishing a religion, the prayers offered by the teachers in this case are not unconstitutional."[3]

In short, he held that the religion clauses of the First Amendment do not apply to the states—a constitutional point long in dispute. The Court of Appeals let Hand's decision pass on to the Supreme Court without comment; eventually the Supreme Court reversed Hand's ruling. *Jaffree* dragged on through the courts. Presently, more than six hundred Mobile parents intervened in the case, alleging that their children in public schools labored under an unconstitutional establishment of secular humanism. Their principal evidence of such an establishment was the substance and tone of textbooks in history, social science, and home economics prescribed by Alabama's state educational authorities for use in public schools.

Now the plaintiff Jaffree had been opposed to religious observances in public schools—and had won his case by an appeal to the Supreme Court. But the plaintiffs, the Christian parents, on the contrary, objected to the omission or denial of the Christian religion in school curricula. Having succeeded in his object, Jaffree now withdrew from the litigation, and the case became an action of Christian parents against the Mobile County school commissioners and, in effect, against the educational bureaucracy of the state of Alabama.

Since 1947, as was mentioned earlier, the Supreme Court has been handing down rulings intended to work a thorough separation between state and church, especially with respect to the subject of religion in schools. But the Court repeatedly has affirmed that the state's neutrality with respect to religion does not mean that federal or state governments may favor a militant secularism in public schools.

The words of Justice Douglas in the *Zorach* case concerning this point, were quoted earlier. His doctrine was reaffirmed in *Abington School District v. Schempp* [4] in phrases that may be applied precisely to the Alabama textbook controversy: "We agree, of course, that the State may not establish a 'religion of secularism' in the sense of affirmatively opposing or showing hostility to religion, thus 'preferring those who believe in no religion over those who do believe.'"

Thus if a federal court in Alabama, as instructed by the Supreme Court of the United States, must forbid the Alabama educational authorities to allow prayer or even momentary meditation in public schools, must not a federal court forbid such school authorities to permit the teaching of a creed called secular humanism, through the compulsory use of certain textbooks? Such was the argument presented by counsel for the group of Christian parents in Mobile.

The trial was lengthy, with many witnesses for plaintiffs and defendants, and involved intellectual complexities. Judge Hand, a jurist of much learning and a gentleman of considerable presence, eventually found it necessary to rule on two principal points—in effect, first, is secular humanism a religion within the first clause of the First Amendment; second, did the textbooks objected to by the Mobile parents impart or advocate a teaching known as secular humanism?

Now a religion is a system of belief and practice, the expounders of which set forth certain doctrines concerning the nature and destiny of mankind, humankind's place in the cosmos, and human moral relationships. Faith in some authority as to the human condition is a mark of every religion. The term implies that a relatively large number of people are joined together in such belief and practice, and that a body of writings or traditions exists to justify, explain, and define a particular religion's doctrines and observances.

Although most religions have been theistic—that is, committed to belief in a supreme being or a number of divine beings—this is not true, strictly speaking, of every variety of religion, ancient or modern; in some creeds, the theistic element may be obscured by the ethical element.

Since the Enlightenment of the eighteenth century, there have arisen religious or quasi-religious movements of a humanitarian character that reject most or all of the dogma of the older Christian churches, but still claim the word religion and sometimes are animated by a religious zeal.

The enlargement of the term *religion* may be observed from early in the eighteenth century to the present. By the time of the adoption of the First Amendment, Americans generally took it for granted that Unitarianism, deism, and Quakerism were coherent forms of religion— although they would not have been held such, in the Western world, a century earlier. During the nineteenth century, dictionaries, and other works of reference extended the term, in recognition of new intellectual currents and a changing climate of opinion.

Thus if we turn to the 1902 edition of *The Century Dictionary*, the most ample of American dictionaries, we find that the first definition of *religion* refers to "superhuman power or superhuman powers," but the second definition therein runs thus: "The healthful development and right life of the spiritual nature, as contrasted with that of the mere intellectual and social powers." In support of this latter definition, *Century* cites Matthew Arnold: "Religion, if we follow the intention of human thought and human language in the use of the word, is ethics heightened, enkindled, lit up by feeling; the passage from morality to religion is made when to morality is supplied emotion." The concept of influence by a transcendent power is absent from this passage from Arnold's *Literature and Dogma*, published in 1873.

As *The Interpreter's Dictionary of the Bible* (1962) points out, the word *religion* occurs infrequently in the Bible itself, and does not signify *faith*: rather, it is a late New Testament word, signifying a "system of doctrine, an organization, an approved pattern of behavior and form of worship." This limited meaning of the word has come back into common use during the twentieth century.

If we turn to the article on the philosophy of religion in the 1974 edition of the *Encyclopaedia Britannica*, we find the recognized term *secular religion*, a twentieth-century development, or "religionless Christianity". This is "a Christianity influenced by its residual social and political ideal, but bereft of its specifically religious practices, doctrines, or institutions. Such practices as traditional intercessory prayers are dismissed as empty approximations to magic; doctrine is condemned as outdated and expressed in terms of past cultures; institutions are criticized as oppressive and conservative." With this secular religion of recent years, we come very close indeed to the secular humanism of the Mobile trial.

Requested at the Mobile trial to name some characteristics of religion, I replied that a religion holds some world view or teaching concerning the cosmos, expounds a moral system, has a body of dogma or fundamental doctrines, and proselytizes with zeal. Counsel for the defendants inquired whether vegetarianism might be a religion; I replied in the negative.

THE TERMS *humanist* and *humanitarianism* have an intricate and confused history. If one turns again to the old *Century Dictionary*, one finds this definition of humanist: "One accomplished in literary and classical culture; especially, in the fourteenth, fifteenth, and sixteenth centuries, one of the scholars who, following the impulse of Petrarch, pursued and disseminated the study and a truer understanding of classical, and particularly of Greek, literature." That sort of humanism, emphasizing our cultural patrimony from the ancient world, was represented in the United States during the first three decades of the twentieth century by such critics and scholars as Paul Elmer More and Irving Babbitt. Such classical humanism had nothing in common with the secular humanism discussed at the Mobile trial.[5]

In my testimony at Mobile, I discussed the origins of American or Religious Humanism in the intellectual movment led by Dewey and his friends. Several authoritative witnesses at Mobile, on either side, testified at length as to the character of secular humanism. As I put it in response to questioning, secular humanism is a creed or world view that holds we have no reason to believe in a creator; that the world is "self-existing"; that no transcendent power is at work in the world; that we should not turn to traditional religion for wisdom, but rather we should develop a new ethics or method of moral science.

In his long opinion after the conclusion of the trial, Judge Hand quoted my response to his inquiry in the courtroom as to my reasons for criticizing secular humanism: "Because it omits what Plato said was the really important thing in all his writings: the doctrine of the soul. We find in secular humanism no recognition of the soul. There is only the human animal: the naked ape, if you will. What really distinguishes us human beings from the brutes is possession of a soul. Thus the development of the spiritual is the highest aim of a good education. That is not taken into account at all by the secular humanists. They think of man as a mechanism, a fleshy computer."

Yet a member of the American Humanist Association—which, in effect, is the church of the secular humanists—is not necessarily a thoroughgoing atheist, and Dewey sought earnestly to retain the label "religious" for this movement, as in the passage from his book *A Common Faith*, quoted earlier. Similarly, in his essay contributed to *Living Philosophies*, Dewey preached a new or renewed faith: "I would suggest that the future of religion is connected with the possibility of developing a faith in the possibilities of human experience and human relationships that will create a vital sense of the solidarity of human interests and inspire action to make that sense a reality. If our nominally religious institutions learn how to use their symbols and enhance such a faith, they may become useful allies of a conception of life that is in harmony with knowledge and social needs."[6]

This secular humanist movement or ideology has various marks of religion. In the sense understood by the Framers of the First Amendment, it appears that secular humanism should be regarded as a religion, both with respect to establishment and to free exercise. The religious and ethical doctrines of Joseph Priestley and of Thomas Paine, during the last quarter of the eighteenth century, were not far removed from what is now termed secular humanism. Yet doubtless Priestley's and Paine's religious radicalism would have been regarded by the Congress that approved the Bill of Rights as falling within the prohibitions and the privileges of the First Amendment.

At Mobile, testimony from the historian James Hitchcock, the psychologist William Coulson, and several other witnesses supported the plaintiffs' contention that secular humanism amounts to a religion, in competition with Christianity, Judaism, and other religions of transcendence. And it is a religion—or an anti-religion, if you will—that eagerly seeks to convert the rising generation to the views held by the American Humanist Association and allied organizations.

Having listened patiently to days of examination and cross examination of the expert witnesses for either side, and having asked them many questions directly, Judge Hand concluded in his opinion that "for the purposes of the First Amendment, secular humanism is a religious belief system, entitled to the protections of, and subject to the prohibitions of, the religion clauses. It is not a mere scientific methodology that may be promoted and advanced in the public schools."

The "values clarification" and "moral development" systems advocated by certain of the textbooks used in Mobile schools, Hand found, are based upon quasi-religious concepts and stand in contradiction of the assumptions of transcendent religions such as Christianity and Judaism. In this he found important the testimony of Paul Vitz, professor of psychology at New York University and the author of a systematic study of bias in textbooks.[7]

"Teaching that moral choices are purely personal and can only be based on some autonomous, as yet undiscovered and unfulfilled, inner self is a sweeping fundamental belief that must not be promoted by the public schools," Judge Hand remarked. "With these books, the State of Alabama has overstepped its mark, and must withdraw to perform its proper non-religious functions."[8]

OF SOME FORTY TEXTBOOKS objected to by the plaintiffs, only one—a history of which the principal author is Daniel Boorstin—was exempted from Judge Hand's order that these books be removed from Mobile schools. The textbooks in question were manuals in the disciplines of home economics, social studies, and history. It may seem odd that the subject of home economics roused the wrath of the Christian parents, but home economics now extends its dominion over sex education, family relations, and much else beyond the confines of cooking and sewing.

The principal charge against the textbooks in history and social studies was that they sinned by omission: next to nothing was said about the influence of religion on American history and society. This exclusion was deliberate. Counsel for the defense did not attempt to justify or to deny those sweeping omissions. Anyone who has taken the trouble to look into the history textbooks used today (with few exceptions) will find it difficult to dissent from Hand's condemnation:

> These history books discriminate against the very concept of religion, and theistic religions in particular, by omissions so serious that a student learning history from them would not be apprised of relevant facts about American history. Even where the factor of religion is included, as in statements that some colonies were founded to obtain religious freedom, there is rarely an explanation of Christianity's involvement. The student would reasonably assume, absent other information, that theistic religion is, at best, extraneous to an intelligent understanding of this country's history. The texts reviewed are not merely bad history, but lack so many facts as to equal ideological promotion. The Court notes that while both sets of defendants conducted an extensive defense of the home economics books against which the plaintiffs' heaviest artillery was trained, they did not even conduct a rear-guard action to ward off the assault on these deplorable history texts.

The five home economics textbooks against which the plaintiffs protested all taught "humanistic psychology," according to the testimony of the expert witnesses. Humanistic psychology is not to be confounded with study of the humanities; the term is more specialized, implying denial of the transcendent. But why should this humanistic psychology be found unconstitutional—or rather, why should it be excluded by court order from Alabama schools? In Hand's words,

> [t]he books teach that the student must determine right and wrong based only on his own experience, feelings and "values." These "values" are described as originating from within. A description of the origin of morals must be based on a faith assumption: a religious dogma. The books are not simply claiming that a moral rule must be internally accepted before it becomes

meaningful, because this is true of *all* facts and beliefs. The books require the student to accept that the validity of a moral choice is only to be decided by the student. The requirement is not stated explicitly. Instead, the books repeat, over and over, that the decision is "yours alone," or is "purely personal" that "only you can decide". . . . This highly relativistic and individualistic approach constitutes the promotion of a fundamental faith claim opposed to other religious faiths. . . . This faith assumes that self-actualization is the goal of every human being, that man has no supernatural attributes or component, that there are only temporal and physical consequences for man's actions, and that these results, alone, determine the morality of an action. This belief strikes at the heart of many theistic religions' beliefs that certain actions are in and of themselves immoral, whatever the consequences, and that, in addition, actions will have extra-temporal consequences.

The home economics books, in short, all advocated an innovating theory of human nature, based upon faith—in effect, the religion of secular humanism. What those textbooks taught was calculated to undo transcendent religions and the moral beliefs derived from those religions. Therefore, Judge Hand reasoned, their prescribed use in Mobile was a violation of the First Amendment. The Alabama educational authorities—whether or not by design—had been engaged in establishing a religion, that of secular humanism.

For his bold opinion, Judge Hand was fantastically reviled by certain publicists and professors. The language of one such critic, Alan Dershowitz, a professor at Harvard Law School, must suffice here for the purpose of illustration. Judge Hand, Mr. Dershowitz wrote in his syndicated newspaper column, is the "Ayatollah Khomeini of the federal judiciary . . . a disgrace to the federal judiciary. He is a constitutional outlaw in robes, a Torquemada of the twentieth century."

Hand's decision was carried by the defendants to the Circuit Court of Appeals—and there overturned. Judge Hand had shipped to that Court of Appeals many crates of exhibits and testimony in *Douglas T. Smith, et al., v. Board of School Commissioners.* Those crates were returned to him in short order—with their seals unbroken. Presumably the judges to whom the appeal had been made preferred not to be confused by evidence.

For lack of funds, the parent plaintiffs did not appeal the case beyond the Court of Appeals to the Supreme Court. In 1983, the report of the National Commission on Excellence in Education, *A Nation at Risk*, had declared that parents are the primary educators of their children. But in overturning Judge Hand's opinion, the Court of Appeals insured that secular humanists would be the primary educators of Alabama children, whether the parents should like it or not.

The body of belief, or non-theistic religion, called secular humanism is not a creation of the Evil Spirit. Some honest and able scholars subscribed to the two Humanist Manifestos. But if secular humanism should triumph totally in schools, immense mischief would be done in the long run to the person and the republic. For the dissolving of religious convictions brings about the decadence of the civil social order. A feeble humanitarianism cannot do duty for a pervasive religious faith.

In conformity to the First Amendment, Judge Hand was saying at Mobile, the state must not impose a non-theistic religion upon public schools, any more than it may impose a theistic religion upon all pupils. The judge's own words put the principle admirably: "If this court is compelled to purge 'God is great, God is good, we thank Him for our daily food,' from the classroom, then this court must also purge from the classroom those things that serve to teach that salvation is through man's self rather than through a deity."

It was not Judge Hand who chose to bring the power of the federal government into the classroom. Perhaps the kindest thing that might be done for the public schools would be to rescue them altogether from the interference of federal courts—which is precisely what Judge Hand tried to accomplish in the original *Jaffree* case of 1982.

Beyond textbooks lies the greater difficulty of imparting through public schools any understanding of ultimate questions and moral norms, if schools are not permitted to touch upon either theistic religions or non-theistic religions. Religious and moral instruction was the primary need that schools were created to satisfy. How worthwhile are schools that ignore altogether such duties?

The purpose of the religion clauses of the First Amendment was to protect religion in America from interference by the general government: to leave to the several states, and to voluntary religious associations, church questions. The assumption behind several recent Supreme Court decisions seems to have been that religion, and Christianity in particular, is suspect, and ought to be subordinated to "overriding public interest." It is conceivable that the Supreme Court, retracing its steps, may come to find in error those decisions which, mindlessly quoting the phrase "wall of separation," would make a presumptuous humanitarianism *de facto* the established church of the United States of America.

15

Pornography and
Free Speech

I N NO STATE OF THE UNION, two centuries ago, would foul
speech or publication have been tolerated by the public
authorities—notwithstanding provisions in state constitutions for
freedom of speech and press. Nor would Congress have
permitted in the District of Columbia or the Territories obscene utter-
ance or pornographic productions.

Freedom to speak and to publish never has been absolute in the
United States. It has been pointed out by several important commentators on the text of the Constitution that the First Amendment's
protections for the spoken and the written word are limited by the article
"the"—that is, "The Congress shall make no law abridging the freedom
of speech, or of the press. . . ." Why not simply the phrase "freedom of
speech," without the article? Because the Framers of the First Amendment,
and the First Congress of the United States, were aware that liberty of
speech can degenerate into license of speech.

What is meant by "the freedom of speech, or of the press"? The article here signifies the degree of freedom of speech and press that already was prevalent throughout the thirteen states in 1789; or perhaps the degree of freedom of speech and press that had prevailed in Britain and the British North American colonies since 1689. The First Amendment, that is, does not affirm any absolute, total right to speak and print, and over the years the federal judiciary has sustained many limitations upon what can be said and printed.

For a representative judge of the formative period of American law—or, at least, those judges influenced by Story and Kent—these questions of obscenity, pornography, and the like could be resolved readily enough through consulting *Of Private Wrongs*, the fourth vol-ume of Blackstone's *Commentaries on the Laws of England*. Blackstone discussed such crimes and follies at the end of his fourth chapter, "Of Offenses against God and Religion"; he was succinct, confining himself to two paragraphs on the whole subject.

Such social misconduct Blackstone defines as "open and notorious lewdness, either by keeping . . . houses of ill fame, which is an indictable offense; or by some scandalous and public indecency, 'or the sale of immoral pictures and prints,' for which the punishment 'at common law' is by fine and imprisonment." Blackstone was careful to preface this chapter on offenses against God and religion by the caution that "All crimes ought . . . to be estimated merely according to the mischiefs which they produce in civil society; and of consequence, private vices, or breach of mere absolute duties, which man is bound to perform considered only as an individual, are not, cannot be, the object of any municipal law; any farther than as by their evil example, or other pernicious effects, they may prejudice the community, and thereby become a species of private crimes."[1] Blackstone took it for granted that Christian sexual morality was applicable to offenses of open and notorious lewdness—supposing that these acts were not mere private vice, but were inflicted in some degree upon the public.

Once upon a time, responsibility for restraining pornographic publications lay within the police powers of the several states. Not until after World War II did federal courts begin to intervene in such concerns, tending to restrain censors rather than pornographers and to enlarge the protections extended by the First Amendment to the media of public expression—which now include, necessarily, television, radio, films, musical records, telephones, and other modes of communication quite unimagined in 1791. Thus, obscenity and salacity have many channels near the end of the twentieth century. And clearly the Supreme Court has been bewildered as to what it should do about pornography and allied afflictions, having handed down decisions that opened the sluices to a flood of obscenity.

Chief Justice Earl Warren once declared that, should he find in his daughter's hands such foul materials as the pornography shown in evidence during one appeal to the Court, he would knock down the pornographer. Nevertheless, as a justice he would not impair the pornographer's right to publish the trash. Many of the Supreme Court's major decisions on appeals of cases involving pornography have seemed no more consistent than was Chief Justice Warren.

Despite such occasional expressions of distaste for dirty pictures and obscene phrases, most justices most of the time have been considerably more concerned for the integrity of the second provision of the First Amendment than for the public and private consequences of indecent publication. The course of the Supreme Court's intervention in the censorship of obscene publications, and the reasoning or prejudices behind the Court's decisions, are matters of some interest—in the light of the consequences of forty years' indulgence of lubricity, as examined in the 1986 report of the Attorney General's Commission on Pornography.

WITH THE WIDESPREAD INCREASE of literacy and the improvement of printing techniques, traffic in pornographic materials has grown ever since late in the eighteenth century. In every country, until very recently, restraints upon obscene publications were employed by the public authorities; nevertheless, under-the-counter traffic in such goods persisted everywhere in some degree, and borderline publications were tolerated much of the time. The grounds for state prohibition of pornography were chiefly three: (1) incitement of crimes against the person that pornography may work, (2) damage done to the family by pornography's attractions, and (3) public duty to protect the emotions and the minds of children from obscene images and concepts.

In America, addiction to pornography—in books, magazines, films, electronic media of communication—was not a really serious affliction until after World War II. As is generally the consequence of war, that great struggle injured public morality in divers ways, arousing sensual appetites and besmirching the moral imagination that nurtures the vision of human dignity. The swift increase in indecent publications shortly after the war's end provoked stronger action by local committees, police forces, and voluntary associations to restrain this traffic. The contest between official or unofficial censors on one side, and pornographers (in uneasy alliance with reputable publishers) on the other was carried into the federal courts—where it still lingers.

About 1947, we were in the green tree; now we are in the dry. Infant television had not yet been seduced into impudicity; radio rarely ventured to titillate. Cable television and VCRs had not been invented; thus the private showing of obscene films required some bother. The glossy "girlie" magazines of the sort now peddled everywhere had not yet been fully developed, although corner newsstands offered a considerable variety of snickering and leering publications, from "humor" magazines to horror pulps, for boys and men who furtively sought that sort of thing. There existed, nevertheless, recognized bounds beyond which such publications rarely ventured: publishers and vendors knew the power of local censors.

Who were these censors, so denounced by the righteous guardians of freedom of the press? Ordinarily these were municipal committees, lawfully chosen, composed typically of clergymen, police officers, married women active in civics, and perhaps a professor or two. These committees almost never made attempts to exercise political censorship; they were concerned with public decency. More tolerant usually than the typical householder in their towns, the members of such committees were sensible enough: "the freedom of speech, or of the press" specified in the First Amendment rarely suffered any abridgment at their hands. Until the late 1940s, no American court, federal or state, suggested in its opinions that obscene publications might appeal to the protections of the First Amendment.

Upon these local committees of censors, however, would descend soon new techniques of color printing, making photographs more exciting than they had been in the sepia tones of the rotogravure sections in Sunday's newspapers. Undressed women in black and white would be converted in the girlie magazines into undressed women in more appealing multicolor. More baneful to the moral imagination, in the long run, would be the new-mode salacious or nihilistic novel.

In 1948, in the case of *Doubleday v. New York*, a state court found that Edmund Wilson's novel *Memoirs of Hecate County*, the potboiling work of a talented man of letters, was obscene; the case was carried to the Supreme Court of the United States on constitutional points. Dividing four to four, the justices in effect sustained the New York Court, letting the suppression of the book stand, but the fact that the Supreme Court had received the appeal on constitutional grounds was ominous for the jurisdiction of state courts and of censorial bodies, when pornography became a subject of litigation.

Strong challenges to almost any form of censorial restraint upon publication were arising in the courts of several states during the four or five years following the end of the war. Perhaps the most significant early action of this sort was a Philadelphia case, *Commonwealth v. Gordon et al.* The vice squad of Philadelphia's police department had seized from fifty-four bookshops copies of four novels alleged to be obscene: books by Ross Lockridge, Calder Willingham, James T. Farrell, and Harold Robbins. Judge Curtis Bok of the Pennsylvania Court of Quarter Sessions found for the bookselling defendants, chiefly accord-ing to the "clear and present danger" doctrine that had been enunciated by Justice Oliver Wendell Holmes. "The only clear and present danger to be prevented by section 524 that will satisfy both the Constitution and the current customs of our era is the imminence of the commission of criminal behavior resulting from the reading of a book," Judge Bok ruled. "Publication alone can have no such automatic effect."

This decision was severely criticized by an eminent authority on constitutional law, Edwin S. Corwin. "This obviously overlooks the primary purpose of governmental interference with the distribution of 'obscene literature,' namely to prevent immature minds from contamination," Corwin wrote. "Dealing with this point Judge Bok protests against putting the 'entire reading public at the mercy of the adolescent mind.' Should, on the other hand, the adolescent mind be put at the mercy of the uninhibited reading tastes of an elderly federal judge?"

Although *Commonwealth v. Gordon* was not appealed, similar cases had begun to move upward in emulation of *Doubleday v. New York* and other early appeals. The rough war years had coarsened the Ameri-can public's literary taste, and a heavy, oppressive sexual obsession could be discerned in many modes of American life. The censors could not stand their ground against a "new morality" that was altering the prejudices, habits, and actions of boys on the street corner and judges on the bench. Alfred Kinsey's *Sexual Behavior in the Human Male* was published in 1948—an absurd book, unscientific, but influential, and useful to various people as an apology for their curious private habits.[2]

Already, in 1948, the Supreme Court of the United States had commenced to rule adversely concerning state statutes meant to restrain obscene publications. Were they consonant with the second provision of the First Amendment? Such questions the Supreme Court had not even asked in earlier eras.

In *Winters v. New York* (1948), the state of New York had made it a felony to print or distribute "any printed matter principally made up of criminal views, police reports, or accounts of criminal deeds, or pictures, or stories of deeds of bloodshed, lust or crime" that might incite to crimes against the person. Six of the nine Supreme Court justices had found this statute unconstitutional, on the ground that it did not establish an ascertainable standard of guilt. The precedent was now established for overturning a state's obscenity statutes through the federal courts; appeals to federal jurisdiction were numerous.

By 1953, uncertainty as to the constitutionality of most state obscenity statutes had dissuaded state prosecutors from proceeding vigorously against many pornographic or quasi-pornographic publica-tions that formerly would have been restrained. The Post Office's censorship of materials sent through the mails also was less strict than it once had been—postal officials perhaps being intimidated by charges of Comstockery that had been echoing for some years. Municipal authorities generally had grown lax in applying their vague powers to preserve public decency, so that drugstore news racks were little harassed in most cities. Police still might suppress the more vile forms of pornography—often in the form of crude "comic" booklets, surreptitiously sold, or they might charge a bookseller with having sold a volume by Frank Harris or Henry Miller.

During 1953 and 1954, marketing of sensational paperbacks con-tinued to swell in volume, and a high proportion of these were sold in part by suggestive or actually pornographic cover designs. Historical romances on the paperback racks, sub-literary, now featured graphic erotic episodes calculated to induce gross fantasies. Editors of large trade publishers increasingly competed in profitable impudicity, often justifying it by the researches, presumably infallible, of Alfred Kinsey.

For people who liked that sort of thing, that was the sort of thing they liked—as Abraham Lincoln had put it. Much more ominous was the debasing of the sentiments and minds of children by the mass-production of "comic" booklets specializing in horror, torture, mon-strosity, exhibitionism, and homicide. As Margaret Mead wrote in 1953, "To the old abused adage, 'To the pure all things are pure,' should be added, 'To the inexperienced, great confusion is possible.'"

Bertrand Russell thought otherwise. Writing in *Encounter* for July 1954, he declared that he would like to see all forms of censorship abolished, in the belief that the resulting flood of pornography would last only a few years, and then the public would lose interest. His view was not sustained by subsequent events.

While this fight about the printed page was at its height, the Su-preme Court intervened in states' endeavors to censor movies. In March 1954, the Court reversed decisions of New York and Ohio courts, denying state censorship agencies power to prohibit the showing of two foreign films—*La Ronde* and *M*. One of these films was concerned with adultery, the other with criminal perversion. The Court held that the term "immoral" was too vague to be accepted as proper ground for suppressing films. This decision followed a precedent established in July 1953, when the Court had denied New York State the power to prohibit the showing of *The Miracle* as an abridgment of free expression. It remained uncertain in 1953 and 1954, nevertheless, how far the Court might push its claim to jurisdiction over state and local cen-sorships.

It was clear enough that the majority of judges in the early 1950s held views of freedom of expression derived from John Stuart Mill and other liberals of the nineteenth century, though brought up to date after a fashion by liberal educators and writers of twentieth-century America. With some honorable exceptions, justices of the Supreme Court have not been original thinkers. Their understanding of human nature, society, and the law itself often has been derived from their non-juridical contemporaries.

To apprehend the mentality of the justices who dealt with obscenity cases forty years ago, one may turn to the expressions of opinion of leading liberal publicists and educators and polemicists of that time. Consider the attitudes toward censorship in 1954 of Fred Millett, an influential educationist, and David Riesman, a much-read sociologist. Writing in the *Bulletin of the American Association of University Pro-fessors*, Millett opposed censorship for any reason. He maintained that the immense sale of salacious publications was simply a consequence of the growth of literacy and secondary education in America: "We can only hope that perhaps in two or three hundred years, secondary education will produce results that are not ignoble." Riesman, in his book *Individualism Reconsidered*, suggested that people who support censorship are "anti-intellectuals" endeavoring to "outlaw the worldly and the educated . . . a sign of their resentment of their inferior status in the traditional hierarchies of prestige and comprehension."

Could neither Millett nor Riesman perceive any reasonable purpose in censorship? Would they have smiled complacently upon Julius Strelcher's obscene publications against German Jews, regarding them merely as a sign of increasing literacy in Germany? The mind has its slums, and the society that does not regard them with some alarm may find itself overwhelmed by its own intellectual proletariat.

The mentality of Millett or Riesman—a set of attitudes Gordon Chalmers called "disintegrated liberalism"—was the mentality of the majority of the men who sat on the Supreme Court in the 1950s. The mentality of the general public, however—at least the mentality of people active in practical politics—was distinctly different from that of the majority of the justices. In reaction against the swelling empire of the pornographers, public pressures grew during 1955 and 1956 for more effective restraints upon that traffic. In New York, Connecticut, Maryland, Washington, Montana, Alaska, Nevada, Ohio, and Texas, state legislatures adopted statutes to check the distribution of obscene publications. Several other states already had enacted such legislation. A number of Post Office suits were filed against publishers and dis-tributors of salacious materials. Voluntary groups organized against pornography were vigorous. The number of court verdicts against publishers and vendors nevertheless was remarkably small. "The most publicized cases of attempts to stop the sale or exhibition of books and films in recent years all resulted in the freeing of the books and the pictures by the courts," J.M. O'Neill wrote in the September 1955 number of *Social Order*.

In 1954, Congress passed a bill prohibiting interstate transportation of obscene matter by common carriers. Difficulties in the way of effective enforcement of this statute were formidable, and the courts fretted about the meaning of "obscene" and other terms in the act. The federal statute of 1950 authorizing the Post Office to refuse to deliver the mail of known mailers of obscene matter was found by the Court of Appeals for the District of Columbia to be confined to "materials already published and duly found unlawful"; it would not justify a Post Office prohibition of future mailings, until each mailing or publication had been inspected and judged on its own peculiar contents. In another 1955 case, that of *Confidential* magazine, the District Court of the District of Columbia ruled that the Post Office could exercise no prior censorship, but must decide on the propriety or obscenity of separate issues after they had been mailed. And in yet other cases, federal courts seem disposed to give the defendant in censorship cases the benefit of whatever doubts might exist.

Playboy magazine, first published in 1954, had attained by the end of 1955 a circulation of nearly half a million copies. (By 1955 some sixty other breast-fetishistic magazines were competing with *Playboy*; pornography production, both soft- and hard-core, was becoming a major industry.) Such glossy popular magazines for men, no matter how nude their female models or how posed, no matter how preten-tiously smutty their stories and articles, had become virtually immune from prosecution at any level of law. Yet all-out pornography involving no question of due process of law under the First Amendment still was held subject to state statutes against published impudicity.

On June 13, 1955 , a test case brought before the Supreme Court of New York was decided against three Times Square booksellers who had sold copies of *Nights of Horror*, a series of fourteen volumes detailing sadism and sexual perversion. The seizure of these books by the New York City police was found lawful and not infringing freedom of the press. If yet other volumes of *Nights of Horror* should be published in the future, the court ruled that they would have to be judged on their merits or demerits: the barn door might be locked only after the horse had been stolen. However horrid these books, "There can be no injunction regarding an unpublished book or pamphlet." In the course of the trial, it was learned that these obscene volumes had been in the possession of the leader of a gang of young "thrill killers" who had committed murder and torture earlier in the year.

During 1956, New York, Kentucky, Rhode Island, and Georgia adopted special statutes checking distribution of indecent and sadistic publications. In that same year, some thirty-four states either adopted such statutes or were preparing to do so. Two important cases arose in Michigan: the banning of the novel *The Devil Rides Outside* in Detroit, and the order of the prosecutor of St. Clair County that wholesalers not distribute publications on the "Publications Disapproved" list of the National Organization for Decent Literature.

All this ferment about pornography burst into the Supreme Court in 1957. There resulted three important decisions, not altogether consistent one with another, which in a rough way established precedents binding upon both federal and state courts—but only until the middle 1960s, when a new round of Supreme Court decisions bewildered judges, lawyers, pornographers, and the annoyed general public.

The first of these cases of 1957 was *Butler v. Michigan*[3], and the

Supreme Court's decision overthrew Michigan's obscenity statute, on the ground that in both the Detroit and the Port Huron (St. Clair County) actions against distribution of certain books, application of the Michigan statute "reduced the adult population of Michigan to reading only what is fit for children." (One recalls Judge Bok's ruling in Philadelphia nearly a decade earlier.) Civil liberties zealots rejoiced at this slap to censors, and Michigan for years thereafter lay open to pornography.

Soon after, however, the same nine justices confounded extremists for freedom of expression by the majority ruling, the opinion for which was written by Justice Brennan, in *Roth v. United States* [4], a federal action, not an appeal from a state court. Samuel Roth, a New York pornographer, was sent to jail, and the Court made it clear (for the time being) that the First Amendment does not confer the least immunity upon pornographers. The word "obscene" is sufficiently clear in meaning, the Court found, to be employed in a statute; but the constitutional test is whether the dominant character of the whole publication appeals to the prurient interest of the average person, applying contemporary standards of the community. Prurience is defined as "a shameful or morbid interest in nudity, sex, or excretion."

In the third important case, involving the infamous *Nights of Horror* series—the case of *Kingsley Book Company v. Brown* [5], appealed from the New York courts—the Supreme Court ruled that courts may rightfully issue injunctions on the complaints of city officials to restrain the selling of allegedly pornographic publications until a prompt decision is reached regarding the character of the suspected material. Justice Frankfurter described as a "filthy business" the trade of Kingsley Books and others purveying the *Nights of Horror* series. A curious array of organizations and persons had filed *amicus curiae* briefs in support of the men in that "filthy business" of *Nights of Horror*: the American Book Publishers Council, the Authors League, *Playboy* magazine, Morris Ernst, and the American Civil Liberties Union. They were chagrined by this decision that impaired the liberties of makers of obscene books.

Because two of these three rulings seemed to impose restraints upon mass produced pornography, various commentators in 1957 reasoned that the Court at length had settled upon certain general principles of law with respect to obscene publication and that state legislatures and police officers now could conform their statutes and enforcement to approved guidelines. *Roth*, it was thought, supplied the norm. [6]

But the *Roth* decision turned out to be no better than an uneasy truce, during which the tendency of the Supreme Court was to diminish the seeming strictness of the opinion in *Roth*, while legislators and law-enforcement people remained confused. Then, in *Jacobellis v. Ohio*[7] and *Memoirs v. Massachusetts* [8], the Supreme Court turned its back on restraining censors rather than on pornographers. Justice Brennan's opinions in both cases established (temporarily) the doctrine that if a publication should have "literary or scientific or artistic value or any other form of social importance" it could not be denied constitutional protection of freedom of the press—no matter how much obscenity it might contain along with the alleged "social importance." Brennan expressed the doctrine as follows in his opinion for the *Memoirs* case: "Three elements must coalesce: it must be established that (a) the dominant theme of the material taken as a whole appeals to a prurient interest in sex; (b) the material is patently offensive because it affronts contemporary community standards relating to the description or representation of sexual matters; and (c) the material is utterly without redeeming social value."

This test made it nearly impossible to prove that any magazine, book, or film was pornographic. In particular, the requirement that material be "utterly without redeeming social value" was welcomed by producers and distributors of indecency, for it was simple to include in their publications short articles or even phrases that might be regarded as social criticism: thus the whole publication would be excluded from restraint.

The practical effect of the Court's *Jacobellis* and *Memoirs* rulings was to break down enforcement of pornography statutes throughout the country. For about six years, all but the most extreme forms of pornographic publication were permitted to flourish; huge fortunes were made in the business. It became difficult to find an ordinary movie that was not unnecessarily ornamented with scenes offensive to persons endowed with what once had been regarded as decent taste, while virtually every sexual perversion could be displayed in "hard core" pornographic films at "adult" theaters.

As George M. Weaver put it in his *Handbook on the Prosecution of Obscenity Cases*, "The three-part test of *Memoirs* signalled an era of minimal obscenity regulation. As the Court later said in *Miller v. California*, the 'utterly without redeeming social value' criterion charged the prosecution with 'a burden virtually impossible to discharge under our criminal standards of proof.'" One year after *Memoirs* (which concerned the publication in Massachusetts of the old salacious novel *Fanny Hill*), the Court began a six-year period in which it summarily reversed findings of obscenity when any five justices, each applying his own test, concluded that the material was constitutionally protected. This approach, together with the *Memoirs* test, made obscenity prosecutions very chancy propositions.

IT WOULD BE WEARISOME to recount in detail these ultra-liberal rulings of the late 1960s and early 1970s. Some justices of that radical era were prudent most of the period, despite the general readiness of the Supreme Court to convert the First Amendment into an edict of license. Justice Byron White, for one, comes off well. Justice William Brennan, on the other hand, was startlingly erratic. He was wrathful at "pandering"—that is, making large sums of money out of selling pornography, but any obscenity *per se* he seemed, in some of his remarks, to regard as inconsequential.

In 1973, the Court temporarily changed direction. In *Miller v. California* [9], the Court's majority established revised tests for obscenity. To be found obscene at law, a publication must be recognized by "the average person" as appealing to prurient interest, taking into account "contemporary community standards": it must depict or describe sexual conduct in "a patently offensive way"; it must lack serious literary, artistic, or scientific value, taken as a whole.

Whatever the deficiencies and imprecision of these rules, they do reject any constitutional protection for unredeemed obscenity and afford some grounds for state and local authorities to prosecute pornographers. No longer does a "social value" gesture enable a mocking publisher to print whatever he relishes in the way of erotica.

For the past twenty-five years, then—a period coinciding with the withering of the radical political movements of the 1960s and 1970s—the Supreme Court has handed down relatively few startling decisions with respect to obscenity. Yet in 1989 there came to the attention of the Court the unpleasant phenomenon of obscene telephone conversations for pay. Might not public authorities interfere with commercial salacity over the wires? Yes, possibly, the Court's majority decided—but only if the calls were obscene. Should the dirty talk be classified as merely indecent, it would be exempt from restraint. What standards might be employed to distinguish the obscene from the indecent, the Court did not condescend to enunciate. Doubtless a huge volume of litigation over this fine distinction will pour into state and federal courts.

The federal courts now tend to relinquish authority in these perplexed cases to the state and local courts from which the Supreme Court had snatched jurisdiction. Yet the language of the federal decisions has deprived state and local authorities of nearly any ground on which actions or materials may be judged obscene or blameless—except the surviving phrase, "affronts local community standards." Though state and local censorships have been slowly re-established to some degree in most states during recent years, after four decades of being knocked about by federal courts, state and local prosecutors are wary of charging pornographers with felonies. The more successful pornographers have acquired fortunes with which to defend themselves and their soiled empires. And the average American citizen cannot recall a time in which most novels were decent enough, most movies were meant to entertain rather than to arouse appetites, television was content to worship Mammon rather than Astarte, video shops did not make indecent films available readily in nearly every neighborhood, the crime statistics for rape were relatively low, and the attorney general did not need to spend much of his time fighting the purveyors of dirty pictures.

Federal judges, from the Chief Justice down to men and women most recently confirmed in their judicial appointments, would like to wash their hands of this distasteful business, the more difficult because the federal judiciary has been unable to arrive at any tolerable definitions of obscenity, pornography, lewdness, and the like—unable, that is, short of repairing to Christian, or at least generally religious, teachings. It no longer seems heroic in a judge to affirm the inalienable right of Mr. Larry Flynt to build a lucrative Empire of Onan at the expense of public morality.

Perhaps hereafter the Supreme Court of the United States will repair to the doctrine of judicial restraint as justification for a dignified withdrawal from confused and contradictory involvement in the exercise of police powers previously reserved to the states and their agencies. Those unhappy four decades of meddling were undertaken by the Court without either legislation by the Congress or prodding by any powerful pressure group—except the lobbyists for pornographers and "civil liberties" fanatics.

Certain lessons may be learned from those decades of the Court's vagaries on pornography, censorship, and "redeeming social value." One thing demonstrated is the imprudence of translating a Bill of Rights protection of the several states against Congress into an unlimited license for the Supreme Court to meddle with states' jurisdictions in such concerns. Another lesson is the inefficacy of substituting personal and shifting value judgments of nine justices—who can form no consensus among themselves—for enduring moral standards derived from religion, philosophy, and a people's customs and conventions. A third profitable reflection is this: in a self-righteous endeavor to guarantee an extreme of liberty to "emancipated" individuals, the judicial branch of government may work sorry harm—possibly irreparable damage—upon the body social.

"The individual is foolish," Edmund Burke wrote, "but the species is wise." The species has been wise in setting itself against corrupting pornography; yet there have been appointed to the Supreme Court, this past half-century, some foolish individuals.

Part V

The Economic Foundations of the Republic

16

John Marshall and the Rise of the Corporation

F
OR MORE THAN A CENTURY AND A HALF, after
the ratification of the Bill of Rights, no great difficulties arose
concerning interpretation of the religion clause, or clauses, of
the First Amendment; "original intent" prevailed. Not until
recent decades did federal courts read into those few phrases prohibitions
against a friendly relationship between church and state.

It was otherwise with those provisions of the Constitution that
concerned economic activity: from the early years of the Republic, when
land speculation, commerce and manufacturing, incorporation, and all
such matters of gain and loss stood in dispute, the federal courts began
to hand down decisions that shaped the American nation economically
and socially. Liberal construction of the Constitution prevailed in such
decisions; and though opponents, chiefly in the Democratic party,
appealed angrily to "original intent," the Supreme Court extended to
property strong protections of the federal government.

In consequence, the Constitution, as interpreted by Chief Justice John Marshall and the majority of his associate justices, has made possible America's present economic pattern—even though that pattern is not at all what most of the Framers expected to come to pass in America. In this present chapter, I offer the reader some reflections on Marshall's decisions and the coming of the corporate economy.

Although joint-stock companies existed in a recognizable form as early as the sixteenth century, the tremendous corporation with which everyone is familiar nowadays came to pass in the nineteenth and twentieth centuries. For such gigantic combinations, artificial creations, to survive and prosper, the enforcement of strong laws is required. Presently the civil social order appears to center round the stock markets, such is the magnitude and influence of commercial corporations. Major political decisions of a country tend to reflect the state of the market. A century and a half ago, Chateaubriand (after praising certain French statesmen of yesteryear) remarked sardonically, "But nowadays statesmen understand only the stock market—and that badly."

Nowhere in the Constitution are joint-stock companies, let alone corporations, specifically mentioned. The protections and privileges of commercial and charitable corporations, rather, are derived from Article I, Section 10, with its clause prohibiting the several states from passing any "Law impairing the Obligation of Contracts. . . ." This is reinforced by the provision in the Fifth Amendment that no person shall "be deprived of life, liberty, or property, without due process of law. . . ." and by the provision in the Fourteenth Amendment, Section 1, that no state may "deprive any person of life, liberty, or property without due process of law. . . ."

It was Chief Justice John Marshall who applied the contract clause to corporations, even when those corporations came into conflict with a state government; and who through certain of his decisions afforded commercial corporations the shelter and refuge of federal courts. The growth of industrial and mercantile corporations in America is related to those rulings at law, even though that growth did not assume tremendous proportions until after the Civil War.

Throughout much of the world, the American corporate structure of business has been emulated, and the huge international corporations of our present decade are rooted in the successes of American grand-scale corporations. So I think it worth our while to examine some of the relationships between the law of the Constitution and that phenomenon of political economy called the business corporation—chiefly through an account of John Marshall's reasoning.

Nowadays the business corporation is regarded as particularly American. But in the year 1800, when John Marshall was appointed Chief Justice, the independent commercial corporation was regarded as particularly un-American. A corporation, in British law and in the law of the early Republic, was an organization granted certain privileges because it was expected to serve public purposes. Roscoe Pound refers severely to "the traditional attitude of our American law toward corporations, thinking of them not as modern business devices but in terms of a medieval jealousy of ecclesiastical and municipal development"—and here Pound refers to cases within our present century. He comments that "The American man of business, the captain of industry, has had as much cause of complaint in this respect as the laborer...."[1] If this suspicion of corporations has survived to our own time, it was far stronger two centuries ago.

In many American minds, about the year 1800, the chartered or registered corporation was linked with repudiated theories of mercantilism and state-granted monopolies. Had not the multifunctioned trading corporations of Canada, chartered by Colbert and his successors, failed wretchedly to bring prosperity to either Canada or France? And surely Americans must reject any such monstrous joint-stock domination as the East India Company, the corruptions of which were being denounced at Westminster by Edmund Burke in the very month when the Constitutional Convention had commenced its deliberations at Philadelphia.

From the ratification of the Constitution to the beginning of the year 1800, state governments granted charters, nevertheless, to some three hundred and thirty-five corporations. Most of these were to banks, companies to construct turnpikes and canals and toll bridges, insurance companies, and other associations presumed to serve a public purpose by satisfying real public needs. During those years, only thirteen of the charters were granted by states to mercantile or manufacturing companies. Incorporation, in short, generally was viewed as a high privilege, not to be rashly permitted.

To aspiring entrepreneurs, the advantages of incorporation were obvious. Unlike a private proprietorship or a partnership, a corporation was immortal, virtually: the death of a shareholder, or of a hundred shareholders perhaps, would not dissolve the corporation, which therefore enjoyed the immense advantage of continuity of operation. Better still, to many investors, was the fact that a stockholder in a corporation would be held liable for the corporation's debts only in a sum equal to his investment in the firm, while a private proprietor or a partner would be held liable by common law and statute for the whole of a firm's indebtedness. Moreover, a corporation might gather up capital for its operations far exceeding what even the biggest limited partnership might succeed in raising. Clearly, incorporation was and is a privilege, conferring benefits not shared by earlier business structures.

Thus voices were raised, Alexander Hamilton's among them, in favor of allowing entrepreneurs to pursue their own advantage through incorporation—on the assumption that this liberal policy would lead, if indirectly, toward greater national prosperity. Pressures for the growth and protection of commercial corporations steadily increased after 1790.

ONE FORM of joint-stock company, the immediate ancestor of the great commercial or industrial corporations, did flourish from the time the Articles of Confederation were drawn up. I refer to the land companies, which bought and sold, during the first several decades of the new Republic, immense tracts of public lands and of lands confiscated during the Revolution.

Such speculation ruined Robert Morris, the financier of the Revolution; it undid Justice James Wilson, as he sat on the Supreme Court. In the fullness of time, one such league of speculators, the New England Mississippi Land Company, would have its curious proceedings carried to the Supreme Court, Chief Justice Marshall there presiding.

Let us imagine ourselves in the small low-domed chamber of the United States Supreme Court, within the Capitol, on March 16, 1810. Mr. Chief Justice Marshall is announcing the Court's decision in the case of *Fletcher v. Peck*, which had roots running so far back as the year 1789.

The great Chief Justice was a slovenly, ungainly, humorous, lovable man; except for his marvellous eyes, to call him "uncouth" was flattery. On the bench, he maintained the Federalist cause that had been overwhelmed at the polls by the American democracy ten years before. In law, he was the disciple of Blackstone; in politics, of Burke.

Marshall's keen intellect, his powers of argument, and his literary talents had baffled President Jefferson's enmity. In *Fletcher v. Peck*, Marshall had found an admirable opportunity to expound his fundamental doctrine of the sovereignty of the American nation, as set against the claim of sovereignty made by the several states, and an opportunity, too, for upholding the doctrine of the inviolable nature of contracts— even contracts to which a state should be a party.

The action known as *Fletcher v. Peck* arose out of the Yazoo land scandals, in which the New England Mississippi Land Company was involved.[2] This was a collusive case intended by both parties to have the result of obtaining from the Congress compensation for the loss of lands claimed by the state of Georgia. Speculators had bribed the representatives in the Georgia legislature—with the exception of one member—to sell those lands (now in Alabama and Mississippi) at a price absurdly low. The succeeding Georgia legislature had rescinded the grant. The question that the Supreme Court had to consider, as Marshall framed it, was whether the "contract clause" of Article I of the Constitution bound a state government, so that a legislature might not abrogate a grant. Behind this question loomed the dispute as to where sovereignty actually reposed—with the several states, or with the American nation as represented in the federal government.

With no dissent from any of his colleagues on the bench, Marshall found that the grant of the Yazoo lands by the state of Georgia was a contract; that contracts, out of social necessity, must be enforced, and property protected against encroachments; that the rescinding of the

Yazoo grants was unconstitutional, under Article I, Section 10, for states, as well as citizens, were bound by the contract clause.

I do not inquire here into the validity of Marshall's reasoning. Of present concern is merely the way in which his famous opinion in *Fletcher v. Peck* enlarged protections for contracts and encouraged the growth of business corporations. In effect, Marshall extended the federal judiciary's enforcement of contracts to state governments. And if the claims of so suspect a stock company as the New England Mississippi Land Company were sustained in effect by the Supreme Court, surely less scandalous companies and corporations might feel reasonably confident of being countenanced by federal courts.

It has been remarked by commentators that Marshall's decision was much influenced by his desire to encourage occupation and development of the empty western lands of the United States. He approved what we now call "venture capital," speculation that usually would produce large returns in goods and services, and such bold investors must be protected against arbitrary interference by public authorities or by rival economic interests. This was part and parcel of Marshall's confident nationalism. The Chief Justice was an evangel of economic progress. The last-ditch opponents of compensating the Yazoo claimants, adversaries by 1810 of both Marshall and Jefferson, were the little band in Congress of the Old Republicans (or Tertium Quids), led by John Randolph of Roanoke, whose marvellous invective for years dissuaded the Congress from granting the Yazoo compensation, *Fletcher v. Peck* notwithstanding.

Marshall, though called the Supreme Conservative by his chief biographer, stood for territorial and economic expansion; Randolph and his planter colleagues, for things established and economic retrenchment. Yet it does not follow that Marshall sanctioned an unrestrained vain-glorious triumph of speculative investors and promoters; more on that point presently.

It might be interesting to trace Marshall's economic views and influence through a diversity of cases at law, but here we must confine ourselves to merely two others. Of *Fletcher v. Peck*, it may be remarked that Marshall's opinion sheltering a joint-stock company encouraged entrepreneurs to demand that the privileges of incorporation be made available generally to investors, rather than restricted, for the most part, to public corporations and companies whose works clearly would provide direct benefits to the public. Only next year, in 1811, the state of New York radically liberalized its statutes of incorporation, passing a general act that virtually abolished restrictions, requiring merely that entrepreneurs or firms submit summary declarations of their economic intentions. Similar general acts of incorporation were adopted in one state or another over the following three decades, so that by the 1850s it was easy to obtain the privileges of incorporation anywhere in the Union. The British Parliament, beginning in 1825, similarly reformed its statutes of incorporation—an instance of how the United States usually had led in the development of corporate structure.

WE NOW TURN to the Dartmouth College case, nine years later. Chief Justice Marshall's opinion in *Dartmouth College v. Woodward* [3] secured the independence of the so-called "private" universities and colleges, whether church-related or wholly secular. Nowadays that independence is encroached upon, increasingly, by both federal and state governments—in part because of the eagerness of many institutions to accept governmental subsidies in one form or another, although some institutions have succumbed to state control regardless. For all that, independent American universities and liberal arts colleges still enjoy a degree of freedom from governmental direction unknown in any other country. Dartmouth College, with Daniel Webster as its orator at the bar, won that liberty for the American higher education in the year 1819.

Somewhat incongruously, the struggle of Dartmouth's trustees to reject the control of a state board of supervisors resulted also in a greater degree of independence and security for America's business corporations. For the decision in *Dartmouth College v. Woodward* was applicable not to charitable corporations only, but to business firms as well.

Marshall and his colleagues ruled in this case that an educational institution privately founded and financed, and employing private teachers, is not converted into a public institution merely because the state has granted that school a charter. On the contrary, the school's charter is a contract which the state may not abrogate, for contracts are protected by the Constitution. Marshall's definition of the corporation is one of the more memorable passages in his *Dartmouth College* opinion:

> A corporation is an artificial being, invisible, intangible, and existing only in contemplation of law. Being the mere creature of law, it possesses only those properties which the charter of its creation confers upon it, either expressly, or as incidental to its very existence. There are such as are supposed best calculated to effect the object for which it was created. Among the most important are immortality, and, if the expression may be allowed, individuality; properties by which a perpetual succession of many persons are considered as the same, and may act as a single individual. They enable a corporation to manage its own affairs, and to hold property without the perplexing intricacies, the hazardous and endless necessity of perpetual conveyances, for the purpose of transmitting it from hand to hand. It is chiefly for the purpose of clothing bodies of men, in succession, with these qualities and capacities, that corporations were invented, and are in use. . . . It is no more a State instrument, than a natural person exercising the same powers would be. . . .

Marshall was not arguing that corporations are unaccountable for their actions or that states should issue charters to corporations lightly. As he put it in his opinion,

> The objects for which a corporation is created are universally such as the government wishes to promote. They are deemed beneficial to the country, and this benefit constitutes the consideration, and, in most cases, the sole consideration, of the grant . . . . The benefit to the public is considered as an ample compensation for the faculty it confers, and the corporation is created. If the advantages to the public constitute a full compensation for the faculty it gives, there can be no reason for exacting a further compensation, by claiming a right to exercise over this artificial being a power which changes its nature, and touches the fund, for the security and application of which it was created.

The privilege of incorporation, in short, ought to be extended to bodies whose work will benefit the public. Marshall was referring immediately to charitable corporations of an educational character. But, as in *Fletcher v. Peck*, Marshall doubtless looked upon honest commercial and industrial companies as conferring public benefits.

What the case of Dartmouth College established was the doctrine that a grant of incorporation is a form of contract, and therefore under the protection of the federal government. Marshall's primary interest in this case was to establish still more firmly his principle that the Constitution protects private property and contract against encroachments of governments—and state governments in particular. For more than half a century this rule, though modified somewhat by later decisions of the Supreme Court, prevailed in interpretations of the Constitution.

It ought not to be supposed that Marshall set free from all restraints either charitable corporations or business corporations, I repeat. For Marshall's opinion in *Dartmouth College v. Woodward*—as Edwin S. Corwin put it some seventy years ago—"leaves it perfectly clear that legislatures may reserve the right to alter or repeal at will the charters they grant."[4] Such reservations, inserted in corporate charters when they are issued, considerably restrain the ambitions and undertakings of business corporations.

The Dartmouth College case was decided in 1819. Eleven years later, in the case of *Providence Bank v. Billings*[5], Marshall found it necessary to check corporations in their assertions of independence from nearly all state controls. During the decade that had intervened, the ruling that corporate charters were protected as contracts had encouraged entrepreneurs as well as public interest corporations to assert that their charters exempted them even from the payment of taxes—which latter claim was made by the Providence Bank. Not so, Marshall ruled: charters must be narrowly construed, and the Providence Bank must pay a state bank tax that the legislature had imposed some thirty years after granting the Bank's charter, for the charter, in Marshall's words, "contained no stipulation promising exemption from taxation. The State, then, has made no express contract which has been impaired by the act of which the plaintiffs complain." Corporations, like individuals, must expect to bear their share of the public burdens. Certain corporations may be exempted from taxation, if the state finds it desirable to exempt them. We all recall Marshall's observation that the power to tax is the power to destroy, and for that reason—though he did not expressly say so in this Providence Bank opinion—churches and colleges may be exempted.

But it is otherwise with most corporations, including banks. Here is Marshall on the subject: "The great object of an incorporation is to bestow the character and properties of individuality on a collective and changing body of men. This capacity is always given to such a body. Any privileges which may exempt it from the burdens common to individuals do not flow necessarily from the charter, but must be expressed in it, or they do not exist."

In his political economy as related to the Constitution, then, Marshall was a strong champion of rights to property and rights of contract, a friend to rapid economic development of the territories of the United States, and a defender of intelligent economic speculation—in which Marshall himself, indeed, engaged. All this is not to say that Marshall had much notion of what astounding consequences his protections for corporations would produce in the long run.

Although *Fletcher v. Peck*, *Dartmouth College v. Woodward*, and certain other Marshall opinions did have the incidental result of encouraging some growth of business corporations, that was not Marshall's primary object; nor did the great commercial and industrial corporations eclipse private proprietorships and partnerships until after the Civil War. (When that day came, the business corporations would tend to turn to the "due process" clauses of the Fifth and Fourteenth Amendments, rather than to the tenth section of Article I of the Constitution, so strongly emphasized by Marshall.) All that Marshall did was to open the way, constitutionally, for corporations to resist the encroachments of state governments. Yet that relaxing of state controls, in the long run, did much to work the transformation of rural and agricultural America into urban and industrial America—with incalculably profound social and moral effects upon the American people.

JOHN MARSHALL'S handsome house, Federalist style, still stands in Richmond, though little remains of the neighborhood that Marshall knew. The Chief Justice was a neighborly, kindly man, never standing on his dignity. He did his own shopping at Richmond's produce market, leisurely chatting with anyone he met. He was shabbily dressed and affably obliging. A newcomer to Richmond, noticing this gaunt and gawky loafer on the market's fringe, promised him a dime if he would carry home a live turkey the gentleman had purchased. The Chief Justice, pocketing his dime, took the bird under his arm and obediently tagged behind his patron to the gentleman's residence.

Marshall was a most eminent Federalist, a pillar of the party that resisted American democracy. So it will not do to fancy that Marshall had much in common with captains of industry, let alone any notion that he was one of Franklin Roosevelt's "malefactors of great wealth." (At one time he had hoped to become wealthy through good sales of his *Life of Washington*, but President Jefferson had prevented that by ordering post offices not to accept orders for the biography.) His own modest investments were in land and agriculture; early most mornings, he walked four miles out of Richmond to his farm. During his later years, the steam engine was only beginning to speed up America. On circuit, the Chief Justice would drive a stick gig, with no servant accompanying him, the hundred and seventy miles from Richmond to Raleigh, a journey that took him a week, sleeping at bad inns.

Our world of corporate ascendancy was not John Marshall's deliberate creation. But judges, even the greatest of them, cannot be expected to foresee the economic, social, and moral milieu that may come to pass a century and a half after they have handed down certain judgments in actions at law, a milieu which their decisions may have had a considerable hand in shaping. Wise by hindsight, what shall we say about the merits of Marshall's decisions concerning those artificial, invisible, intangible, immortal "persons" called corporations?

When Chief Justice Marshall died in 1835, American manufacturing and commerce were vastly greater than they had been when he was appointed to the Supreme Court in 1800, but that growth is not to be attributed in any substantial degree to his decisions concerning corporations. It had been Jefferson's Embargo, Madison's Non-Intercourse Act, and the War of 1812 that had compelled Americans to turn their hands to the manufacture domestically of a great many goods during the Napoleonic era. The Virginia Dynasty of presidents, Marshall's adversaries, champions of rural and agricultural interests, paradoxically had carried on policies which stimulated American manufacturing more than high protective tariffs could have done. They ushered in the American economy that Hamilton and Marshall had hoped to introduce.

The booming economic development of the year 1835, nevertheless, was greatly troubled by excessive speculation and inflated prices—and, before long, ominous labor disputes. Much of this difficulty grew out of the increased size and number of business corporations, especially those chartered to build railroads and canals. The Baltimore and Ohio Railroad had reached Fredericksburg in December 1831: with that event, the country went wild about railroad stock and other investments in corporations. Few people nowadays read McMaster's masterful *History of the People of the United States*, but a great deal directly relevant to our present discontents may be gleaned from those eight volumes. Consider these passages concerning speculation in corporate stocks and in land at the hour of Marshall's death:

> Under the influence of a wild desire to grow rich without the toil of labor, men of every trade and occupation forsook their usual pursuits, hastened to the exchange and the auction block, and there risked the savings of a lifetime, the hoardings of a few years of prosperity, or the wealth from a former generation on the chances of a day or an hour. Shopkeepers, small tradesmen, clerks, factory hands from town and country, farmers, members of the learned professions, students in law offices, mingled with speculators and capitalists to try their fortune and invest their funds with even more eagerness than in other days they had beset the lottery offices. . . . At a public meeting held at Philadelphia to consider the "system of gambling in stocks," a resolution was adopted denouncing the practice as harmful to business, trade and commerce, by causing frequent and serious agitation in the money market and blunting the moral sense of young men, and a

committee was appointed to suggest remedies and report at a future meeting. Instances were cited of bank clerks who had misused funds, of tradesmen who had been ruined, and of young men of means who had lost their all in the wild desire to become suddenly rich. But all to no avail.[6]

That was in the year 1835. Such speculative phenomena, leading to great economic reverses, have occurred from time to time ever since that date, of course, most notably in 1929; most recently in October 1987, on a less alarming scale.

It was no part of John Marshall's intention to bring about financial profligacy—quite the contrary. Yet Marshall was one of those resourceful gentlemen who cleared the way for the present political economy and the present society of these United States. Is the great commercial or industrial corporation conservative in its nature? A small book called *The Capitalist Manifesto*, published three decades ago, argues that the widespread ownership of stocks and bonds refutes Marx and brings about social stability. But ownership of a few shares of stock, or of a bond, or of a savings account, creates no great personal loyalties, either to a corporation or to the state, and as great "conglomerate" corporations acquire a larger and larger proportion of the means of production and of the service industries, the individual may feel smaller and smaller, and grow bitterly resentful. Then the ideologue may appear to lead the resentful toward the purported earthly Zion.

Karl Marx predicted that under the capitalistic system all production would be concentrated, with the passing of the years, into fewer and fewer firms—until there should be monstrous oligopolies or monopolies, managed by a commercial bureaucracy. In such circumstances, a *coup d'etat* by the proletariat would meet with little resistance, all sympathy for the monopolists having been drained away; and seizure of the means of production would be quite simple. As mergers of industrial firms have gone on apace in recent years in America, and "conglomerates" have bought up, ravenously, a congeries of enterprises, some Americans have begun to take alarm.

The impression remains fairly widespread, nevertheless, that to be conservative and to put one's faith in great corporations is not only possible, but essential. A young woman at a college in North Carolina, who invited me to speak at a symposium, took it for granted that I would defend the big corporation at all points: "Why, that's what conservatism is!" She appeared to be astonished when I declined the opportunity.

Marshall, the "Supreme Conservative," was no more a friend to oligopoly or monopoly than was Adam Smith; he believed in putting down all combinations in restraint of trade. Yet no man can govern posterity. The opinions of eminent judges may be converted, with the passage of time, into sanctions or prohibitions remarkably inconsonant with the principles or prejudices of the black-robed authority on the bench.

I conclude this chapter with a tribute to John Marshall—a tribute written by that most formidable Virginian jurist Spencer Roane. At the ferocious height of his argument with Marshall, respecting the Chief Justice's decision in the case of *McCulloch v. Maryland* (1819), Judge Roane said of his great adversary's opinion that it was very able:

> This was to have been expected, proceeding as it does from a man of the most profound legal attainments, and upon a subject which had employed his thoughts, his tongue, and his pen, as a politician, and an historian for more than thirty years. . . .
>
> It is not in my power to carry on a contest upon such a subject with a man of his gigantic powers. [7]

It might be amusing to behold certain present or recent justices of the Supreme Court confronted, in dispute over questions of original intent, by the ghost of Chief Justice John Marshall.

17

Christian Doctrine and Economic Order

NY POLITICAL CONSTITUTION develops out of a moral order; and every moral order has been derived from religious beliefs. That truth, of which we have been reminded in recent decades by such historians as Christopher Dawson Eric Voegelin, and Arnold Toynbee, was little regarded by the political economists of the first half of the nineteenth century.

Christian orthodoxy, nevertheless, has not forgotten the relationships among Christian doctrine, moral habits, political structures, and economic systems. In the United States, from the 1840s to the 1870s, the American Constitution and the American economy were analyzed acutely by that Christian thinker of remarkable endowments, Orestes Brownson.

That philosopher and polemicist, whose quest for certitude had led him from Congregationalism successively to Presbyterianism, Universalism, humanitarianism, Unitarianism, Transcendentalism, socialism, atheism, and revolutionary plotting, at length—disillusioned with democratic politics and humanitarian notions of perfectibility—had entered the Catholic Church. As John Henry Newman (with whom he engaged in controversy) had set himself in opposition to the Utilitarian notions then being thrust upon England, so in America Brownson thundered against the materialism and the moral individualism of his countrymen.

I think it worth our while to pay attention, belatedly, to what Brownson said about constitutions and economic doctrines, for much of what Brownson predicted has come to pass. Before taking up Brownson, however, we may glance briefly at the economic circumstances of the United States during the middle decades of the nineteenth century.

A gigantic territorial expansion was in progress, and large commercial and industrial development paralleled the acquisition of territory—although not on such a scale, during the 1840s and 1850s, as was to occur shortly after the Civil War. This was the age of the coming of the railroads, the invention of a hundred instruments for efficient agricultural and industrial production, and thousands of important entrepreneurial successes.

In the preceding chapter I touched upon the impetus given to the growth of corporations by the decisions of Chief Justice Marshall. The corporate structure of business was given still freer rein by Chief Justice Roger B. Taney—who, however, repeatedly declared that corporate charters should be granted only when they would be in the public interest, which overrode special interests. Not until after the Civil War, despite the striking increase in incorporations during the 1850s, would commercial corporations eclipse public interest corporations and begin to supplant private proprietorships and partnerships in firms that required very large sums of capital.

America's booming prosperity, already envied in much of the world, was not primarily in consequence of natural resources; the beneficent influence of the federal Constitution loomed much larger as a cause. For the Constitution had made possible a national market, extending even by the 1840s over an area greater than that of Europe. The federal government's power to regulate interstate commerce, a principal objective of the Framers, had been meant to reduce barriers to trade among the several states, and Marshall's decisions had enforced such freedom of trade. Moreover, Congress's powers to grant patents and copyrights, to establish post offices and post roads, to issue money, to establish uniform bankruptcy laws, and to promote the general welfare—all these constitutional provisions encouraged investment and productivity. The federal system of courts and the military strength of both federal and state governments were guarantees of property and contract.

In such circumstances, hard work offered large rewards; so did extravagant speculation. Tocqueville describes American avarice in the years when Orestes Brownson still was a radical: "A native of the United States clings to this world's goods as if he were certain never to die; and he is so hasty in grasping at all within his reach that one would suppose he was constantly afraid of not living long enough to enjoy them. He clutches everything, he holds nothing fast, but soon loosens his grasp to pursue fresh gratifications." The democratic character of American society encourages such economic appetites, Tocqueville remarks in another passage: "Democracy encourages a taste for physical gratification; this taste, if it becomes excessive, soon disposes men to believe that all is matter only; and materialism, in its turn, hurries them on with mad impatience to these same delights; such is the fatal circle within which democratic nations are driven round."[1] That fatal circle is grimmer still in the America of today.

Democratic materialism had its clerical apologists. One thinks of the title of a book, published in 1836, by the Reverend Thomas P. Hunt: *The Book of Wealth: in Which It is Proved from the Bible that It Is the Duty of Every Man to Become Rich*. What Max Weber calls the Protestant Ethic was sufficiently evident in such publications. Only two delegates to the Constitutional Convention in 1787 had been Catholics, and by 1840, Catholics still had next to no influence upon American thought or policy—although the Irish had begun to pour in to build the railroads.

But in the year 1844, Orestes Brownson, becoming a Catholic communicant, began to criticize the American republic and the American economy in the light of Catholic moral and social doctrine. His arguments remain pertinent to our present discontents.

TO UNDERSTAND the nature of national constitutions, one ought to read Brownson's book *The American Republic*, published in 1865. In that book and some of Brownson's other writings, one encounters a coherent application of Catholic moral and social teachings to the American Republic—an undertaking resumed, nearly a century later, by Father John Courtney Murray, in his book *We Hold These Truths: Catholic Reflections on the American Proposition*.

Brownson emphasizes that there exists in every nation, distinct from the formal constitution, an "unwritten" constitution made up of custom, usage, moral habit, and religious assumptions. Such an unwritten or informal constitution operates in the United States. If some new written constitution conflicts seriously with the old unwritten constitution of a country, that new formal constitution will be ineffectual. This is true in America as elsewhere. Brownson points out in *Liberalism and the Church*, written in 1869, that the Constitution of the United States is superior to the constitutions of other nations because it is founded upon a conviction (not mentioned in that written Constitution) of Christian origin, bound up with natural law:

> The peculiarity of the American Constitution . . . is not merely in asserting the equality of all men before the law, but in asserting their equal rights as held not from the law, but from the Creator, anterior to civil society, and therefore rights which government is bound by its very constitution to recognize and protect to the full extent of its power. This view of rights you will not find in the Greek and Roman republics. Under them man was held to exist for the state, and had no rights but such as he held from it. You will not find it in the Roman Empire. . . . [2]

Distinguishing between what he calls "the providential constitution of the people" and what he calls "the constitution of the government," Brownson proceeds in *The American Republic* to a close analysis of the written Constitution of the United States, and of Secession and Reconstruction. He finds the Constitution of 1787, joined with the providential or unwritten constitution of the American people, as good a constitution as any nation has known, for it maintains in balance or tension the claims of freedom on the one hand and of authority on the other: "No government, whose workings are entrusted to men, ever is or can be practically perfect—secure all good, and guard against all evil. In all human governments there will be defects and abuses, and he is no wise man who expects perfection from imperfection. But the American Constitution, taken as a whole, and in all its parts, is the least imperfect that has ever existed, and under it individual rights, personal freedom and independence, as well as public authority or society, are better protected than under any other. . . ."[3]

But those sentences were written before Reconstruction, engineered by the Radical Republicans, was imposed upon the states that had made up the Confederacy. Brownson had been an ardent opponent of slavery, a strong supporter of the Union, and at one time had called himself a Radical Republican. The ruinous measures vengefully thrust upon the South, however, roused Brownson's anger and sorrow. In the pages of *Brownson's Quarterly Review*, he denounced the Fourteenth and Fifteenth Amendments as destructive of the old Constitution's purpose. Those amendments had been unconstitutionally incorporated in the Constitution, and behind them loomed democratic despotism. As Brownson put it, "Fanatical humanitarianism triumphed, and the Union ceased to be a union of states. The people, irrespective of state organizations, became practically sovereign, and the federal republic became a consolidated republic, or centralized democracy, 'one and indivisible.'"[4]

To apprehend Brownson's argument, we need to digress for a few paragraphs concerning the Fourteenth and Fifteenth Amendments.

Drawn up by the Radical Republicans, dominant in Washington after their thrashing of President Andrew Johnson, the Fourteenth Amendment was a lengthy and most controversial addition to the Constitution. It was meant, among other purposes, to punish the people of the defeated Confederacy.

Section I of the Amendment declared that all persons born or naturalized within the United States are citizens of the United States "and of the States wherein they reside." This sentence guaranteed that Negroes would be treated as full citizens. The following sentence apparently was meant to provide that black Americans would receive equal treatment; but another motive of the Radical Republican politicians (or some of them) who backed this amendment was to extend the guarantees of the Fifth Amendment (previously applying only to the federal government) to the several states. This would mean that the federal government might restrain state regulation of trade and industry. The debatable passage runs as follows: "No State shall make or enforce any law which shall abridge the privileges or immunities of citizens of the United States; nor shall any State deprive any person of life, liberty, or property, without due process of law; nor deny to any person within its jurisdiction the equal protection of the laws."

The federal courts did not at once proceed to interpret this "due process" clause of the Fourteenth Amendment to mean that the federal government might restrain state legislatures in their regulation of business. Indeed, in the Slaughterhouse Cases (1873), the Supreme Court firmly rejected the argument that the Fourteenth Amendment had extended the due process clause of the Fifth Amendment to the governments of the several states, in the sense of enlarging the jurisdiction of the federal government. Yet by 1884, the Supreme Court had changed its mind, and ever since then the federal courts have intervened in many economic concerns previously reserved to states' jurisdiction. As Edward S. Corwin summarizes this development in his analysis of the Fourteenth Amendment, "What induced the Court to dismiss its fears of upsetting the balance in the distribution of powers under the Federal System and to enlarge its own supervisory powers over state legislation were the appeals more and more addressed to it for adequate protection of property rights against the remedial social legislation which the States were increasingly enacting in the wake of industrial expansion."[5]

Although Brownson did not live to see the extension of the due process clause to the state governments, he gloomily expected such a result of the Fourteenth Amendment. "The great fault of our statesmen has been to make what should be a great agricultural and commercial people unnaturally a great manufacturing people," he wrote to his son in 1871. Reconstruction of the South had become reconstruction of the American economy by special interests: "The great industrial corporations have got the control and the government is simply its factor."[6]

Dr. James McClellan, an able latter-day disciple of Justice Story, looks upon the Reconstruction Amendments much as Brownson did:

> Beginning with the Reconstruction Amendments, which enlarged the powers not only of the federal courts but of Congress as well, the radical Republicans cut the heart out of federalism by stripping the states of their sovereignty respecting citizenship, state criminal procedures, and voter qualification. Using an interpretive device known as the doctrine of incorporation, the federal courts later used the Due Process Clause of the 14th Amendment to obliterate the reserved powers of the states respecting nearly all of the liberties enumerated in the Bill of Rights, thereby accomplishing a complete nationalization of all civil liberties and overturning the main purpose of the first ten amendments. [7]

The centralizing Radical Republicans professed to be concerned for the liberties of black Americans. So they were, surely; men's motives are mixed. With few exceptions, the Radical Republicans were a self-righteous crew. All in all, despite its words about "due process," there is an unpleasant ring of arbitrary power about the Fourteenth Amendment. This was the first amendment to conflict clearly with the provisions of the original seven articles of the Constitution: for the whole tendency of Fourteenth Amendment was to centralize political power in Washington and to favor the North over the South. With the Fourteenth Amendment, the powers of the several states began to dwindle. For the defeated eleven states of the Confederacy to be readmitted to the Union, they were required first to ratify this Amendment, much though the people of those eleven states might dislike its provisions. Also there were loud complaints that political trickery and intimidation had been employed to secure ratification of the Amendment. About the Fourteenth Amendment, then, there still hangs a cloud, and Brownson, in the pages of his *Review*, parts vehemently with the dominant Republicans who framed that amendment.

As for the Fifteenth Amendment, which deprived the states of power to determine who should vote, Brownson thundered that this "is to destroy the state as a body politic." These two amendments, Brownson wrote, are revolutionary in their character and tendency, and destructive of the providential or unwritten constitution of the American people, according to which, though one people, they are organized as a union, not of individuals, but of states, or political societies, each with an autonomy of its own. . . . Give to congress or the Union the power to determine who shall or shall not be the political people of a state, and the state no longer exists; you merge the state in the Union, obliterate state lines, and convert the republic from a federal into a centralized or consolidated republic, or a pure democracy in which constitutions count for nothing, and the majority for the time have unlimited power. [8]

Our present subject being the relationships between the Constitution and political economy, however, we must turn from Brownson's convictions about sovereignty and the franchise to his economic principles. What economic consequences did Brownson expect from the Reconstruction Amendments? And how would those consequences accord with the Church's teachings about social order?

BROWNSON HAD COMMENCED his career as a polemicist when the doctrines of Bentham, the Philosophic Radicals, and the economists of Manchester were in the ascendant. In his early years as a political radical, and in his later years as a political conservative, he rejected Utilitarian economics. The reason for this is sufficiently given in some remarks by an imaginary priest in Brownson's late book *Liberalism and the Church*. Brownson's spokesman says,

The political economists consider man only as a producing, distributing, and consuming machine, and seek only to get the greatest possible supply with the greatest possible demand. I, by my profession, if not by my sympathy with my fellow men, am led to look upon man as having a sentient, intellectual, and moral nature, and I seek for him the greatest possible sum of virtue and happiness. It is not likely, then, that the political economists and I should think alike. It adds not to the well-being of the poor that the aggregate wealth of a nation increases, if they are all the time growing poorer, and find it every day more difficult to supply their wants, or to obtain by honest industry their bread. Under the new system, it may be that wealth increases, but the tendency in the great industrial nations is to concentrate it in fewer hands, or in huge overgrown corporations, which in your country [the United States] are stronger than the government, and control, not always the elections, but the legislative assemblies, both state and national.[9]

Here, as again and again in his writings, Brownson reaffirms the venerable doctrines of charity, family, community, and responsibility that the Church had enunciated over the centuries. His response to the evangels of the Dismal Science is like that of Coleridge and Southey in England. When we turn to the question of wants, we find Brownson reasserting the Christian teaching that is thoroughly forgotten in our age. Brownson's imaginary priest from Europe, in *Liberalism and the Church*, rejects the liberals' notion that the gratification of wants is always a good:

> I was taught that to make a man happy we should study not to increase his stores, but to diminish his desires. The political economists study to increase a man's desires, and to develop new wants in him, in order to increase as much as possible consumption, which, in turn, will increase the demand, and the increased demand will stimulate increased production. The demand creates the supply, and the supply stimulates competition, which, in turn, creates an increased demand. This, if I understand it, is the essence of your modern science of political economy. But what is the gain to the laborer? . . . . The more wants one has that he is unable to satisfy, the more he suffers.[10]

The artificial stimulation of wants is evil, Brownson reminded his readers; while "poverty is no evil," he insisted. (Brownson himself had much practical experience of poverty, early and late in life.) Liberalism, obsessed by its economic calculations, leads mankind toward a materialistic hell in which the whole of life is an exercise in getting and spending.

These being Brownson's convictions, we need not wonder that the treatment of the southern states during Reconstruction, and the Four-

teenth and Fifteenth Amendments, made him almost despair for the
American Republic. He perceived in the measures of the Radical
Republicans a design to crush the agricultural South, to employ the
power and resources of the federal government for the stimulation of
heavy industry, to concentrate power in a central government and in
great profit-making corporations, to gratify special economic interests
at the general expense.

The due process clause of the Fourteenth Amendment, only eight
years after Brownson's death, was being interpreted by the Supreme Court
as binding upon the states in economic concerns—so, in effect, sheltering
commerce and industry from the regulation of state legislatures.
Brownson anticipated and scorned the twentieth-century American
slogan that "the business of America is business." In the rich he would
put no trust—not in those rich who meant to grow richer through
speculation and misinterpretation of the Constitution.

As he had written in *The American Republic*, discussing enlargement
of the franchise, "The men of wealth, the business men, manufacturers
and merchants, bankers and brokers, are the men who exert the worst
influence on government in every country, for they always strive to use it
as an instrument of advancing their own private interests. They act on
the beautiful maxim, 'Let governments take care of the rich, and the rich
will take care of the poor,' instead of the far safer maxim, 'Let government
take care of the weak, the strong can take care of themselves.'" [11]

What Brownson expresses in these passages is not socialist ideology;
it is the Christian teaching of the common good. What Brownson
preached to his countrymen was restraint of appetites and concern for
the general welfare. The high exhortation often attributed to President
John F. Kennedy, "Ask not what your country can do for you, but what
you can do for your country," actually is borrowed from one of Brownson's
addresses by Mr. Arthur Schlesinger, Jr., whose first book had been about
Brownson, and who wrote the President's inaugural address.

Few used such language during what Mark Twain called the Gilded
Age, when speculation in gold and railway stocks might bring almost
overnight wealth beyond the dreams of avarice: Henry Adams and Charles
Francis Adams, Jr., describe most memorably the avarice of that age.

But Brownson, when a radical and when a conservative, thought first of the laboring classes in any debate over the state of society.

Although Brownson's social and economic beliefs were rooted in Catholic doctrine, Brownson was no theocrat: he did not fancy that the Church should give marching orders to the captains and the kings. A passage in *Liberalism and the Church* might almost have been written by Father John Courtney Murray:

> The Church is not the state nor the framer of its constitution, and she has not and never has pretended to have temporal authority in the temporal order. She is a spiritual kingdom— the kingdom of God on earth—and she leaves to the civil and political order that which God himself leaves to it—human free will. She has always asserted the great principle which the American people more successfully than any other have carried out in their political constitution, but it has never been her mission to apply them practically out of her own order. Our Lord did not come as a temporal Messiah. The efforts to defend these principles, even in their spiritual application, has raised an almost universal clamor against her for encroaching on the province of the civil power, and are the basis of the principal charges her enemies even now allege against her. What then would have been the outcry, had she attempted to organize political society in accordance with these principles! The relation between Church and State here, which so well meets her wants, can subsist only where the state is founded on the recognition of the freedom of conscience, and the equal rights of all, which it is bound to protect and defend. Never in the Old World has it been humanly possible to found the state on the American doctrine of equal rights embodied in the American Constitution.[14]

The Church's social teachings, then, are to work within and through the established political institutions of the United States—not advanced in a presumptuous spirit of hostility to the written or the unwritten constitution. "The American constitution is not founded on political atheism. Something of Christian tradition lives among us and is kept alive by the common law and the judicial department of the government." So Brownson wrote in his *Review*, in the spring of 1873.[13]

But would the swelling apparatus of the federal government—even the federal judiciary—remain friendly enough to the Church? Toward his end, Brownson had grave misgivings as to that. "The church wants freedom in relation to the state—nothing more," he had written in *The American Republic*, "for all her power comes immediately from God, without any intervention or mediation of the state." [14] Would that freedom endure?

Among the consequences of the Civil War and Reconstruction had been the enfeebling of the old Constitution, the subjugation of the agricultural economy, the corruptions of the Gilded Age, and the triumph of a secular order with Protestant roots but divested of faith in a transcendent order. Between 1860 and 1870 a revolution had been worked, and Brownson found that revolution to be an American variant of Jacobinism. This thoroughly secularized American state would not remain neutral on moral questions. As the general government consolidated its power over the years, it would interfere increasingly with the concerns of the Church. Brownson's prediction is attaining fulfillment at the end of the twentieth century.

Might the Church withstand such pressures? Indeed, might the Church cohere long in the licentious American democracy with its ungoverned appetites and its revolt against authority? "There is a subtle influence at work which undermines the authority alike of the parent and of the magistrate, with Catholics as with non-Catholics," Brownson wrote to his son in 1870. "Catholics as well as others imbibe the spirit of the country, imbibe from infancy the spirit of independence, freedom from all restraint, unbounded license. So far are Catholics from converting the country, they cannot hold their own." [15]

The endeavor to humanize the economy is as necessary nowadays as it was in Brownson's time. Yet how much of the providential constitution, the unwritten constitution, still operates within American society? Is the providential constitution a ghost merely? If so, can the written Constitution be long for this world?

18

Ideology and Property

THE CONSTITUTION, as interpreted by the courts, upheld the claims of the possessors of property during the very years when property was fiercely assailed by European ideologues. In Europe, revolutionary ferment disrupted great states, in 1830 and 1848 particularly; yet America was spared ideological passions of that sort until much later in the century.

The Civil War, of course, did as much mischief as might any social revolt, but neither the partisans of the Union nor those of the Confederacy intended a radical reconstitution of American society. Decades would elapse before the *Communist Manifesto* and other socialist tracts would exert any influence in the United States, and even then, social revolutionaries would be few and bitterly disliked by the general public.

In the preceding chapter we touched upon Orestes Brownson's stern criticism of American materialism and avarice. Yet Brownson, so much concerned for the laboring classes, denounced socialism only a few months after the *Communist Manifesto* had been promulgated. Brownson wrote at the end of 1848:

> Undoubtedly Christianity requires us to remove all evil, and in seeking to remove evil we follow the Christian principle; but what the socialists call evil, what the people in revolt are seeking to remove, is not evil. Nothing is evil but that which turns a man away from his end, or interposes a barrier to his advance toward it. Nothing but one's own sin can do that. Nothing, then, but sin is or can be evil, and that is evil only to him who commits it. Take all those things which socialists declaim against,—monarchy, aristocracy, inequalities of rank, inequalities of riches, poverty, want, distress, hunger, starvation even,—not one of them, nor all of them combined, can harm the just man, or prevent, except by his own will, any one from the fulfillment of his destiny. If one is prepared to die, he may as well die in a hovel as a palace, of hunger as of fever. Nothing can harm us, that does not separate or tend to separate us from God. Nothing but our own internal malice can so separate us, and it is always in our power, through grace, which is never withheld, to remove that at will. [1]

Such thoroughgoing rejection of the socialist ideology on Christian principles was general among the Irish Catholics who by the time of the Civil War had come to form a very large part of the American working class, some of whom had fought Union regiments in the streets of New York, opposing conscription. That is an important reason, among other reasons, why not until the 1880s and 1890s did outbursts of ideological fury occur in the United States.

If conservatism is the negation of ideology, the United States has been the most conservative of lands. During the French Revolution and the Napoleonic era, in America there were no counterparts of the Jacobins, and no enthusiasts for military rule. If there existed a discontented submerged class, it had consisted of the black slaves, more or less outside the civil social order and unable to take any part in politics, or even to hope for a successful insurrection. Besides, ownership of real property extended to a higher proportion of the general population than in any other country; and those who did not own property, aspired to accumulate it. Nobody demanded a new constitution, or radical political and economic alterations—not until the 1880s, that is.

From the end of the Civil War until well into the twentieth century, most federal judges upheld a strongly individualistic concept of property. In effect, they agreed with Sir Henry Maine, their contemporary, that "Nobody is at liberty to attack several property and to say at the same time that he values civilization. The history of the two cannot be disentangled."[2] Various school and college textbooks declare that such American judges were much influenced by the doctrines of Herbert Spencer, that individualistic philosopher now so thoroughly forgotten; but that is true only in part. For the American champions of private property drew their arguments from many sources, among them Roman law, common law, Utilitarianism, the writings of Edmund Burke, and the historical jurists, especially Maine. And they could refer to the authority of the Framers of the Constitution, who to a man had been mindful of the need for security of private property, and to that of the chief commentators on the Constitution, Joseph Story and James Kent, emphatic defenders of property rights.

Thus a long series of decisions by federal judges prevented state and local governments from interfering much with established rights of property-holding or with economic competition. These decisions were handed down, with some boldness, at times of widespread distress in the American economy, when national labor unions were taking form, and when episodes of ideological violence had broken out during labor disputes.

For illustration, let us turn backward a century to the era of Grover Cleveland. On May 14, 1884, occurred the famous Panic of that year: nearly ten thousand banks failed across the land. Two months later the Democrats nominated Cleveland for the presidency; he won in November. The depression that followed the Panic led to massive strikes, more strikes being organized during 1886 than during any other year of the nineteenth century. By April 1885, President Cleveland proposed to Congress a federal commission to deal with the labor question. On May 4, 1886, at Haymarket Square in Chicago, police broke up a huge anarchist rally. Bombs thrown at the police killed eleven people and wounded a hundred, and later four anarchist leaders were hanged for murder. To a great many people, it seemed as if the ideological passions of Europe would sweep across America too, and indeed President Cleveland would be confronted by worse disorders in 1894.

Yet during those years the federal courts, as if bent on proclaiming "the sanctity of private property," handed down decisions detested by the militant anarchists. On May 10, 1886, in the case of *Santa Clara County v. Southern Pacific Railroad*, the Supreme Court ruled that a corporation is a person, protected under the due process clause of the Fourteenth Amendment. On October 25 of the same year, in *Wabash, St. Louis and Pacific Railway Company v. Illinois*, the Supreme Court found that a state may not constitutionally regulate even that portion of interstate commerce which occurs within the state's borders—in effect, sheltering the railways against state regulation or interference with their property. These two decisions undid the earlier rulings in the Slaughterhouse cases and similar rulings that the Fourteenth Amendment was not intended to bind the several states—a point on which I touched previously.

Or a decade later, in 1894 and 1895, the time of the march of Coxey's Army upon Washington and the fierce Pullman strike in Chicago, we find the Supreme Court handing down decisions calculated to enlarge the federal government's protection of financial and industrial firms from state regulation, and to sanction the employment and enforcement of federal injunctions against strikers interfering with interstate commerce. During the 1880s and 1890s, such federal courts' decisions are too numerous for me to cite here, let alone analyze. But I suppose that no historian of American law would dispute my statement that the Supreme Court, throughout those years, tended to make the federal government the giant guardian of private property—and especially, perhaps, of private property in its corporate form.

State regulatory commissions and state legislatures could be wheedled or bullied during those years into measures favored by labor unions or by organizations of discontented farmers, not to mention more radical groups. Even Congress might find it prudent to yield to popular demands of the hour that conflicted with corporations' interests, but the Supreme Court stood firm against any hint of socialistic measures. Not until 1905, with Justice Oliver Wendell Holmes's dissent in *Lochner v. New York*, was a strong voice raised in the Supreme Court to suggest that judges ought to give less weight, under the Fourteenth Amendment, to the claims of property. Not until years after that did the Supreme Court begin to find occasionally against the due process doctrine regarding property that had taken shape early in the 1880s. Indeed, the Supreme Court may be regarded as in general siding with the claims of the owners of private property right down to 1935—when, in *A. L. A. Schechter Poultry Corporation v. United States* (the famous "sick chicken" case) the Court undid the National Industrial Recovery Act. Thereafter, as President Franklin Roosevelt threatened to appoint new justices, the decisions of the Court concerning private property began to take a different tack. By 1937, large scale federal regulation of industry and commerce had got underway without resistance by the Supreme Court. We are still in the era that then commenced.

How was it that for six decades or longer the Supreme Court of the United States had maintained a protection of private property against governmental regulation, under the Constitution, exceeding in thoroughness the rights or privileges of private property in any other country—and that in a time of the growth of socialist and anarchist concepts and parties in Europe and Britain? A time, indeed, of economic protests, both urban and rural, in the United States?

The large majority of American citizens believed in an economy of private ownership and competition. As George Santayana was to write later, "It will take some hammering to drive a coddling socialism into America." The socialist ideology never attained a really popular following. So although suspicion and resentment of the "trusts" and "robber baron" capitalists were widespread, and certain decisions of the Supreme Court might be reproached by a fair number of citizens, still both attachment to property rights and respect for the Court averted any obdurate resistance to the decisions in Washington.

Gradually there arose, nevertheless, the concept of a distinction between "property rights" and "human rights," a thesis sanctioned by

President Woodrow Wilson, and gaining currency rapidly after the year 1914. It was argued that the federal courts tended to be very mindful indeed of the property rights of stock holders, bondholders, and large proprietors, but insufficiently mindful of the claims of the humble and those not well endowed with the goods of fortune. The Great Depression, bringing such protests to a head, opened the way for the election of Franklin Roosevelt and, early in his second administration, for Supreme Court decisions more to the taste of the advocates of "human rights."

In jurisprudence, actually, no line of demarcation is drawn between alleged "property rights" and alleged "human rights." For all civil social rights are human rights, and only human beings enjoy rights. God has no rights: he possesses infinite powers. The state has no rights: the state holds earthly power. Property has no rights: inanimate things cannot plead in courts of law. In truth, the right to hold property is a very important human right; the great critic Paul Elmer More remarks that so far as civilization is concerned, *the rights to property are more important than the right to life.*[3] If the holding of property becomes insecure, all civilization is shaken.

No such thing as an absolute right ever existed: for one man's assertion of his right soon infringes upon some other man's assertion, every right is married to the performance of some duty; and the common good, on occasion, must transcend some individual's claim of right. Yet so recently as the 1950s my friend Richard Weaver, the author of *Ideas Have Consequences*, tried to maintain that there should be an absolute right of property, and a good many other Americans seem to have thought so. Certainly the federal courts, for more than half a century, accorded to private property privileges unconceded in most modern countries. Until 1899, in the United States, a man might build on the edge of his property a wall quite as high as he liked, maliciously, to cut off his neighbor's "air, light, and view"—this under a claim of common law—so nearly absolute were property rights. (In Scotland, for instance, such an act, malicious or not, would have been actionable under the doctrine of "ancient lights"—that is, closing up access to light from existing windows.) It seems to me that for the common good some diminishing of the individualistic privileges of property owners was required fairly early in the twentieth century. For one thing, the circumstances of tenancy of property in an eighteenth-century New England village, say, were rather different from the circumstances of tenancy of property in late twentieth-century Chicago.

Nevertheless, the federal courts' zeal in protecting private property for more than half a century did increase the prosperity and productivity of the American economy, doubtless. It sheltered industry and commerce from excessive regulation and interference from state and local governments, more susceptible to populist pressures than was the federal government. Thus such protective decisions encouraged the growth of large efficient corporations possessed of an ample capital. Huge personal fortunes were accumulated under such a system with its very rapid growth, but as Tocqueville reminds us, it is better for a society, often, that there should exist a few huge fortunes rather than a multitude of petty competences. For with great wealth great things may be accomplished, while mere widespread affluence is wasted in petty and ostentatious consumption. Some of the men who enriched themselves by unscrupulous speculation during that era were sufficiently repellent: we encounter their portraits in the Adams brothers' *Chapters of Erie.* Yet others were men of talent and taste and generosity. At any rate, in terms of political economy, the period of the courts' solicitude for property rights was an era of successful productivity. Interpretation of the Fourteenth Amendment to favor the cause of commerce and industry on a large scale, however dubious in terms of stare decisis, had strong utilitarian advantages.

Yet it brought certain disadvantages to American society. For it reinforced the materialism and obsession with accumulating wealth that Tocqueville and Brownson had reproached among Americans. It helped to make possible an inordinately swift concentration of capital (from abroad, in part, because European investors could rely upon the "sanctity" of property in America) that financed forced-draft industrialization at the expense of agriculture and rural life in the United States. It increased the powers of the federal government at the expense of state and local authority—which seemed agreeable enough to men of large means at that time; but later such centralization could, and did, work in a less pleasing way.

Rather gradually, economic doctrines of *laissez-faire* and sedulous safeguards for private property declined on the federal bench, although not really overthrown until 1937. In 1916, Louis Brandeis had told the Chicago Bar Association that with respect to static property, the courts had "applied complacently eighteenth-century concepts of the individual and of the sacredness of private property." No one would accuse the Supreme Court, nowadays, of any such archaisms.

IT HAS BEEN ARGUED by some historians that the reforms of President Franklin Roosevelt, including his intimidation of the Supreme Court, prevented the rise of subversive ideological factions in the United States. Certainly Roosevelt himself feared that national demagogues or fanatics might rise up, as they had in Europe; he took Huey Long for one such, rather improbably. For my part, I do not believe that any socialist or fascist revolution could have come to pass in America because of the Great Depression: like the British, the American people are not ideologically inclined. Let me add, nevertheless, that one reason why ideology never has taken deep root among the citizenry of the United States is this: the Constitution may be adapted to altered social circumstances without resort to force or even to extreme language.

During the decades we have been describing, it was the intention of the Supreme Court to protect private property against spoliation by government. That intention has been difficult to discern during the past quarter of a century. Instead there have tended to dominate the Court, when private property has been in question, doctrines of "compelling necessity" or "overriding interest" on the part of agencies of the state. Permit me to turn to a few illustrations of this change of mind and heart.

The most conspicuous example of the Supreme Court's attitude toward property, during the past quarter of a century, is its sustaining of the massive "urban renewal" programs. The Housing and Development Act of 1965, the Demonstration Cities and Metropolitan Development Act of 1966, and subsequent national "urban renewal" programs set in motion immense schemes of demolition in nearly all American cities, and lesser (though costly) schemes of rebuilding. These overwhelming abrupt changes in urban landscapes involved the use of the power of eminent domain to acquire whole urban neighborhoods (with some monetary compensation to owners of property, of course, but through compulsory purchase), bulldoze large tracts, and then sell the vacant sites (when possible) to "developers" who might make a great deal of money out of their new developments. It is not possible to assess the social consequences of this alleged "renewal." It must suffice to mention that George Romney, on leaving the governorship of Michigan to take a cabinet post in Washington, declared on television that the principal causes of the devastating riots in Detroit during 1967— the evidence of which still stares at us—had been the consequences of urban renewal and federal highway building in the city, destroying long-settled neighborhoods. In Detroit, Newark, and other devastated cities, a cry of the rioters of 1967, while hurling gasoline bombs at vacant buildings, was "Instant urban renewal!"

Now the confiscations and demolitions of urban renewal, and the similar clearances required for driving huge highways through old cities, involved the compulsory transfer of many thousands of private properties, residential or commercial, from the hands of their proprietors— first to some local "renewal" authority, in the case of the "Metropolitan Development" or "Title I" projects, and then from that public authority to some other "private" proprietor, usually a development corporation. In short, the government (ordinarily local government subsidized by federal funds) took real property away from hundreds of thousands of owners and sold or transferred those properties to other persons.

In Grover Cleveland's time, any such undertaking would have been denounced by public men as "socialistic"—even an income tax of 4 percent being called socialistic in Cleveland's time—and, if enacted into statute, would have been found unconstitutional, very promptly, by the federal courts. It is otherwise in our time, for federal district and appeals courts, in nearly all instances, from 1965 to the present, have declined to impede urban renewal projects on constitutional grounds. And when plaintiffs against urban-renewal authorities have endeavored to carry their plaints to the Supreme Court of the United States, that Court consistently has decided not to assume appellate jurisdiction in such cases.

From time to time, over the years, I have become involved in such disputes at law—particularly when I wrote a nationally-syndicated newspaper column. I once took up the cause of Miss Frederika Blankner, a patriotic old lady who lived in a downtown hotel in Chicago and owned a small apartment building on the South Side, near the University of Chicago. The Chicago urban renewal bureaucrats coveted that apartment building, and Miss Blankner fought hard to retain it. All of her tenants were blacks. *Sub rosa*, the University of Chicago had concluded with the city's administration, then headed by Mayor Daley, a plan to demolish a great many buildings in the vicinity of the University, push out their black tenants, and "restore" the neighborhood to middle class occupancy.

Miss Blankner tried to maintain her building in good condition, despite the endeavors of city building inspectors to declare it unfit for habitation, and she had decent tenants. At great expense to herself, she fought the case in city courts, state courts and federal courts. Twice she got so far as an appeal to the Supreme Court of the United States, but both times that Court refused to take jurisdiction. Having fought the good fight, and lost, Miss Blankner died. Her inherited apartment building was demolished by the civic improvers. So much for the rights of small proprietors, or of poor tenants, under the present view of private property entertained by the federal courts.

Or take the case of the historic town of Galena, Illinois, in which I had a more successful part. Galena's old streets down by the river are a joy to the friends of historic preservation, but some local developers late in the 1960s got up a design, with federal funds available, to wipe out those handsome and interesting old streets and build on the site a shopping center of the usual dreary pattern, with a gigantic drug store as its center and sprawling parking lots. I fought the proposal in my column, which was widely read in Dubuque and Galena. My opposition was reproached by the "renewing" element of Galena, which had obtained control of the town government. "How could I possibly take up the cause of the oldfangled possessors of property in downtown Galena?" a haughty progressive woman inquired of me by letter. Those opponents of renewal were merely the proprietors of the hotel where Lincoln had stayed, and an elderly lawyer, a bookseller, an antique-dealer, and other insignificant folk. "What right have those people to stop progress?" my neoterist correspondent demanded.

I replied to her that those obscurants happened to own the properties in question: such was their right, guaranteed by state and federal constitutions. This story has a happy ending: the obscurants succeeded in blocking that urban renewal scheme at the last hour, and the mayor of Galena was turned out of office.

There is no end of such illustrations of political and judicial indifference to the prescriptive rights of individual owners of real property. Until a very few years ago, there used to exist in Detroit a quarter called Poletown. There thousands of people, most of them poor, most of them of Albanian or other eastern European stock, were pushed out of their houses, against their will, to make way for a new General Motors plant that allegedly would benefit Detroit. Two Catholic churches, together with hundreds of houses, were swept ruthlessly out of existence. Yet soon the new industrial plant was malfunctioning, and General Motors Corporation was seeking remission of taxes on that vast property—which it had acquired rather cheaply through the device of compulsory purchase and resale by the public authority.[4]

My present purpose, however, is not examination of urban blunders, but rather comparison of the constitutional interpretations of yesteryear, concerning property, with the constitutional interpretations of our present era. A juridical individualism has given way to a juridical collectivism—employing this latter term as it is used by A. V. Dicey and other scholars in the law. From the judges' conviction that the possessor of property enjoys rights almost absolute, we have shifted by degrees to the judges' submission to the doctrine that the community's "overriding interest" leaves every household at the mercy of the highway engineer or the grand scale developer.

Somehow this radical change of constitutional interpretation has been accomplished without the triumph of any radical ideology. It is not socialists, anarchists, or communists who have undone that understanding of property rights expounded by Justice Story and Chancellor Kent. Rather, the reduction of the protections to private property—at least, protections to the property of individuals of modest means—has resulted from an alliance between the "professional" urban planners and those wide-awake commercial developers and industrial firms who are looking for the main chance. Such powerful interests, with their allies of the "concrete lobby" and other economic groups that profit from demolition and building, can persuade Congress and state and local authorities to exercise the ancient power of eminent domain in ways that would have infuriated the gentlemen who framed the Constitution in 1787.

And the courts, perhaps influenced by social thinkers very different from Herbert Spencer, find it prudent not to intervene in favor of small proprietors. Thus the United States shifts, if more slowly than most of the world, toward centralization, consolidation, status as opposed to contract, and dimmed prospects for the man of property and the venerable right to dwell undisturbed in one's own house.

Epilogue

The Constitution and the Antagonist World

O NCE UPON A TIME it was the assumption of most of the people in the world that the fundamental constitution of their society would endure to the end of time, or at least for a very great while, or certainly for the lifetime of those who recently had become adults. But events since 1914 have destroyed that expectation, mercilessly, in country upon country, culture after culture.

Whole peoples have been uprooted or transplanted, or perhaps extirpated; complex patterns of life have been devastated or totally supplanted; political systems have vanished almost without trace; classes have been effaced, ancient rights abolished, the cake of custom ground to powder. Constitutions written and unwritten have been subverted almost overnight by conventions of political fanatics, and innovating substitute constitutions in their turn have been expunged within a few years, making way for yet more novel political structures—no less

evanescent. Even Britain has experienced much constitutional alteration during the past quarter of a century, especially in local government.

Among great powers, only the American Republic has not deliberately altered its general frame of government—neither the formal
written Constitution of the United States nor the unwritten constitution that, in the phrase of Orestes Brownson, "is the real or actual
constitution of the people as a state or sovereign community and constituting them such or such a state." I say "deliberately," implying that
the American people, as represented in the Congress and in the state
legislatures, have not approved very large changes in the political
structure. Nor have they, as a people, endorsed large innovations in
the complex of customs, conventions, and prescriptions that compose
the unwritten constitution. It is true that several amendments to the
federal Constitution have been ratified, but none of these, not even
the two extending the franchise, greatly altered the general political
structure. Many state constitutions have been revised, and of course
technological, economic, demographic, and moral alterations outside
the strictly political pattern have produced large social consequences.
Nevertheless, the formal federal Constitution framed in 1787 still
functions for the most part, and the large majority of American citizens
still take for granted the mass of customs, conventions, mores, and
social beliefs that amount to an unwritten constitution, and which
generally are older than the written Constitution of 1787. In short,
Americans have known no political revolution, either violent or
accomplished without bloodshed, for two centuries; nor have we
consciously swept away old ways of living in community so that we
might conform to some brave new ideological design.

Americans stand politically strongly attached to old ways of managing public affairs, rejecting all proposals for thoroughgoing constitutional revision, holding inviolate documentary and even architectural
symbols of the national experience. Probably the considerable majority
of Americans today assume that our national constitutions will endure
for time out of mind, that the political order, at least, which the present
generation knows will be known also by their grandchildren and great-
grandchildren, that in time past other nations may have fallen low

even as Nineveh and Tyre, but that the United States of America, as a
system of order and justice and freedom, is immutable.

This is a natural presumption, the power and prosperity of this
nation in the closing years of the twentieth century considered. Not
since 1814 has the continental United States had to repel foreign troops.
There has not occurred no catastrophic interruption of domestic tranquillity since 1865, and the American economy has become a cornucopia,
with only infrequent, occasional, and partial interruptions of its bounty.
How could this constitutional order ever come to an end?

Such, no doubt, were the sentiments of the inhabitants of the
Roman empire near the end of the Antonine age, although already
Marcus Aurelius had great difficulty in raising revenue sufficient to
defend the northern frontiers and greater difficulty still in repelling,
sword in hand, the barbarian hosts. Roman history no longer being
taught in American schools, the public is unaware of such parallels.
There are few readers of such studies as Freya Stark's *Rome on the
Euphrates*, which traces convincingly the fashion in which a great power
decayed for lack of imagination.

In my seemingly complacent account of America's conservative
ways, then, I have omitted something important: the strong tendency
of our courts of law, the Supreme Court of the United States in particular, to remold our political and social institutions nearer to the
judges' hearts' desires. The courts, joined by the Congress, the state
legislatures, and the executive branch, busily have conferred new rights,
entitlements, and privileges upon large classes of citizens. New constitutional rights are discovered or proposed annually; next to nothing is
said about constitutional duties. Most professors and publicists still
appear to fancy that more emancipation from oldfangled moral restraints, not to mention more generous public largesse—so like the
old Roman liturgies—would relieve us of worry and work. Yet just
now we perhaps perceive a reaction against large scale constitutional
alteration by a judicial aristocracy or council of elders—the Ephors of
Washington.

But I lack time to cry O tempora! O mores! adequately. Kipling's
lines must suffice, a single stanza:

> On the first Feminian Sandstones we were promised the Fuller
> Life
> (Which started by loving our neighbour and ended by loving his
> wife)
> Till our women had no more children and the men lost reason
> and faith,
> And the Gods of the Copybook Headings said: "The Wages of
> Sin is Death."

No civilization endures forever; no national constitution can of itself sustain a people bent upon private pleasures, asking not what they can do for the country, but what the country can do for them. So I venture upon some speculations concerning the future of American politics—signifying by the word *politics* not partisan controversies, but constitutional establishments, custom and convention, political principles.

I SPECULATE in the manner of Edmund Burke, at once the most imaginative and most practical of writers and doers in our political tradition of the English-speaking peoples: Burke, the philosopher in action. I do not mean that you and I can peer through dead men's eyes. Rather, I am asking you to put on the mind of Burke with me, to look at the future of American politics as he looked at the future of European politics in his day—with wonderful prescience, as affairs turned out.

I choose Burke as our guide for this time travel because, in the words of Harold Laski, "Burke has endured as the permanent manual of political wisdom without which statesmen are as sailors on an uncharted sea." Or, to quote Woodrow Wilson, "Burke makes as deep an impression upon our hearts as upon our minds. We are taken captive, not so much by his reasoning, strongly as that moves to its conquest, as by the generous warmth that steals out of him into our hearts."

In his *Reflections on the Revolution in France*, his *Appeal from the New to the Old Whigs*, his *Thoughts on the Present Discontents*, and other writings and speeches, Burke has much to say about constitutions, the

British Constitution in particular—though not one word, friendly or hostile, about the American Constitution of 1787. Very succinctly, though I hope not superficially, I offer you some observations of Burke upon healthy and unhealthy constitutions of government. We will confine ourselves to four of Burke's constitutional arguments; then let us try to apply these reflections, so far as they are pertinent to our own age, to prospects for the constitution (in its larger sense) of the United States.

Burke's first constitutional principle is that a good constitution grows out of the common experience of a people over a considerable elapse of time. It is not possible to create an improved constitution out of whole cloth. As he declared in his "Speech on the Reform of Representation" (1782), "I look with filial reverence on the constitution of my country, and never will cut it in pieces and put it into the kettle of any magician, in order to boil it, with the puddle of their compounds, into youth and vigor. On the contrary, I will drive away such pretenders; I will nurse its venerable age, and with lenient arts extend a parent's breath."[1] An enduring constitution is the product of a nation's struggles. Here Burke is echoed by one of his more eminent American disciples, John C. Calhoun, in his *Disquisition on Government*: "A constitution, to succeed, must spring from the bosom of the community, and be adapted to the intelligence and character of the people, and all the multifarious relations, internal and external, which distinguish one people from another. If it do not, it will prove, in practice, to be, not a constitution, but a cumbrous and useless machine, which must be speedily superseded and laid aside, for some other more simple, and better suited to their condition."[2]

A truth that Burke emphasizes almost equally with the preceding "organic" concept of constitutions is the necessity of religious faith to a constitutional order. "We know, and, what is better, we feel inwardly, that religion is the basis of civil society, and the source of all good, and of all comfort," he writes in *Reflections on the Revolution in France*. "We know, and it is our pride to know, that man is by his constitution a religious animal; that atheism is against, not only our reason, but our instincts; and that it cannot prevail long." An established church is required—parallel with "an established monarchy, an established aristocracy, and an established democracy. . . . All persons possessing any portion of power ought to be strongly and awfully impressed with an idea that they act in trust, and that they are to account for their conduct in that trust to the one great Master, Author, and Founder of society."[3] The first clause of the First Amendment to the Constitution, and the American circumstances which produced that clause—Burke's "dissidence of dissent, and the Protestantism of the Protestant religion"—had forestalled any established national church in the United States, three years before Burke published his *Reflections*. But the First Amendment, and curious interpretations of its first clause by the Supreme Court in this century, leave us today in some perplexity.

A third point in Burke's constitutional principles which needs to be noted here is his emphasis upon the function of a natural aristocracy, in which mingle both "men of actual virtue" (the "new" men of enterprising talents) and "men of presumptive virtue" (gentlemen of old families and adequate means). It is this aristocracy, "the cheap defense of nations," that supplies a people's leadership. (In a more grudging fashion, a similar apology for aristocracy is advanced by John Adams.) Burke asserts also the necessity for an "establishment of democracy"; he is the most practical eighteenth-century advocate, indeed, of popular government. Nevertheless, "A true natural aristocracy is not a separate interest in the state, or separable from it," Burke writes in his *Appeal from the New Whigs*. "It is an essential integrant part of any large body rightly constituted."[4]

Fourth, Burke contends that the good constitution maintains a balance or tension between the claims of freedom and the claims of order. Natural law is a reality, and from natural law flow certain natural rights. But government does not exist merely to defend claims of personal liberty. The Rights of Man claimed by the French revolutionaries are impossible to realize, unlimited, in any civil social order. "By having a right to everything they want everything," Burke writes in his *Reflections*:

> Government is a contrivance of human wisdom to provide for human wants. Men have a right that these wants should be

provided for by this wisdom. Among these wants is to be reckoned the want, out of civil society, of a sufficient restraint upon their passions. Society requires not only that the passions of individuals should be subjected, but that even in the mass and body, as well as in the individuals, the inclinations of men should frequently be thwarted, their will controlled, and their passions brought into subjection. . . . In this sense the restraints on men, as well as their liberties, are to be reckoned among their rights. [5]

On no point of political theory in America does greater confusion exist than upon this question of "human rights" as set against the need for restraints upon will and appetite.

So much for four principles of constitutional order that recur in Burke's speeches and writings over three decades. Let us now see how far the American constitution, both written and unwritten, accords with these principles, and how strongly prepared the American constitutional order may be to withstand powerful challenges in the dawning years.

CONSIDER FIRST BURKE'S CONVICTION—well sustained by the painful experience of Europe after the two World Wars and by the emergent nations of Africa and Asia—that any sound national constitution must be the fruit of long experience, tried and tested, that "paper constitutions" are not worth the paper they have been written upon, and that sudden, sweeping, large scale alterations of an old constitution almost certainly must destroy its ancient virtues rather than lopping off its acquired vices. May we apply these admonitions to the written Constitution of the United States in our present circumstances?

There exists today no popular demand for abrogating the Constitution of 1787 in general and substituting some new fundamental law. But there do exist strong movements to make specific important changes in the Constitution—changes or amendments, however, the intention of which is to return interpretation of the Constitution to what was the common understanding or usage until recent decades. Thus the pressure for formal alteration of the Constitution is conservative, not innovative. The principal constitutional amendments proposed at present are designed to compel Congress to balance the federal budget, to make abortion unlawful (reversing Supreme Court decisions of recent years), to permit prayer in public schools (so reversing other Supreme Court decisions), to return to legislative bodies jurisdiction over the apportionment and boundaries of legislative districts (which until 1962 remained a "political question" outside the jurisdictions of federal courts). The popular movement is therefore not for striking down old constitutional provisions or interpretations, but for returning to precedents only very recently overthrown by federal judges. In short, there exists no clear and present danger of a discarding of the old Constitution by the people, by the Congress, or by the executive branch.

Innovative alteration of the Constitution has been the work, instead, of a majority of the justices of the Supreme Court within the past forty years, chiefly. Possessing powers not conferred upon the chief judicial body of any other country, the Supreme Court has made itself into a reforming council, politicized. The phrase "judicial usurpation," nowadays employed by opponents of certain Supreme Court decisions, almost certainly would have been employed similarly by Burke in his time had the British judiciary then possessed authority sufficient to undo acts of Parliament—which of course the British judges did not have, and do not possess today.[6] In his "Speech on the Economical Reform," in 1780, Burke remarked that "the judges are, or ought to be, of a reserved and retired character, and wholly unconnected with the political world." Twenty-two years ago, my friend C.P. Ives commented on this passage from Burke, "What Burke would have thought when justices of the highest court felt compelled to campaign, at least quasi-politically, in defense of their own prior decisions as judges, it is not hard to infer."

A second constitutional convention could be called, but a second convention would possess arbitrary power to amend the old Constitution as the delegates might think fit or to sweep the Constitution altogether away, supplanting it by a new creation—which is precisely what the delegates to the Convention of 1787 did to the Articles of Confederation. Should a new convention be summoned, grandiose proposals for constitutional innovation might be put forward forcefully by persons and interests whose intellectual mentors would be not Edmund Burke or John Adams, but Jean-Jacques Rousseau or Jeremy Bentham, given to abstraction and levelling innovation. Sentimental egalitarianism on the one hand, dull utilitarianism on the other, might undo the prudent work of the Federalists, breaking that long continuity of law and political institutions that runs back beyond the beginning of American history. Thus men and women respectful of the established Constitution should bear in mind that a second national convention, even though brought about by a conservative impulse, might have radical consequences—of a populist cast, or of a centralizing cast, or of both afflictions blended.

Second, what of the religious basis of the American order? Joseph Story and James Kent, the great early commentators upon American constitutional law, pointed out that although America has no national establishment of religion, American laws and social institutions rest upon the moral postulates of the Christian religion. Sometimes, since the 1940s, the Supreme Court's majority, and a good many other federal and state judges, have seemed to hold that religion of any sort is suspect and should be excluded from public life.

If the latter understanding prevails in the interpretation of the written Constitution and works changes in our unwritten constitution of custom and convention, then very grave consequences are liable to develop. One of them would be the steady increase of fraud and violent crime, not to be adequately held in check by police powers, for religious belief is sufficiently enfeebled in our time already, with ineluctable moral consequences, and disapprobation by the state would work yet more mischief. Another consequence would be an increased danger from virulent ideology of one sort or another, for ideology rushes in to fill the vacuum left by the decay of religion. In foreign affairs, the decline of Americans' religious belief would mean an increase of the appeals of Marxism and of Marxist powers. A third consequence, intended to diminish the effects of the two afflictions just described, might be the systematic development of a "civil religion" of Americanism, a kind of Americanist ideology built of bricks from the yard of John Dewey and his disciples—dull, unimaginative, materialistic, and in the long run destined to ignominious failure.

In a time when telephone companies look forward to profits to be made from "dial-a-porn" services (within federal regulations, of course), and when all the police powers of federal and state and local governments do not suffice to put down an enormous traffic in narcotics, some freethinking spirits may begin to apprehend the truth in Burke's declaration that the state is built upon religious consensus. If we inquire whether the constitutions of government in the United States will endure a hundred years from now, the speculative answer must depend in no small part on whether there still will subsist, a century from now, widespread belief in a transcendent order. It may not be in the power of the political authority to renew the religious understanding, but at least the political authority can refrain from accelerating the decay of religious learning.

Third, what are we doing in America to develop people of virtue and wisdom sufficient to lead the democracy and sustain our old constitutional order of justice and freedom? The alternative to an aristocracy (the leadership of the best in the public interest) is an oligarchy (the leadership of the rich in their own interest). It is inane merely to chant, with Carl Sandburg, "The People, yes!" A people deprived of honest, able, and imaginative leadership will come to ruin.

The popular and journalistic response, in 1983, to the United States Commission on Excellence in Education did hearten some of us, for temporarily it overcame the educationists' denunciations of "elitism" and showed that a considerable part of the public has become aware of our American failure to develop right reason and moral imagination, scientific understanding and political knowledge, among the rising generation; our failure to provide, if you will, sufficient opportunity for the healthful growth of a natural aristocracy, which is essential to the survival of a democracy. But the administration of proposed educational reforms has fallen back into the hands of the very foundation bureaucrats, accrediting agencies, departments of public instruction, pillars of the National Education Association, and all those dull dogs of Holy Educationism who prate endlessly of "equity" (meaning enforced educational mediocrity) and shudder internally at the mention of "excellence" (which would eliminate the oligarchs of the educationist empire, should excellence actually be achieved). We may make some improvements in schooling at every level, but they will be small ameliorations, as matters drift at present.

The principal purpose of what has been called liberal education was to develop a considerable body of young people who would become molders of public opinion and leaders of community—the natural aristocracy, which is something different from the "meritocracy" and specialized elite that grow up in the twentieth-century welfare state.

But how much truly liberal education do we undertake nowadays? We still go through the motions—and then a large proportion of young people who have been endowed with the degree of bachelor of arts go on to work toward the degree of M.B.A., as if liberal learning were irrelevant to the real world. What we require more urgently than we do routine business skills is young men and women of courage and imagination, who know that life is for something more than consumption.

The Constitution is not sustained by intellectual mediocrity, obsession with creature comforts, and "four legs good, two legs bad" praise of an abstract democracy. If we neglect the talents of the ablest of the rising generation, we are left in the long run with what Tocqueville called democratic despotism—a regime of stagnation and dull uniformity—if not with something still worse than that.

Finally, it is even truer today than it was in Burke's time that those who begin by claiming everything will end with nothing at all—not even a Republic. An effectual "welfare rights" lobby piles up incredible federal deficits and national debts, as if wealth were a mere matter of printing presses and new debt ceilings. Presently such claims of entitlements make it difficult to maintain the common defense. The Bill of Rights is invoked as if it really were a suicide pact—from those who would defend to the death the inalienable right of a mugger to buy a "Saturday night special," to those humanitarians who insist that even imminent peril to public health must not be permitted to impede exercise of the inalienable right to engage in sexual perversions.

Great states with good constitutions develop when most people think of their duties and restrain their appetites. Great states sink toward their dissolution when most people think of their privileges and indulge their appetites freely. This rule is as true of democracies as it is of autocracies. And no matter how admirable a constitution may look upon paper, it will be ineffectual unless the unwritten constitution, the web of custom and convention, affirms an enduring moral order of obligation and personal responsibility.

THE RUIN or the recovery of America's constitutions, and the general future of American politics, will be determined more by choices than by circumstances. Here I have done no more than to suggest what some of those choices must be. "Not to lose ourselves in the infinite void of the conjectural world," Burke wrote near the end of his life in the *First Letter of the Regicide Peace*, "our business is with what is likely to be affected for the better or the worse by the wisdom or weakness of our plans." To shape the American political future through prudent and courageous choices is yet within the realm of possibility. "I despair neither of the public fortune nor of the public mind," Burke continued. "There is much to be done undoubtedly, and much to be retrieved. We must walk in new ways, or we can never encounter our enemy in his devious march. We are not at an end of our struggle, nor near it. Let us not deceive ourselves; we are at the beginning of great troubles." [7]

As it was with Britain in the closing years of the eighteenth century, so is it with America in the closing years of the twentieth. As did the British then, we confront an armed doctrine and are divided in our own counsels. And yet our own general complacency scarcely is shaken: most of us behave as if nothing very disagreeable ever could happen to the Constitution of the United States, and as if the political future of this nation would be a mere alternation of Republican and Democratic presidential victories, somewhat less interesting than professional baseball and football.

The crash of empires and the collapse of constitutions have blinded and deafened most of the world since 1914. Only American territories and American laws have stood little touched amidst the general ruin. It is not accident that will preserve them for posterity. Of those Americans who dabble in politics at all, many think of such activities chiefly as a game, membership on a team, with minor prizes to be passed out after the latest victory. Yet a few men and women, like Burke, engage in politics not because they love the game, but because they know that the alternative to a politics of elevation is a politics of degradation. Let us try to be of their number.

Notes

Introduction

1. Russell Kirk, *Rights and Duties: Reflections on Our Conservative Constitution* (Dallas, Texas: Spence Publishing Company, 1997), p. 4. Hereafter, RD.

2. Ibid., p. viii.

3. Ibid., p. 26.

4. Kirk, *The Conservative Mind: From Burke to Eliot*, 7th ed. (Chicago: Regnery Books, 1986), p. 340. Hereafter, CM.

5. RD, p. 16.

6. CM, p. 158.

7. Joseph Story, *Commentaries on the Constitution of the United States*, intro. Ronald D. Rotunda and John E. Nowak (Durham, N.C.: Carolina Academic Press, 1987), III.xliv §979.

8. CM, p. 459.

9. Kirk, *The Roots of American Order* (Malibu, Calif.: Pepperdine University Press, 1978), p. 471. Hereafter, RAO.

10. RD, p. 250.

11. Ibid. Emphasis added.

12. RD, p. 251.

13. Ibid., p. 260.

14. Ibid, p. 4.

15. RAO, p. 5.

16. Interestingly, Kirk goes so far to suggest that, had large numbers of English-speaking Catholics settled in North America, the hypothetical Catholic colonies would have been rather like the actual Protestant colonies in 1775. See RAO, p. 237. Kirk's point is that order is not reducible to its discrete elements (e.g., ecclesiastical affiliation).

17. RD, p. 228.

18. Orestes Brownson, *The American Republic: Its Constitution, Tendencies and Destiny*, new ed. (New York: P. O'Shea, 1866), p. 5

19. U. S. Constitution, art. 1, sec. 8.

20. See "The Case For and Against Natural Law," in Kirk, *Redeeming the Time*, Jeffrey O. Nelson, ed. (Wilmington, Delaware: Intercollegiate Studies Institute, 1997), pp. 196-212; See also RD, pp. 126-138.

21. Notice, for example, that Kirk himself is drawn into the controversies of the Court, and has surprisingly little to say about state constitutions.

22. 381 U.S. 479 (1965): 484.

23. Ibid.: 487. (Goldberg J., concurring.)

24. William J. Brennan, Jr. "The Constitution of the United States: Contemporary Ratification" *South Texas Law Review* 27 (1986): 434.

25. In *Planned Parenthood v. Casey*: "the Court's legitimacy depends on making legally principled decisions under circumstances in which their principled character is sufficiently *plausible to be accepted by the Nation.*" *Planned Parenthood v. Casey*, 505 U.S. 833 (1992): 866 . Remarking that "Liberty must not be extinguished for want of a line that is clear," the authors of the joint opinion in *Casey* declare that "it falls to us to give some real substance" to individual liberties. Ibid.: 869. We have here in a nutshell the new model of constitutional change—one that bespeaks Brennan's notion of "contemporary ratification." The Court gives new substance to the Constitution, and then awaits a verdict from the people.

26. Both indeed are Catholics, with a deep suspicion of positivism.

27. RD, p. 253.

28. Letter to James Madison, September 6, 1789. *Thomas Jefferson: Writings* (The Library of America, 1984), p. 959.

29. Brennan, p. 438.

30. Ibid., p. 444.

31. If Jefferson's radical concept of generational usufruct is combined with a decidedly non-Jeffersonian principle of judicial supremacy, the result would be more or less like Brennan's judicial philosophy.

32. 491 U.S. 110 (1989): 141. (Brennan J., dissenting).

33. Depending upon the particular object of change, the legislator may be more entitled than the judge to change society. That does not mean that such change is wise. In *The Conservative Mind*, Kirk presents the six canons of radicalism. See #6, p. 27: "The aim of the reformer, moral and political, is emancipation—liberation from old creeds, old oaths, old establishments."

34. RD, p. 7.

35. Ibid., p. 208.

36. Because society has an inherent value, Kirk can say "[c]onservatism never is more admirable than when it accepts changes that it disapproves, with good grace, for the sake of a general conciliation." CM, p. 47. The unwritten constitution, on Kirk's view, consists of many compromises reached for the common good; and because the common good is real value, these compromises are not just exercises of cunning or temporary accommodations to society. Can a liberal of Brennan's convictions sincerely hold that it is a virtue to compromise for the good of the whole?

37. Robert Bork, "Natural Law and the Constitution," *First Things* (March 1992): 16.

38. CM, p. 8.

39. RAO, pp. 108-111.

40. RD, p. 137. In the original text, only the word *authority* is italicized. I have taken the liberty to italicize the preposition *for*. It brings out even more clearly the full sense of the sentence. Rather than conceiving of two authorities contesting for the same turf, it is better to think of the positive law making the natural law effective, and of human legal art assisting the general ends of nature.

41. James Madison, a slave holder, argued at the Constitutional Convention that it would be "wrong to admit in the Constitution the idea that there could be property in men." Max Farrand, ed., *The Records of the Federal Convention of 1787*, vol. 2 (New Haven: Yale University Press, 1937), p. 417. His point is that it is one thing to compromise on the issue of slavery, but quite another thing to embed in the Constitution a principle violative of natural rights.

42. RD, p. 130.

43. Ibid., p. 40.

44. On several occasions, Kirk insisted to this author that Brownson's "The Higher Law" is the best work of its kind produced by an American mind. And although he has the reader look at the American experiment through the "eyes of Burke," he could have said just as well through the eyes of Brownson.

45. This discussion leaves to one side the related, but different question of a truly private judgment of conscience in the light of the natural law. Brownson and Kirk address the problem of a public authority imposing the natural law against the positive law of the Constitution. This is an entirely different problem than

the predicament of a judge who decides to recuse himself from a case, or even from the situation of a person who invokes the higher law as a ground for conscientious disobedience.

46. RD, p. 130-31.
47. Ibid, p. 20.
48. Ibid, p. 136.
49. Ibid, p. 236.
50. Ibid, p. 256.
51. Ibid, p. 30.
52. Ibid.
53. Ibid, p. 8.
54. Ibid, p. 229.
55. Ibid, p. 207.
56. Ibid, p. 231.
57. RAO, p. 419.
58. Ibid, p. 471.
59. RD, pp. 260-261.
60. Ibid., p. 261.

1. Conserving Order, Justice, and Freedom

1.   See H. M. Lydenberg, ed., *What Did Macaulay Say about America?* (New York: New York Public Library, 1925).

2.   Henry Maine, *Popular Government* (Indianapolis: Liberty Classics, 1976), p. 204.

3.   Ibid., pp. 242-43.

4.   Ibid., pp. 253-54.

5.   James Bryce, *The American Commonwealth*, new edition, vol. 1 (New York: Macmillan, 1919), p. 361.

6.   James Wilson, quoted in Bryce, p. 361, n.

7.   Bryce, p. 362.

8.   Ibid., p. 361.

9.   Ibid., p. 362.

10. Ibid., p. 403.

11. Ibid., p. 407.

12. Ibid., p. 407-8.

13. Daniel Boorstin, *The Genius of American Politics* (Chicago: University of Chicago Press, 1953), pp. 185-87.

14. Alexis de Tocqueville, *Democracy in America*, ed. J. P. Mayer (Garden City, N.J.: Doubleday, 1969), pp. 150-51.

2. The Controversy over Original Intent

1.   Fitch's steamboat and the incident of its demonstration to delegates to the Convention are described by John Bach McMaster, with his usual vividness, in *A History of the People of the United States from the Revolution to the Civil War*, vol. 1 (New York: Appleton, 1901), pp. 432-36.

2.   John Randolph of Roanoke, "Speech on Surveys for Roads and Canals," January 30, 1824, in the *Annals of Congress*, Eighteenth Congress, 1296-1311; reprinted in Kirk, *John Randolph of Roanoke, A Study in American Politics*, 3rd ed. (Indianapolis: Liberty Press, 1978), pp. 430-32.

3.   On this question of the appellate jurisdiction of the Supreme Court, see Ralph Rossum, *Congressional Control of the Judiciary: The Article III Option* (Cumberland, Va.: Center for Judicial Studies, 1988), which discusses both sides of the dispute.

3. The Rights of Man or the Bill of Rights?

1.   Friedrich Heer, *The Intellectual History of Europe*, vol. 2, *The Counter-Reformation to 1945*, trans. Jonathan Steinberg (Garden City, N.J.: Anchor Books, 1968), p. 209.

2.   Carl Becker, *The Declaration of Independence: A Study in the History of Political Ideas* (New York: Knopf, 1922), pp. 231-32.

3.   Lord Acton, *Lectures on the French Revolution*, ed. Figgis and Laurence (London: Macmillan, 1916), p. 107.

4. A Revolution Not Made, but Prevented

1.   E. J. Payne, *Burke: Select Works*, vol. 2, *Reflections on the Revolution in France* (Oxford: The Clarendon Press, 1898), pp. xiv, 304n. See Edmund Burke, *Appeal from the New to the Old Whigs*, in *The Works of the Right Honourable Edmund Burke*, vol. 6 (London: Rivington, 1826), pp. 159-179.

2.   Ibid., pp. 36-37. In Burke's era, Whigs approved of the Revolution of 1688, and Fox's Whigs thought of the French Revolution as a Gallic equivalent of what had occurred in Britain a century earlier. But the employment of the word "revolution" was ambiguous; Sir Joseph Jekyll, lawyer and Whig politician, early in the eighteenth century, did not use the word in its sense of coming full cycle, but thought of it as signifying radical and violent overturn; so he distinguished the triumph of William and Mary from the evil of genuine revolution. Burke found it awkward, but necessary, to make the same distinction. In short, the history of *revolution* is complex etymologically.

3.   Maurice Ashley, *The Glorious Revolution of 1688* (New York: Scribner's, 1966), p. 198.

4.   Woodrow Wilson, "Edmund Burke and the French Revolution", *The Century Magazine*, September 1901.

5.   Ross J. S. Hoffman, *Edmund Burke, New York Agent* (Philadelphia: American Philosophical Society, 1956), p. 191.

6.   Boorstin, *The Genius of American Politics*, pp. 68-69.

7.   Ibid., pp. 94-95.

8.   Clinton Rossiter, *Seedtime of the Republic: The Origin of the American Tradition of Political Liberty* (New York: Harcourt, Brace, 1953), pp. 270, 395.

9.   H. Trevor Colburn, *The Lamp of Experience: Whig History and the Intellectual Origins of the American Revolution* (Chapel Hill: University of North Carolina Press, 1963), p. 190.

10.   Burke, *Appeal from the New to the Old Whigs*, pp. 122-23.

11.   Becker, *The Declaration of Independence*, pp. 219-20.

12.   Boorstin, p. 76.

13.   I commend two books on this subject: Crane Brinton, *The Anatomy of Revolution* (New York: Prentice-Hall, 1938); D. W. Brogan, *The Price of Revolution* (London: Hamish Hamilton, 1951).

14.   John Randolph, in *Proceedings and Debates of the Virginia State Convention of 1829-30* (Richmond, 1830), pp. 312-21; reprinted in Kirk, *John Randolph of Roanoke*, p. 214.

5. A Natural Aristocracy

1.   Burke, *Appeal from the New to the Old Whigs*, pp. 217-218.

2.   James Fenimore Cooper, *The American Democrat*, intro. H. L. Mencken (New York: Knopf, 1931), pp. 112-13.

3.   For the religious professions of the Framers, see M. E. Bradford, *A Worthy Company* (Marlborough, N.H.: Plymouth Rock Foundation, 1982).

4.   On knowledge of the classics in eighteenth-century America, see Richard M. Gummere, *The American Colonial Mind and the Classical Tradition* (Cambridge, Mass.: Harvard University Press, 1963); also Gummere's *Seven Wise Men of Colonial America* (Harvard University Press, 1967).

5.   Thomas Fuller, *The Holy State and the Profane State* (Cambridge: Williams, 1648), pp. 138-41.

7. Men of Property

1.   Bryce, pp. 22, 23, 24, notes.

2.   Wilson mordantly attacked Edmund Burke's politics. See Robert Green

McCloskey, ed., *The Works of James Wilson*, 2 vols. (Cambridge, Massachusetts: Harvard University Press, 1967).

    3.   Forrest McDonald, *We the People: The Economic Origins of the Constitution* (University of Chicago Press, 1958), p. 350. This book, and two others by McDonald—*E Pluribus Unum: The Formation of the American Republic*, 2d ed. (Indianapolis: Liberty Press, 1979), and *Novus Ordo Seclorum: The Intellectual Origins of the Constitution* (Lawrence: University Press of Kansas, 1985)—establish Dr. McDonald as a leading historian of the Constitution.

    4.   Ibid., p. 355.

    5.   Bradford, pp. ix-x.

8. John Locke and the Social Contract

    1.   Gottfried Dietze, *The Federalist: a Classic on Federalism and Free Government* (Baltimore: Johns Hopkins Press, 1960), p. 325.

    2.   Louis Hartz, *The Liberal Tradition in America: An Interpretation of American Political Thought Since the Revolution* (New York: Harcourt, Brace, 1954), pp. 32, 308.

    3.   Richard Hofstadter, *The American Political Tradition and the Men Who Made It* (New York: Knopf, 1948), p. vii.

    4.   Leo Strauss, *Natural Right and History* (Chicago: University of Chicago Press, 1953).

    5.   John Rawls, *A Theory of Justice* (Cambridge, Mass.: Harvard University Press, 1971); Robert Nozick, *Anarchy, State, and Utopia* (New York: Basic Books, 1974).

    6.   Maurice Cranston, "The Politics of John Locke," *History Today* 11, no. 9 (1952): 662; see also Cranston, *John Locke, a Biography* (Oxford: Oxford University Press, 1985).

    7.   Rossiter, pp. 358-59.

    8.   Ibid.

    9.   See Gilbert Chinard, *Thomas Jefferson: The Apostle of Americanism* (Ann Arbor: University of Michigan Press, 1957), particularly Book Two, Chapter 1, "Jefferson and the American Revolution"; also Chinard's edition of Jefferson's Commonplace Book.

    10.   John Adams, elsewhere in the ten volumes of his works, gives another list consisting of "Sidney, Locke, Hoadley, Trenchard, Gordon, and Plato Redivivus"; but, putting these aside, he devotes three whole chapters to Marchmont Nedham. See the first volume of *A Defence of the Constitutions of Government of the United States of America*, in *The Life and Works of John Adams*, C. F. Adams, ed., vol. 4 (Boston: Little, Brown, 1851), pp. 3-133; quotation on p. 4.

11. Irving Brant, *James Madison: The Nationalist, 1780–1785* (Indianapolis: Bobbs-Merrill, 1948), p. 415.

12. William Lee Miller, *The First Liberty: Religion and the American Republic* (New York: Alfred A. Knopf, 1986), pp. 139, 145.

13. Ellis Sandoz, *A Government of Laws: Political Theory, Religion, and the American Founding* (Baton Rouge: Louisiana State University Press, 1990), p. 23.

14. The latest edition of Madison's Notes is the best: James McClellan and M. E. Bradford, eds., *Debates in the Federal Convention of 1787 as Reported by James Madison;* vol. III of *Jonathan Elliot's Debates in the Several State Conventions on the Adoption of the Federal Constitution* (Richmond, Va.: James River Press, 1989).

9. Edmund Burke and the Chartered Rights of Englishmen

1. Adams, *Defence of the Constitutions of Government of the United States of America,* in *Works,* vol. 4, pp. 463–64.

2. Bradford, "The Best Constitution in Existence: The Influence of the British Example on the Framers of Our Fundamental Law," *Brigham Young University Studies* 27 (1987): 51–66.

3 . *The Annual Register* for the years and subjects in question now is reprinted in a useful large volume edited by David R. Murdoch, *Rebellion in America: A Contemporary British Viewpoint, 1763–1783* (Santa Barbara, Calif.: Clio Books, 1984).

4. See Griffith J. McGhee, *The Life and Correspondence of James Iredell,* vol. 2 (New York: Appleton, 1858), as well as the correspondence of James Iredell in the State Archives of North Carolina, Raleigh.

5. American historians' plagiarism from Burke's *Annual Register* was exposed in historical journals so early as 1889—although Marshall's *Life of Washington* went undetected until much later. A recent summary of this influence is contained in Harvey Wish's book *The American Historian* (New York: Oxford University Press, 1960). See also Peter Stanlis, "Burke's *Annual Register* and American History," *The Burke Newsletter* 4, no. 2 (1962–63): 179–81.

6. Reinhold Niebuhr, "English and German Mentality—A Study in National Traits," *Christendom* 1, no. 3 (1936): 466.

7. Bryce, pp. 427–32.

8. Maine, *Popular Government* (Indianapolis: Liberty Classics, 1976), pp. 212–15.

9. William Holdsworth, *The History of English Law,* vol. 9 (London: Methuen, 1938), p. 137.

10. Stanley Pargellis, "The Theory of Balanced Government," in Conyers Read, ed., *The Constitution Reconsidered,* revised ed. (New York: Harper Torchbooks, 1948), pp. 37–49.

11. Bryce, p. 77.

12. Maine, *Popular Government*, p. 247.

13. Holdsworth, *English Law*, p. 279.

14. For Burke's influence on Story, see McClellan, *Joseph Story and the American Constitution* (Norman: University of Oklahoma Press, 1971), and R. Kent Newmyer, *Supreme Court Justice Joseph Story: Statesman of the Old Republic* (Chapel Hill: University of North Carolina Press, 1985).

15. Burke, *Appeal from the New to the Old Whigs*, pp. 261-62, 265.

10. Natural Law and the Constitution

1. Robert H. Bork, *The Tempting of America: The Political Seduction of* the *Law* (New York: The Fress Press, 1990), p. 209; see also Robert H. Bork, "Mr. Jaffa's Constitution," *National Review* (1994): 61. This article contains an overwhelming devastation of Harry Jaffa's notions of natural law in the Declaration of Independence as binding upon the Constitution.

2. See Becker, particularly Chapter 6.

3. A. P. D'Entreves, *Natural Law: An Introduction to Legal Philosophy* (New Brunswick, N.J.: Transaction Publishers, 1994), pp. 108-16, 120.

4. Orestes A. Brownson, "The Higher Law," in *Essays and Reviews* (New York: D & J Sadlier, 1870), pp. 349, 355-56.

5. Ibid., p. 357.

6. Ibid., p. 359-60.

7. Ibid., p. 363.

8. Ibid.

9. Ibid., p. 364.

10. Russell Hittinger, "Liberalism and the American Natural Law Tradition," *Wake Forest Law Review* 25 (1990): 429.

11. Hittinger, "The Natural Law in the Positive Laws," *Review of Politics* 55 (1993): 22.

12. Ibid., pp. 27-8.

11. The Christian Postulates of English and American Law

1. Henry Maine, *Early History of Institutions* (William S. Hein & Co., 1987), pp. 60, 55-58, 56, 104-05, 337, 338.

2. Roscoe Pound, *Interpretations of Legal History* (William Gaunt & Sons, 1980), pp. 24-25.

3. J. C. Gray, *Nature and Sources of the Law*, 2d ed, (Peter Smith, 1972), pp. 308-09.

4. Ibid., p. 306.

5. Ernst Troeltsch, *Social Teaching of the Christian Churches*, trans. Olive Wyon (Westminster John Knox Press, 1992), p. 160.

6. *Taylor's Case*, 1 Ventris 293 (1676).

7. *Rex v. Woolston*, 2 Strange 832 (1729).

8. 13 U. S. 43 (1815).

9. 43 U. S. 127.

10. *People v. Ruggles*, 8 Johnson 290, 293-94 (N.Y. 1811).

11. *Reynolds v. United States*, 98 U. S. 145 (1879).

12. Joseph Story, *Commentaries on the Constitution of the United States*, vol. 1 (1833), p. 459.

13. *Vidal v. Girard's Executors*: 198.

14. John C. H. Wu, *Fountain of Justice* (1955), p. 215.

15. Huntington Cairns, *Law and Its Premises* (1962), p. 10.

16. Ibid., p.26.

12. Politics and Religion

1. Story, *Commentaries,* as quoted in Edward S. Corwin, ed., *The Constitution of the United States of America: Analysis and Interpretation* (Washington, D.C.: Government Printing Office, 1952), pp. 758-59.

2. Tocqueville, *Democracy in America,* ed. Phillips Bradley, vol. 1 (New York: Knopf, 1948), p. 305.

3. 343 U. S. 313-14 (1952).

4. Aleksandr Solzhenitsyn, "The Templeton Address," *National Review* 35, no. 14 (1983): 873-876.

5. T. S. Eliot, "Thoughts after Lambeth," in *Selected Essays, 1917-1932* (New York: Harcourt, Brace, 1932), p. 332.

6. Solzhenitsyn.

7. A good recent study of the relations between politics and religious belief and institutions in the United States, from the seventeenth century to recent years, is A. James Reichley, *Religion in American Public Life* (Washington, D.C.: The Brookings Institute, 1985).

13. A Christian College in the Secular City

1. See James Serritella, "Tangling with Entanglement: Toward a Constitutional Evaluation of Church-State Contacts," *Law and Contemporary Problems* 44, no. 2 (1981).

2. See P. Skerry, *Christian Schools, Racial Quotas, and the IRS* (Washington, D.C.: Ethics and Public Policy Center, 1980).

3. *Wisconsin v. Yoder,* 406 U. S. 205 (1972).

4. *Kentucky State Board for Elementary and Secondary Education v. Rudasill,* 48 U. S.L.W. 3733 (1980).

5. *NLRB v. Catholic Bishop of Chicago,* 440 U. S. 490 (1979).

6. *Grace Brethren Church v. California,* CV 79-93 MRP (C. D. Cal. 1979).

7. *Lemon v. Kurtzman,* 403 U. S. 602 (1970).

8. 330 U. S. 1 (1947).

9. 343 U. S. 306 (1952).

10. *Lemon v. Kurtzman.*

11. Ibid.

12. *Meek v. Pittenger,* 421 U. S. 349 (1974).

13. Ibid.

14. *Wolman v. Walter,* 433 U. S. 229 (1977).

15. *Levitt v. Committee for Public Education,* 413 U. S. 472 (1973).

16. *Committee for Public Education & Religious Liberty v. Nyquist,* 413 U. S. 756 (1973).

17. *Board of Education v. Allen,* 392 U. S. 236 (1968).

18. *Wolman v. Walter; Committee for Public Education & Religious Liberty v. Regan,* – U. S. –, 100 S. Ct. 840 (1980).

19. *Wolman v. Walter.*

20. Ibid.

21. *Lemon v. Kurtzman,* in dicta.

22. *Tilton v. Richardson,* 403 U. S. 672 (1971).

23. *Hunt v. McNair,* 413 U. S. 734 (1973).

24. *Shelton College Catalogue, 1980-81,* p. 9.

25. Superior Court of New Jersey, Chancery Division, Cape May Court, Docket No. C-1088-79E, November 15, 1979.

26. *Shelton College Catalogue, 1980-81,* p. 10.

27. William Bentley Ball, letter to author. Emphasis in original.

28. New Jersey, *Statutes, Annotated* (West 1968), 18A: 68-6.

29. Ibid.

30. *Shelton College v. State Board of Education,* 48 N. J. 501 (1967).

31. Ibid.

32. 482 F. Supp. 968 (D.N.J. 1980), *affirmed;* Slip Opinion, 3dCir. (April 14, 1981).

33. Verified Complaint for Temporary Restraining Order, Declaratory Judgment and Preliminary and Permanent Injunction, filed in *Shelton College v. State Board of Education* (D. N. J., November 19, 1979), p. 12.

34. Superior Court of New Jersey, Chancery Division, Cape May Court, Docket No. C-1088-79E, December 10, 1980.

35. Ball's discussion included *Walz v. Tax Commission,* 397 U. S. 664 (1970), *Lemon v. Kurtzman, State of New York v. Cathedral Academy,* 434 U. S. 125 (1977),

and several other cases.

36. Brief for Defendants, *New Jersey State Board of Higher Education v. Board of Directors of Shelton College* (Superior Court of New Jersey, Chancery Division, Cape May Court, Docket No. C-1088-79E 1980), pp. 39-41.

37. *New Jersey-Philadelphia Presbytery of Bible Presbyterian Church v. New Jersey State Board of Higher Education*, 740 F.2d 957 (1984), affirmed; *New Jersey-Philadelphia Presbytery of Bible Presbyterian Church v. New Jersey State Board of Higher Education*, 469 U. S. 1107 (1985), certiorari denied.

38. The "Humanist Manifesto" of 1932 is reprinted in D. Faber, ed., *The Christian Challenge* (1980).

39. Max Picard, *The Flight from God* (Chicago: Regnery Books, 1949).

40. *Stone v. Superintendent of Public Instruction of Kentucky*, 66 L.Ed.2d 199 (1980).

41. *Virginia Declaration of Rights*, article XVI (adopted June 6, 1776).

14. An Establishment of Humanitarianism?

1. 136 U. S. 1 (1890).

2. A good, succinct treatment of this subject is by Joseph R Costanzo, "Prayer in Public Schools," in his *Political and Legal Studies*, vol. 2, *Studies in American Constitutional Law* (West Hanover, Mass.: Christopher Publishing House, 1982), pp. 259-74.

3. *Jaffree* is discussed judiciously by Professor John S. Baker, Jr., in his address "The Religion Clauses Reconsidered: The Jaffree Case" published in *The Assault on Religion: Commentaries on the Decline of Religious Liberty*, ed., Russell Kirk (Lanham, Md.: University Press of America, 1986), pp. 33-49.

4. 374 U. S. 203 (1963).

5. The distinction between different schools of humanism in America is discussed by Russell Kirk in his introduction to Irving Babbitt, *Literature and the American College: Essays in Defense of the Humanities* (Washington, D.C.: National Humanities Institute, 1986), pp. 9-16.

6. John Dewey, in *Living Philosophies* (Cleveland: World Publishing Company, 1941), pp. 21-35.

7. See Paul C. Vitz, *Censorship: Evidence of Bias in Our Children's Textbooks* (Ann Arbor: Servant Books, 1986).

8. The full text of Judge Hand's opinion, with appendices, is printed in *American Education on Trial: Is Secular Humanism a Religion?* with an introduction by Richard John Neuhaus (Washington, D.C.: Center for Judicial Studies, 1987). All quotations of Judge Hand in this chapter are taken from that pamphlet.

15. Pornography and Free Speech

1.   William Blackstone, *Commentaries on the Law of England,* vol. 4 (London, 1769), pp. 64, 41.

2.   For criticisms of Kinsey's first volume, see Reinhold Niebuhr, "Sex Standards in America," *Christianity and Crisis,* May 24, 1948; and Russell Kirk, "Statistics and Sinai," *The South Atlantic Quarterly,* April, 1949; reprinted in Kirk, *Beyond the Dreams of Avarice: Essays of a Social Critic* (Chicago: Henry Regnery Company, 1956). See also Niebuhr, "Sex and Religion in the Kinsey Report," *Christianity and Crisis,* November 2, 1953.

3.   352 U. S. 380 (1957).

4.   354 U. S. 476 (1957)

5.   *Kingsley Books Inc. v. Brown,* 354 U. S. 436 (1957).

6.   The principal actions at law concerning pornography during the 1950s are discussed in greater detail by Kirk in articles on "Censorship" in *Collier's Year Book,* volumes for 1953, 1954, 1955, 1956, and 1957.

7.   378 U. S. 184 (1964).

8.   383 U. S. 413 (1966).

9.   413 U. S. 15 (1973).

16. John Marshall and the Rise of the Corporation

1.   Roscoe Pound, *The Formative Era of American Law* (Boston: Little, Brown, 1938), pp. 84, 128.

2.   See G. Peter McGrath, *Yazoo: The Case of Fletcher v. Peck* (New York: Norton, 1966); also John Randolph of Roanoke, Debate on the Yazoo Claims, February 1, 1805, printed in Russell Kirk, *John Randolph of Roanoke* (Indianapolis: Liberty Press, 1978), pp. 311-23; T. P. Abernathy, *The South in the New Nation, 1789-1819* (Baton Rouge: Louisiana State University Press, 1961); and Abraham Butler, *Georgia Speculation Unveiled* (Hartford: Babcock, 1797; Reader Microprint, 1966).

3.   4 Wheat. 518 (1819).

4.   Edwin S. Corwin, *John Marshall and the Constitution* (New Haven: Yale University Press, 1920), p. 168.

5.   *Providence Bank v. Billings,* 4 Pet. 514 (1830).

6.   John Bach McMaster, *A History of the People of the United States, from the Revolution to the Civil War,* vol. 6 (New York: Appleton, 1906), pp. 335-38.

7.   Roane, quoted in Albert J. Beveridge, *The Life of John Marshall,* vol. 4 (Boston: Houghton Mifflin, 1919), p. 313.

17. Christian Doctrine and Economic Order

1. Tocqueville, *Democracy in America*, ed. Phillips Bradley, vol. 2 (New York: Knopf, 1948), pp. 136, 145.
2. Brownson, *Liberalism and the Church* (New York: Sadlier, 1887), pp. 98-99.
3. Brownson, *The American Republic: Its Constitution, Tendencies and Destiny*, reprint (Clifton, N. J.: Augustus M. Kelley, 1972), pp. 275-76.
4. Brownson, "Constitutional Guaranties," *Brownson's Quarterly Review*, April 1874, in *Works of Orestes Brownson*, vol. 18 (Detroit, 1882-87), p. 257.
5. Edwin S. Corwin, ed., *The Constitution of the United States of America: Analysis and Interpretation* (Washington, D.C.: Government Printing Office, 1953), p. 974.
6. Quoted in Hugh Marshall, *Orestes Brownson and the American Republic* (Washington, D.C.: Catholic University Press, 1971), p. 264.
7. James McClellan, "The Constitution from a Conservative Perspective," *The Heritage Lectures*, No. 157 (Washington, D.C.: Heritage Foundation, 1988), p. 6.
8. Brownson, "Constitutional Guaranties," pp. 254-55.
9. Brownson, *Liberalism and the Church*, pp. 39-40.
10. Ibid., pp. 40-41.
11. Brownson, *American Republic*, p. 383.
12. Brownson, *Liberalism*, pp. 95-96.
13. Brownson, "The Democratic Principle," *Brownson's Quarterly Review*, April, 1873, *Works*, vol. 18, p. 226.
14. Brownson, *American Republic*, p. 427.
15. Quoted by Marshall, p. 284.

18. Ideology and Property

1. Orestes Brownson, "Socialism and the Church," in *Essays and Reviews, Chiefly on Theology, Politics, and Socialism* (New York: Sadlier, 1880), p. 506.
2. Henry Maine, *Village Communities in the East and West*, 3rd ed. (London: John Murray, 1876), pp. 238-39.
3. Paul Elmer More, *Aristocracy and Justice*, Shelburne Essays, seventh series (Boston: Houghton Mifflin, 1915), p. 136 (emphasis in original).
4. The Supreme Court of Michigan sustained the City of Detroit in its transfer of land in Poletown to General Motors Corporation. But in June 1989, the Michigan Court of Appeals, in a similar case involving Chrysler Corporation, found that such arbitrary transfer of real property from one owner to another is

"an abuse of power" which (in the words of a dissenting opinion in the Supreme Court's Poletown case) "means that there is virtually no limit to the use of condemnation to aid private businesses."

Epilogue: The Constitution and the Antagonist World

1.   Edmund Burke, "Speech on a Motion Made in the House of Commons, the 7th of May 1782, for a Committee to Inquire into the State of the Representation of the Commons in Parliament," in *Works*, vol. 6, p. 153.

2.   John C. Calhoun, *A Disquisition on Government*, in *Calhoun: Basic Documents*, ed. John M. Anderson (State College, Pa.: Bald Eagle Press, 1952), p. 79.

3.   Burke, *Reflections on the Revolution in France*, pp. 106-10.

4.   Burke, *Appeal from the New to the Old Whigs*, p. 217.

5.   Burke, *Reflections*, pp. 70-71.

6.   For analysis and criticism of the Supreme Court's enlargement of its powers, see Raoul Berger, *Government by Judiciary: The Transformation of the Fourteenth Amendment* (Cambridge, Mass.: Harvard University Press, 1977); Christopher Wolfe, *The Rise of Modern Judicial Review: From Constitutional Interpretation to Judge-Made Law* (New York: Basic Books, 1986); Carrol D. Kilgore, *Judicial Tyranny* (Nashville: Thomas Nelson, 1977).

8.   Burke, *Two Letters Addressed to a Member of the Present Parliament on the Proposals for Peace with the Regicide Directory of France*, in *Select Works*, vol. 3, pp. 4-5, 10.

Index

A

A. L. A. Schechter Poultry Corporation v. United States, 241

Abington School District v. Schempp, 185

Abolition of Man, The, Lewis's, 128

Abolitionists, 132-33

abortion, 136, 256

Act of Settlement, 48

Acton, John, first baron, 43,

Adams, Charles Francis, Jr.,234

Adams, Henry, 236

Adams, John, xv, 3, 50,65, 86-87, 105, 111, 123, 254, 257

Adams, John Quincy, 123, 129

American Book Publishers Council, 204

American Civil Liberties Union, 73-74, 182, 204

American Commonwealth, The, Bryce's, 10-13

American Democrat, The, Cooper's,65

American Humanism, see secular humanism

American Humanist Association, 182, 188-89

American Political Tradition and the Men Who Made It, The, Hofstadter's, 96

American Republic, The, Brownson's, 230-31, 234, 236

American Revolution, see Revolution, American

Americanism, 257

Ames, Fisher, viii, 42, 153-54

Amish, 167

Anarchy, State, and Utopia, Nozick's, 98

Anbury, Thomas, 116

animal rights, 75

Annapolis Convention on trade, 1786, 81

Annual Register, Burke's,69, 114-16, 119, 123

Anti-Federalists, 19, 36, 89

Apollo, 146-47, 149

Apostle's Creed, 68, 146, 170

Appeal from the New to the Old Whigs, Burke's, 55-56, 64-65, 113, 124

Aquinas, Thomas, 101, 127, 143

archonocracy, 31

Aristotle, 31, 106, 108, 127

Arkes, Hadley, 127

Arnold, Matthew, 186

Articles of Confederation, 19-20, 77, 81, 216, 256

Ashley, Maurice, 51

atheism, 177, 225, 253

Athenians, 5

Attorney General's Commission on Pornography, 1986, 196

Aurelius, Marcus, 251

Austin, John, 136

Authors' League, 204

and pornography, 194-208
power of, 24-31, 138
and property, 240-41, 244, 246
and religion, 157, 167-69, 172, 176-77, 181-82,
    184-85, 193, 254, 257

T

Talleyrand, Charles Maurice de, 21
Taine, Hippolyte Adolphe, 35
Taney, Roger B., 226
Tao, 128
Taylor, John, of Caroline, 65
Taylor's Case, 144
"Templeton Address," Solzhenitsyn's, 159, 164
Tempting of America, The, Bork's, 137
Ten Commandments, 62
Terrett v. Taylor, 144
"Theory of Balanced Government, A," Par-
    gellis's, 120
Theory of Justice, A, Rawls's, 97-98
Third Amendment, see Constitution, U.S.
Thomas, Clarence, xx, 126, 137
Thoughts on Government, Adams's, 105
Thoughts on the Present Discontents, Burke's, 51,
    114, 120, 122
Tocqueville, Alexis de, xv, 3, 6, 13, 15-16, 35, 53,
    80, 85, 156-57, 227, 243, 259
Toynbee, Arnold, 147, 225
Treatise of Human Nature, A, Hume's, 106
Troeltsch, Ernst, 143
Tucker, St. George, 22
Tugwell, Rexford Guy, 62
Twain, Mark, 234
Two Treatises of Civil Government, Locke's, 97-
    98, 100-04, 108-09, 113

U

United Nations, 42
Universal Declaration of Human Rights,
    United Nations, 42
Union, the, 16, 154, 229, 231-32, 237-38
University of Chicago, 246
unitarianism, 186, 225
urban renewal, 244-47
U.S. Post Office and censorship, 200, 202-03
utilitarian economics, 232
utilitarianism, 90, 226, 239, 257

V

values clarification, 189, 191
Vandals, 7
Venetian Constitution, 99
venture capital, 216
Vergil, 69
Vidal v. Girard's Executors, 144-45
Virginia Convention of 1829, 71

Virginia Declaration of Rights, 72-73, 75, 77, 178
Vitz, Paul C., 189
Voegelin, Eric, 147, 225
Voltaire, 36-37, 39, 62

W

*Wabash, St. Louis and Pacific Railway Company
    v. Illinois*, 240
Waite, Morrison Remmick, 145
Walker, Graham, 127
Wall Street Journal, 73
War of 1812, 91, 222
War of Independence, 35, 47-48, 59, 114
Warren, Earl, 196
Washington, George, 3, 17, 28, 40, 50, 60, 66, 77,
    82, 90, 116, 123, 164-65
Wealth of Nations, The, Smith's, 86, 88
Weaver, George, 206
Weaver, Richard, 242
Weber, Max, 227
Webster, Daniel, 144, 219
Westminster Confession of Faith, 170
*We Hold These Truths: Catholic Reflections on the
    American Proposition*, Murray's, 228
*We the People: The Economic Origins of the Con-
    stitution*, McDonald's, 84
Whigs,
    American, 53, 104
    English, 37, 47-53, 55, 98-102, 107-08, 113-14,
        124
    interpretation of history, 50-51
    Rockingham, 52, 112, 115, 122
White, Byron, 206
William and Mary, 47-48
William III, of Orange, 51, 98
Williamson, Hugh, 116
Wilson, Edmund, 198
Wilson, James, 25-26, 38, 66, 80, 82-84, 89, 116,
    214
Wilson, Woodrow, 52, 59, 242, 252
Winters v. New York, 199
Wisconsin v. Yoder, 176
Woolston's Case, 144
Wright, Louis B., 103
Wu, John C. H., 146
Wythe, George, 66

Y

Yates, Robert, 23

Z

Zorach v. Clauson, 157, 168, 185

About the Authors

Russell Kirk (1918-1994)—literary and social critic, historian of ideas, political philosopher, man of letters—rose to prominence in 1953 following the publication of his landmark book, *The Conservative Mind*. Hailed by *Time* and *Newsweek* as one of America's leading thinkers, for forty years Kirk stood at the center of the conservative intellectual movement in America.

Kirk was president of two educational foundations, the founding editor of *Modern Age* and *The University Bookman*, and the only American to have earned the highest arts degree of Scotland's senior university—doctor of letters of St. Andrews. The author of over thirty books, hundreds of articles, and award-winning fiction, he was the recipient of numerous honors and fellowships. In 1989, he received the Presidential Citizens Award.

His other books include *The Roots of American Order, Eliot and His Age, Edmund Burke: A Genius Reconsidered,* and *The Sword of Imagination,* memoirs he completed shortly before his death.

For more than two decades, Kirk hosted seminars and research scholars at Piety Hill, his ancestral home in rural Michigan. Shortly after his death, the Russell Kirk Center for Cultural Renewal was founded at Piety Hill to continue his work.

Russell Hittinger is Warren Professor of Catholic Studies and Research Professor of Law at the University of Tulsa. He is the only person ever to have studied at Piety Hill as a student and returned as a faculty member.

Mitchell S. Muncy is editor in chief of Spence Publishing Company.

Colophon

This book was designed and set into type by Mitchell S. Muncy,

with cover art by Stephen J. Ott,

and printed and bound by Thomson-Shore, Inc., Dexter, Michigan.

The text face is Adobe Caslon,

designed by Carol Twombly,

based on faces cut by William Caslon, London, in the 1730s,

and issued in digital form by Adobe Systems,

Mountain View, California, in 1989.

The paper is acid-free and is of archival quality.

DATE DUE

MAR 1 2011			